BELIEVERS
AND
BELIEFS

BELIEVERS AND BELIEFS

A PRACTICAL GUIDE TO RELIGIOUS ETIQUETTE FOR BUSINESS AND SOCIAL OCCASIONS

GAYLE COLQUITT WHITE

BERKLEY BOOKS, NEW YORK

This book is an original publication of The Berkley Publishing Group.

BELIEVERS AND BELIEFS

A Berkley Book / published by arrangement with
the author

PRINTING HISTORY
Berkley trade paperback edition / December 1997

The Putnam Berkley World Wide Web site address is http://www.berkley.com

ISBN: 0-425-16002-5

BERKLEY®
Berkley Books are published by The Berkley Publishing Group,
a member of Penguin Putnam Inc.,
200 Madison Avenue, New York, New York 10016.
BERKLEY and the ''B'' design
are trademarks belonging to Berkley Publishing Corporation.

PRINTED IN THE UNITED STATES OF AMERICA
10 9 8 7 6 5 4 3 2 1

To Bob, Bobby, and Margaret, and in memory of my dad

ACKNOWLEDGMENTS

For the last eight years, the editors of the *Atlanta Journal-Constitution* have allowed me to cover the best beat on the newspaper. Several years ago, a coworker told me he never minded being asked to fill in for me on religion stories. "You meet some of the nicest people," he said. It's true. And many of them answered my inane and naive questions for this book directly, have been interviewed for articles that contributed to the research, or actually reviewed chapters of the manuscript. While I was not able to incorporate all their suggestions, their advice was invaluable. My apologies in advance to anyone I left out or to anyone whose statements I misinterpreted.

Thanks to my coworkers at the *Atlanta Journal-Constitution* who have shared the background of their faith and/or expertise with me: Gerdeen Dyer, Ron Feinberg, Jim Galloway, the Rev. Amy Greene and Tyrone Terry.

Thanks to the national and local religious communicators and officials whose work made this possible. Some I consider friends as well as sources. They are arranged in order by chapter: Paul Hippman and Riaz Khadem of the Baha'i faith; Michael Zenkai Taiun Elliston of the Soto Zen Center; Sue MacLachlan and Clifton Irby, Church of Christ, Scientist; P.V. Rao of Emory University and the Atlanta Hindu Temple; Santosh Kothari of the Jain Society of Atlanta; officials of the Watchtower Bible and Tract Society; Sunny Stern of the American Jewish Committee; Donald LeFevre and Michael Leonard of the Church of Jesus Christ of Latter-day Saints; Shirlene Flory of the Reorganized Church of Jesus Christ of Latter-day Saints; Qur'an Sabir of the Atlanta Masjid of Al-Islam; the Japanese Consulate of Atlanta; Jasbir M. Singh and D.S. Bhatia of the Sikh Study Circle; Chi Hung Hwang of the Taipei Economic and Cultural Office in Atlanta; Pallan

Ichaporia, visiting professor of Iranian Studies at the University of Maine and Ali Jafarey of the Zoroastrian Assembly; W. Maurice Abbott, Jr., and Martin Butler of the Seventh-day Adventist Church; Tom Lichti of Menno-Hof; the Rev. Dwight "Ike" Reighard, former president of the Southern Baptist Convention Pastors' Conference and the Georgia Baptist Convention; Linda Myers Swanson and Julie Garber, Church of the Brethren; Monsignor Peter Dora of the Roman Catholic Archdiocese of Atlanta; Hans Holznagel of the United Church of Christ; Bill Long of the North Atlanta Church of Christ; Clifford Willis of the Christian Church (Disciples of Christ); Dr. William Franklin of General Theological Seminary; James Solheim of the Episcopal Church; Ann E. Haffen of the Evangelical Lutheran Church in America; Lutheran Ministries of Georgia; Tom McAnally of the United Methodist Church; Alice Smith of North Georgia United Methodist Communications; Mark Westmoreland of *The Advocate*; Father Homer Goumenis of the Greek Orthodox Cathedral of Atlanta; Juleen Turnage of the Assemblies of God; David Krosh of the Church of God, General Conference; Jet Harper, James Hudnut-Beumler and T. Erskine Clarke of Columbia Theological Seminary; Jerry van Marter of the Presbyterian Church (U.S.A.); Perry Treadwell of the Atlanta Friends; and to others who answered my questions but whose names I neglected to record.

Thanks to Phyllis Tickle who urged me to attempt this and Gary Laderman, professor of religion at Emory University, who affirmed its usefulness.

Thanks to the *Atlanta Journal-Constitution*; to the Religion Newswriters Association; to the staff at the Columbia Theological Seminary library; and — although they did not help directly with this book — to the News Research staff of the *AJC* who have helped so many times for articles that contributed to the research.

Thanks to the authors of all the books, pamphlets and denominational press releases that fill my shelves and files as I cover religion.

Thanks especially to my agent, Greg Johnson of Alive Communications, for keeping the faith; and to editor Denise Silvestro and the copyeditors and designers at Berkley who patiently turned it into a book.

On a personal note, thanks to all my family, the moms, the aunts, Margaret, Bobby, and especially Bob, who did everything else so I could do this; to Barry and Connie, and Tina and Phil, the Cantina Crowd, and the English-Manderson group for being there; to the four churches that have shaped my life: Prospect Methodist; First United Methodist in Barnesville; Rehoboth Presbyterian in Decatur; and First Presbyterian, Atlanta, and to all the people who have nurtured me through them. Most of all, thanks be to God.

—Gayle White
August 19, 1997

CONTENTS

INTRODUCTION

MY Jewish boss's father just died. Should I take food to his family?

Can I take communion at my friend's Catholic wedding?

If you call a male Episcopal priest Father, what do you call a female priest?

Why won't the Jehovah's Witness girl in my daughter's class pledge allegiance to the flag?

These are some questions that readers, coworkers and friends have asked me as religion writer for *The Atlanta Journal-Constitution*.

Within a family of faith, religion represents a common link to the past and future. But religion can also be a wall that divides. Misunderstanding about beliefs and practices can cause animosity and intolerance.

In an increasingly multicultural world, our coworkers and neighbors—even members of our families—may be part of belief systems that are new to us. As we share each other's lives, we are invited to mark each other's milestones. And many of these are grounded in our religions.

How do we behave? What's the etiquette of interfaith relationships? How can we celebrate the things we have in common and respect the things that make us different?

Great reference works are available that tell us the histories and theological intricacies of the world's religions. Other volumes are available about specific religions, frequently written by and for scholars or practitioners.

This book is an overview. I hope it will serve as an introduction to what our neighbors believe and how they practice their faith, and as a guidebook to more extensive information. The reading lists at the end of each chapter and the general reference list at the end of the book offer suggestions for further study of works that were valuable in preparing this volume.

The first part of this book contains chapters on major world religions and on some American-born sects that incorporate aspects of Christianity. Confucianism, practiced in China along with Taoism and Buddhism, is excluded because it is often regarded as more a philosophy than a religion. Unitarianism, with few requirements and little dogma, is also missing.

Despite the growth of multiculturalism, an overwhelming percentage of people in the United States identify with some Christian group, and the second part of this book covers Christianity in its many forms.

Etiquette tips are listed wherever there is specific advice to give.

I hope this guidebook will help people in all walks of life understand each other's religions. It should be a handy reference for libraries, schools, newspapers, social secretaries, caterers and anyone in a business that might serve people from various backgrounds. I hope it can also be used by teachers and students as a supplementary text for classes on world cultures and religions.

Mostly, though, it is intended for people who want to talk intelligently about religions and interact comfortably with their acquaintances of other faiths.

BAHA'IS

*"Know thou assuredly that the essence of all
the Prophets of God is one and the same."*
—Baha'u'llah

THE Baha'i faith, less than two hundred years old, is relatively new among the world's religions. Its major teaching is religious unity. Baha'is believe that God sends prophets or messengers for each age, and thus Buddha, Moses, Muhammad and Jesus Christ are all regarded as the religious leaders for their ages.

The Baha'i faith claims some five million followers in more than two hundred countries and territories.

SYMBOL

The nine-pointed star is the symbol of the Baha'i faith. The number nine is believed to symbolize completeness.

ORIGINS

The Baha'i faith is most closely identified with a Persian man who took the name Baha'u'llah, meaning "Glory of God," but the religion actually traces its roots back a little earlier to a man named Siyyid Ali-Muhammad, who claimed in 1844 to be the Bab, or the gate, to the future. Bab predicted that a great prophet would soon follow him.

Bab claimed both his parents were direct descendants of Muhammad. Perhaps not surprisingly, the Islamic leaders in control of Persia resented his proclamation and had him assassinated in 1850. Although a few of his followers fought back, many of those who were not killed with him fled to what is today Iraq.

One of those who escaped was Mirza Husayn Ali. Born in 1817, he was from a wealthy Persian family. At age twenty-seven, he was introduced to the Bab's writings and took as his new name Glory of God or Baha'u'llah.

After the Bab's execution, Baha'u'llah was imprisoned along with others who had attempted to exact revenge on those who killed their leader. He avoided death, but his home was raided, its finery taken by the raiders, and he was exiled from Persia. He fled to Baghdad in Mesopotamia, now Iraq.

In 1863, he declared to a small group of fellow Babis, or followers of the Bab, that he was the messenger the Bab had predicted and soon after, he declared publicly that he was God's messenger, sent to bring unity to the world. Many former Babis accepted his claim and took the name Baha'is. He taught his followers to treat other religions with respect.

Baha'u'llah died on May 29, 1892, and his son, known as Abdul-Baha, or Servant of Baha, became leader of the Baha'is, and traveled around the world spreading the faith. He appointed his Oxford-educated grandson, Shoghi Effendi Rabbani, to follow him.

Since the death of Shoghi Effendi Rabbani in 1957, Baha'is have been governed by an elected nine-man International House of Justice as outlined in the writings of Baha'u'llah.

HOLY TEXTS

The writings of Baha'u'llah are the primary scriptures of the Baha'i faith. Followers believe his works were inspired by God. Among the best known of the more than one hundred works are:

The Kitab-i-Aqdas, or **The Most Holy Book**—Considered the most important of the scriptures, this was written while Baha'u'llah was in prison in Palestine. In it, he lays out the world order he would like to bring about.

Kitab-i-Iqan, or **The Book of Certitude**—This contains Baha'u'llah's teachings on God and religion.

The Hidden Words—The most popular of Baha'u'llah's work, this is a collection of verses that represent the essence of spiritual teachings of all religions.

DOCTRINE

God—Baha'is are monotheistic, believing in one God who created the universe. But they believe God has come to humankind through many different messengers—from Abraham to Zoroaster—who have founded the world's great religions. These messengers are human but manifest the attributes of the divine.

Good Deeds—Baha'is believe the highest form of worship is service to others.

Creation—The one God is the creator and ruler of the universe.

Humankind—Humans exist on earth in physical bodies, but they are actually spiritual beings with immortal souls that distinguish them from animals. All humankind should be united.

Angels—Angels are those who, through love of God, have excelled beyond human limitations and exist without human traits.

Sin—Baha'is have no concept of original sin. Evil is considered to be the absence of good.

The Devil—There is no evil in creation, but good can be used for ill. Baha'is do not accept the idea of a devil or Satan.

Judgment—Ultimately, one's fate after death depends on the use of this life. People who followed the will of God will be close to him after death, while others will be far from him.

Heaven—The paradise that awaits after death is considered indescribable and unknowable. In general, the faith teaches that people who have nurtured the proper qualities in this life will become closer to God after death.

Hell—The punishment for those who fail to develop the proper qualities in mortal life is remoteness from God in life and after death.

Miracles—There are no supernatural events, but there are events whose origins are beyond present human ability to understand.

Messiah—Baha'u'llah claimed to be sent by God to achieve world peace and unity. He said he was the figure awaited by all the world's major religions.

DOCTRINES SPECIFIC TO BAHA'I

The principles of the Baha'i faith are:

- The unity of humankind
- Universal peace upheld by a world federal system
- A common foundation of all religions
- Compatibility of science and religion
- Equality of men and women
- Elimination of prejudice
- Universal compulsory education
- Spiritual solutions to world problems
- Adoption of a universal auxiliary language

Because followers of the Baha'i faith are working for world unity, they do not participate in political parties, but may vote. Baha'is are expected to register as noncombatants in the military service.

The Baha'i faith accepts the Ten Commandments but expands its moral code, also forbidding promiscuity, gambling, alcohol, drugs, and gossip

Baha'is are obligated to leave a written will upon death.

CALENDAR

The Baha'i year is made up of nineteen months of nineteen days each. Each month is named after a quality of God. Four Intercalary Days (five in Leap Year)

are added between the eighteenth and nineteenth months so that the year will be the same length as that of the solar calendar. The year begins with the Spring Equinox on March 21st.

Splendor—Mar. 21–April 8
Glory—April 9–April 27
Beauty—April 28–May 16
Grandeur—May 17–June 4
Light—June 5–June 23
Mercy—June 24–July 12
Words—July 13–July 31
Perfection—Aug. 1–Aug. 19
Names—Aug. 20–Sept. 7
Might—Sept. 8–Sept. 26

Will—Sept. 27–Oct. 15
Knowledge—Oct. 16–Nov. 3
Power—Nov. 4–Nov. 22
Speech—Nov. 23–Dec. 11
Questions—Dec. 12–Dec. 30
Honor—Dec. 31–Jan. 18
Sovereignty—Jan. 19–Feb. 6
Dominion—Feb. 7–Feb. 25
Intercalary Days—Feb. 26–Mar. 1
Loftiness—Mar. 2–20

RELIGIOUS FESTIVALS AND HOLIDAYS

The Baha'i faith recognizes nine holy days on which followers should not work:

Feast of Naw-Ruz—March 21. This is the Baha'i New Year celebration.

Three days during the Feast of Ridvan—April 21–May 2. This period marks the anniversary of the Declaration of Baha'u'llah. The specific days of celebration are April 21, April 29 and May 2.

Anniversary of the Declaration of the Bab—May 23. On this day, Siyyid Ali Muhammad declared himself to be the Bab, or the Gate.

Anniversary of the Ascension of Baha'u'llah—May 29. The anniversary of the death of the founder of the faith in 1892.

Anniversary of the Martyrdom of the Bab—July 9. In 1850 on this date, the Bab, forerunner of Baha'u'llah, was executed.

Anniversary of the Birth of the Bab—Oct. 20.

Anniversary of the Birth of Baha'u'llah—Nov. 12.

The Period of the Fast is an important time of reflection for Baha'is. This runs for the last month of the Baha'i year, beginning March 2 and going for nineteen days. During this time, Baha'is are to refrain from eating or drinking from sunrise to sunset and devote their time to reflection. People under fifteen or over seventy, pregnant women, nursing mothers, those who are sick and those who must perform hard physical labor are excused.

Cards and gifts are not usually exchanged for Baha'i holy days. Friends should respect Baha'is' and offer encouragement and support during fast time. Wishes of Happy New Year are appropriate on March 21.

Two days are observed by Baha'is, but are not considered holy:

- **Day of the Covenant**—Nov. 26. Marks the appointment of Abdu'l-Baha, Baha'u'llah's oldest son, as preserver of the Covenant with God after his father's death.
- **Anniversary of the Ascension of Abdu'l-Baha**—Nov. 28. Marks the death of Baha'u'llah's son and successor.
- **The intercalary days, known as Ayyam-i-ha**, are a period of joy when people send cards and gifts, especially to the poor.

Cards and gifts may be given during the intercalary days.

ATTITUDE TOWARD OTHER HOLIDAYS

Baha'is may observe the holidays of the culture in which they live or work as they wish.

TITLES

There is no Baha'i clergy. There are no particular forms of address for Baha'i officers.

COMMUNITY WORSHIP

The Nineteen Day Feast—Held once every nineteen days on the beginning of a new month, this day is the closest equivalent of a Baha'i Sabbath. It is the time when the local Baha'i community gathers to worship, have fellowship and conduct business.

Baha'is have built at least one temple on each major continent. All have nine sides and nine entrances and all have central domes. All are open to people of any religion.

In most communities, services are held in more modest quarters. Worship consists of music without accompaniment of instruments, and recitation of Baha'i scriptures and scriptures of other religions.

Usually, only Baha'is attend the Nineteen Day Feast, although the non-Baha'i community may be invited on certain occasions. Non-Baha'is should not participate in the business portions.

PRIVATE WORSHIP

Followers of the Baha'i faith are expected to pray and read the scriptures daily, including reciting one of three obligatory prayers. They are encouraged to face Baha'u'llah's resting place in Israel as they pray. Before each prayer, they wash their faces and hands. At the end of each day, they are encouraged to reflect on the day's actions. In addition, all work performed well, especially for others, is considered worship.

Hosts entertaining a Baha'i should offer an opportunity to perform the ritual washing and prayer.

DRESS

There are no specific dress requirements for followers of the Baha'i Faith.

DIETARY LAWS

Consumption of alcohol is prohibited.

Alcohol is an inappropriate gift for Baha'is.

PLACE OF CHILDREN

Children are allowed to participate in Baha'i activities. The Baha'i faith places great emphasis on learning and requires a secular, as well as a religious, education for everyone. At fifteen, children are expected to observe the nineteen-day month of fasting and reflection.

ROLES OF MEN AND WOMEN

As a principle, men and women are regarded as equal. In fact, according to Baha'i writings, girls should be given preference over boys for educational resources. However, membership in the Universal House of Justice, the governing body of Baha'is, is limited to men. This limitation was specifically prescribed in the writings of the founder of the faith, Baha'u'llah.

HOUSEHOLD

Many Baha'is have in their home a framed representation of Baha'u'llah's name written in Persian. Otherwise, there are no special religious objects.

MILESTONES

Birth—There is no ceremony for infants.

Cards and gifts are appropriate for a new baby.

Marriage—Both parties and their parents must consent to marriage, according to Baha'i law. Because of the Baha'i emphasis on world unity, marriages across racial lines are encouraged.

For the wedding ceremony itself, the local Baha'i governing assembly appoints two witnesses to the marriage. In their presence, the couple must recite: "We will all, verily, abide by the will of God."

Otherwise, Baha'i weddings often reflect the culture in which they are held.

Weddings vary greatly. Guests are expected to participate as they feel comfortable and enjoy the festivities. Gifts and cards are appropriate.

Death—Baha'is do not have bodies embalmed unless legally required, and that they be buried, not cremated. The law of the faith says that a corpse should not be carried more than an hour's journey from the place of death for burial. The *Prayer for the Dead* should be said at the burial of any Baha'i over fifteen years old.

Cards, food, flowers and other expressions of sympathy are appropriate, as is visiting or calling the family.

CONVERSION

A declaration of the Baha'i faith may be made at any time to any Baha'i in any form, stated or written. Registering as a Baha'i is considered a formal commitment to the faith. Local administrators sign and forward a registration form to the national office.

MAJOR ORGANIZATIONS

National Spiritual Assembly of the Baha'is of the United States
536 Sheridan Road
Wilmette, Illinois 60091

FURTHER READING

Esslemont, J. E. *Baha'u'llah and the New Era*. third revised edition, Wilmette, Ill.: Pyramid Publishers, 1970.

Gaver, Jessyca Russell. *The Baha'i Faith*. New York: Hawthorne Books, Inc., 1967.

Hatcher, William S., and Martin, J. Douglas. *The Baha'i Faith*. San Francisco: Harper & Row, 1985.

BUDDHISTS

*"I go for refuge to the Buddha; I go for refuge to
the teachings; I go for refuge to the community."*
—*Universal Statement of Buddhism*

Some people debate whether Buddhism is a religion at all, or simply a philosophy.
Some people who practice aspects of Buddhism claim other theologies. Neverthe-
less, Buddhism is considered one of the world's five major religions—with Hinduism, Judaism, Islam and Christianity. There are an estimated three hundred
million Buddhists in the world, mostly in Asia.

Some schools of Buddhism are becoming increasingly popular in the United
States both because of immigration and because of the number of American converts or practitioners.

SYMBOL

The symbol of Buddhism is the eight-spoked wheel.

ORIGINS

Buddha actually means "the awakened one," but is also the title that was
given to Siddhartha Gautama, known as Siddhatta Gotama, born about 566 B.C.E.
into a royal family in what is now Nepal.

According to some, the prince's mother, the incredibly beautiful Queen Ma-
hamaya, dreamed on the night of his conception that a white elephant had entered
her womb—a sign that her child would be special. Others say that shortly after his
birth, a soothsayer prophesied that Siddhartha would be either a great king or a
man of great holiness.

Siddhartha's mother died shortly after his birth. His father's wealth and power ensured that Siddhartha grew up surrounded with luxury. He was protected as much as possible from any unpleasantness.

Despite his apparently pleasant life, at about age twenty-nine, Siddhartha grew restless and began to venture off the palace grounds. On his excursions, he saw images that changed the course of his life and led to the establishment of Buddhism:

- On his first outing, he is said to have seen an old man with a bent back and learned that everyone who does not die young eventually weakens and loses youthful beauty.
- On his next trip, he saw a diseased man covered with flies and learned that disease does not discriminate but can attack anyone.
- His third venture exposed him to a corpse being carried to cremation surrounded by mourners, a sight that impressed him with the inevitability of death.
- On his fourth time out of the palace, he met a wandering holy man collecting alms.

While the first three sights impressed him with humankind's lack of control over destiny, the fourth is said to have shown him the measure of peace that can come when one accepts this inevitability and searches for satisfaction in the spiritual realm.

Siddhartha left home, cut off his hair and beard, exchanged his elaborate clothes for simple robes and began his spiritual search. After several false starts, including a period of self-mortification and asceticism that left him emaciated, Siddhartha sat alone and motionless under a fig tree contemplating the situation. According to tradition, Mara, the Evil One, called up demons to challenge him and beautiful spirits to deter him from the path to enlightenment. But Siddhartha persisted. Enlightenment came to him as the morning star rose after a full moon. He suddenly was able to recall his past lives and he realized the secrets of the universe.

After his awakening, Siddhartha, now the Buddha, encountered some former companions from his days as an ascetic. Realizing his transformation, they became his first followers.

The Buddha continued to travel and teach both men and women for more than forty years, living modestly and depending on alms. He died at the age of eighty, possibly of food poisoning, while lying on his right side with his head resting on his hand—a pose often portrayed in Buddhist art. With his last breaths, he instructed his followers to work out their own liberation.

The Buddha named no successor and left no documents, but his followers had memorized his words and continued to teach. With the conversion of Ashok, king of northern India, in about the third century B.C.E., Buddhism gained a boost. A community of monks and nuns was established that spread the doctrine as far as Persia. By the first century A.D., Buddhism was known in China, and moved from there into other parts of Asia. Buddhism eventually developed into different schools, each with its own traditions.

HOLY TEXTS

Buddha's teachings were passed on orally for many years but now the *sutras*, or Buddha's teachings, and the *sastras*, or commentaries, fill volumes.

DIVISIONS

Over a few centuries after the death of Siddhartha, Buddhism divided into several schools. The three main paths, or vehicles, of Buddhism are:

Theravada—literally "way of the elders." Theravada is the dominant form of Buddhism in Bangladesh, Burma, Cambodia, Ceylon, Kampuchea, Laos, Sri Lanka and Thailand. Theravadans emphasize the religious life of monks and nuns, and see monastic vows as necessary to become an *arhat* or fully liberated saint. Laypeople take food and clothes to monks in practices of generosity they hope will help them have a rebirth as a monk or nun, and hence stand a better chance of achieving enlightenment.

Theravadans tend to see Buddha as a human, historical figure and to emphasize the individual struggle for enlightenment over the interconnectedness of humankind.

Mahayana—literally, the "greater vehicle." Mahayana is most popular in China, Japan, Korea, Mongolia and Tibet. This school takes a transcendental approach to Buddhism, regarding the historical Buddha and the ancestral line of teachers that followed as enlightened figures who can assist those still struggling along the path to Nirvana. The Mahayana school emphasizes the ability of everyone, not just monks and nuns, to find liberation, and teaches that people are interdependent and obligated to help each other along the path.

For Mahayanas, the ideal is the *bodhisattva*, or "enlightenment being," who postpones entering nirvana in order to work for the enlightenment of all of humankind. Bodhisattvas may be future buddhas who are living on earth as men and women, or those who have attained buddhahood but have not entered complete nirvana. In either case, they are motivated by altruism to help save others.

Within Mahayana Buddhism, there are different historic subschools with origins in different countries or regions. In the West, the best-known of these subschools is Zen Buddhism, which rejects religious ritual, reasoning and dogma but stresses self-realization through expansion of consciousness.

Vajrayana—literally, "diamond" or "indestructible." This school arose largely in northeast and northwest India, but moved into Tibet, China and Japan. The goal of its followers is buddhahood within a single lifetime. The Vajrayana school incorporates magical practices and highly developed rituals. Practitioners of this form of Buddhism often chant special syllables, or mantras. They meditate on designs called *mandalas*, which symbolize cosmic forces. And they use hand gestures called *mudras*. A well-known branch of Vajrayana Buddism is Lamaism, or

Tibetan Buddhism, which regards logic as an aid to understanding. The Dalai Lama is the spiritual leader. Each dalai lama is considered a reincarnation of his predecessors, and is expected to be able to identify his successor.

DOCTRINE

God—Buddha himself did not claim divinity nor did he point to any other deity.

Good Deeds—Doing kindness to others helps elevate the condition that one will be born into after the next rebirth.

Creation—Buddha did not teach that creation was divine.

Humankind—Because of a lack of enlightenment, humans are trapped in *karma*, a series of causes and effects, actions and reactions.

Angels—Some branches of Buddhism teach that spiritual guides help humans on the path toward enlightenment.

Sin—Buddhism readily recognizes the shortcomings, temptations and selfish natures of humans but says they can be overcome by following the proper path.

The Devil—Mara, sometimes depicted with one hundred arms riding on an elephant, symbolizes the evil temptations that can conquer human beings.

Judgment—Actions in this life determine the state of birth in the next. Thus judgment is rendered in an evolutionary process through a series of lifetimes.

Heaven—Buddhists attempt to achieve a state of nirvana, or absolute peace in the absence of suffering. It is regarded as the culmination of a process that may have lasted many lifetimes.

Hell—There is no Buddhist version of hell or eternal punishment.

Miracles—Buddhists have no doctrine of miracles, but believe one's thoughts and actions determine consequences.

The Messiah—There is no messiah figure in Buddhism.

DOCTRINES SPECIFIC TO BUDDHISM

FOUR NOBLE TRUTHS

It is said that the Buddha outlined these truths to his first followers shortly after his enlightenment:

- Suffering is inherent in life.
- Craving sensual pleasure causes suffering.
- Nirvana—release from suffering—comes about by the elimination of selfish, sensual and material desires.
- The path leading to the end of suffering is eightfold. It is not linear, but all parts are integrated.

THE EIGHTFOLD PATH
1. Understanding—A correct outlook based on the Four Noble Truths
2. Intention—The wish to avoid harm
3. Speech—Avoidance of slander, gossip and falsehood
4. Conduct—Moral action
5. Livelihood—Employment that is not harmful to others
6. Effort—Attempting to focus the mind on good thoughts
7. Mindfulness—Integration of feelings and thought
8. Contemplation—Disciplining the mind through meditation

Buddhism teaches that to succeed on the eightfold path and realize liberation, one must overcome three poisons: ignorance, hatred, and desire.

One must embrace the three essential components of Buddhism, also known as the Three Jewels or Three Refuges: *Buddha*—the enlightened one; *Dharma*—the universal truth of his teachings; and *Sangha*—the followers living in harmony with these truths.

Buddhist ethical conduct requires abstention from some traits and cultivation of others:

- Avoid harm; practice kindness
- Avoid taking what is not given; practice generosity
- Avoid sexual misconduct; practice contentment
- Avoid false speech; practice truthfulness
- Avoid intoxicants; practice awareness

Buddhists undertaking a religious life as monks or nuns should be prepared to abide by five additional precepts:

- Abstention from untimely meals
- Abstention from dancing and music
- Abstention from personal adornment and perfume
- Abstention from high seats
- Abstention from silver and gold

CALENDAR

Buddhists use the lunar calendar, beginning the year with the full-moon day on which the Buddha was said to be born.

The lunar months, beginning with the full moon in May, are:

Vesaka   Kattika
Jethamasa   Maghasira
Asalha   Phussa
Savana   Magha
Potthapada   Phagguna
Assayuja   Chittamasa

RELIGIOUS FESTIVALS AND HOLIDAYS

Buddhist festivals vary by country and tradition, but many are held on full-moon days. Here are some more common ones among the largest divisions:

THERAVADA FESTIVALS
Wesak—The main festival of Theravada. Celebrates the birth, death and enlightenment of Buddha at once on the full-moon day of the second lunar month. People wear white and give alms. Flags, lanterns and flowers are a part of the festivities.

Kathina—Almsgiving. People give cloth to monks for robes and fasten money to a money tree.

TIBETAN FESTIVALS
Losar—New Year. A fifteen-day festival in February, this commemorates Buddha's life until his enlightenment. On the last day of the old year, people eat dumplings stuffed with different ingredients, not distinguishable until they are tasted. The stuffing of the dumpling one happens to eat foretells the type of year to come. A lump of coal in a dumpling means a bad year. Leftovers are collected and put by the roadside to draw evil spirits from the old year out of the home. Monks carry big cones with death's-heads on top, representing the community's accumulated evil, to be burned.

Saga Dawa—Celebrated on the fifteenth day of the fourth month, this holiday recognizes Buddha's birth, death and enlightenment. Buddhists forgo meat, light lamps and make their way clockwise around Buddhist monuments by lying down, standing up where the head is, and lying down again. The most devout pledge seven days of fasting and silence.

ZEN FESTIVALS (JAPAN USES THE WESTERN CALENDAR)
Vaishakha Festival—On the eighth and ninth day of the second lunar month, this festival celebrates the month in which Buddha was born and acknowledges Buddha's enlightenment and his death.

Ullambana—Also known as the Festival of the Hungry Ghosts, this celebration for the soul of the departed is widely observed in Japan and China on the fifteenth day of the seventh lunar month. It includes visits to the temple.

In most cases, guests only have to enjoy the festivities. If they enter some parts of the temples, guests will be expected to remove their shoes.

ATTITUDE TOWARD OTHER HOLIDAYS

Buddhists typically celebrate the holidays of the culture in which they live and work.

TITLES

Priest—leads worship in a temple.
President, superintendent or abbot—presides over a Buddhist center.
Lama—teacher or guru in Tibetan Buddhism.
Roshi—a Zen master.

COMMUNITY WORSHIP

On the days of the full moon, many Buddhist visit temples to pledge eight vows—five of which apply to every day and three specifically for the full-moon day:

- Not to do harm
- Not to steal
- Not to lie or defame anyone
- Not to use intoxicants
- Not to be sexually promiscuous
- Not to eat after noon on the full-moon day

- Not to use cosmetics or scents on the full-moon day
- Not to sit or recline in luxury on the full-moon day

Other Buddhists visit centers regularly to study and meditate as part of a group. At a meditation center, they bow to each other and to the statue of Buddha in the room, and kneel on cushions, spending time in silent meditation. A leader will ring a bell to indicate the beginning and end of meditation time.

Guests should sit silently during times of meditation. If the group chants to prepare for meditation, a guest may join in. Guests should not enter or leave while a group is meditating.

PRIVATE WORSHIP

Many Buddhists meditate at home sitting or kneeling on cushions. Some Buddhists use prayer beads to keep their focus as they meditate. Tibetan and Chinese prayer beads usually have 108 beads; Japanese may have fewer.

Friends should be silent and respectful when a Buddhist is meditating. If entertaining a Buddhist guest in the home, hosts should offer a place and time for meditation.

DRESS

Buddhists may wear the customary clothes of the culture in which they live. On full-moon days when they visit the temple, they usually wear plain white clothes. Buddhist monks traditionally shave their heads and wear distinctive orange-red robes. Buddhists usually remove their shoes for worship or meditation.

In most Buddhist temples and centers, shoes are removed. Watch other worshipers and follow their lead. In any event, it would not be wrong to remove your shoes, but it might be wrong to keep them on. Loose, comfortable clothes are best for guests who expect to kneel and participate.

DIETARY LAWS

Different branches of Buddhism have different dietary laws; some require vegetarianism. In general, Buddhists are encouraged to eat healthy, locally grown foods.

If entertaining Buddhists for a meal, it is best to ascertain whether they are vegetarians. If that cannot be determined, offer a variety of foods so that meat can be gracefully avoided.

PLACE OF CHILDREN

Most sects of Buddhism have no initiation ceremony for children, although some Japanese Buddhists have a brief ceremony known as a *jukai*. *Jukai* means "receiving the precepts" or officially becoming a lay Buddhist. In the ceremony, a person commits to practice Buddhism, avoid evil, do good and strive for enlightenment.

ROLES OF MEN AND WOMEN

Although both men and women can be part of Buddhist religious orders, nuns are usually given work that is subservient to monks. Both men and women are regarded as able to achieve ultimate liberation, however.

Within the family, husbands are expected to be respectful and faithful and to support their wives; women are expected to be diligent in performance of household duties, hospitable to relatives and faithful to their husbands.

When greeting a Buddhist, it is best to wait to see whether a hand is offered. In some cultures where Buddhism is popular, touching is considered inappropriate. A bow is always appropriate.

HOUSEHOLD

Buddhist families often have home shrines that feature a statue of Buddha prominently displayed. The family may offer flowers, candles, incense and food as gestures of worship.

Guests in a household should show respect for the family Buddha.

MILESTONES

Birth—A pregnant woman may visit a temple to ask monks to bless her child. After its birth, the child is taken again to the temple for a blessing.

Guests are not usually included at the blessing of a new baby. Gifts and cards are appropriate for the baby and its parents.

Marriage—Buddhism considers marriage a civil, not a religious, ceremony, but weddings may include chanting from the scriptures.

Gifts and cards are acceptable for the bride and groom.

Death—Although birth and marriage are marked with little or no religious ceremony in Buddhism, death is observed with greater ritual. Buddhists see death as a transition to rebirth unless one has achieved nirvana, the end of suffering and the end of the birth-death-rebirth cycle.

Dying people should have Buddhist scripture recited to them to remind them of the Buddha's teaching and encourage them for the transition from one life to the next. Buddhists believe that a person's attitude in death will help determine the condition into which he is reborn.

The body of the deceased may stay with relatives until it is cremated—the usual method of disposal—usually three days after death. Funerals are conducted by monks, who chant scripture and remind those present of the impermanence of each life.

In many Buddhist traditions, relatives are also expected to arrange a memorial service after cremation that will include charitable gifts. The ceremony may be repeated on the anniversaries of a death. Some Buddhist traditions have ceremonies seven days and ninety days after the death as well.

Most Buddhist funerals include an open casket. Guests should view the body and bow slightly. Cards, flowers and donations to charities are appropriate remembrances, but food should not be taken to the bereaved family. In fact, it is considered inappropriate to communicate with mourners until after the funeral.

CONVERSION

People usually become Buddhists by studying with a teacher or attending a center or temple. There is no form of baptism, but a student may receive the precepts and a Buddhist name in an initiation ceremony.

MAJOR ORGANIZATIONS

Buddhist Church of America
1710 Octavia Street
San Francisco, California 94109

Tibet House
241 E. 32nd Street
New York, New York 10016

Atlanta Soto Zen Center
1404 McLendon Avenue, N.E.
Atlanta, Georgia 30307

FURTHER READING

Aitkin, Robert, and Steindl-Rast, David. *The Ground We Share, Everyday Practice Buddhist and Christian.* Liguori, Mo.: Triumph Books, 1994.

Erricker, Clive. *Buddhism, a Teach Yourself Book.* Lincolnwood, Ill.: NTC Publishing Company, 1995.

Hope, Jane, and Van Loon, Borin. *Introducing Buddha.* Totem Books, 1995

Humphries, Chistmas. *Popular Dictionary of Buddhism.* London and Dublin: Curza Press Ltd., 1975.

Percheron, Maurice. *Buddha and Buddhism.* London: Longmans, Green and Co. Ltd., 1957.

Thurman, Robert A. F. *Essential Tibetan Buddhism.* San Francisco: HarperSan Francisco, 1995.

Thurman, Robert A. F. *Inside Tibetan Buddhism.* San Francisco: Collins Publishers, 1995.

FOR CHILDREN

Samarasekara, Dhanapala, and Samarasekara, Udeni. *I am a Buddhist.* New York: Franklin Watts Inc., 1986.

CHRISTIAN SCIENTISTS

"Truth, in divine Science, is the stepping-stone
to the understanding of God."
—Mary Baker Eddy

THE Church of Christ, Scientist, better known as the Christian Science church, is an American movement born of a woman. From its Mother Church in Boston, the church has established 2,300 branch churches in more than sixty countries. The church does not count members, but claims thousands of followers.

Christian Scientists believe the spiritual has power over the physical and that healing can come through prayer and spiritual communion with God. They reject the term "faith healing," but say healing comes when a sick or injured person becomes more fully aligned with God.

Christian Scientists usually make news because of their refusal to accept medical treatment from physicians or hospitals. Especially when children are involved, their reliance on church-related practitioners sometimes becomes controversial.

SYMBOL

A cross and crown surrounded by a circle appears on the official versions of the writings of Mary Baker Eddy, the founder of Christian Science, as a symbol of the church.

ORIGINS

Mary Baker Eddy, was a sheltered, sickly child. The youngest of six children, born in 1821 to strict, religious parents, she was raised on a farm in Bow, New Hampshire. She grew up in the Congregational church and joined as a teenager, despite steadfastly refusing in an interview with church elders to endorse the doctrine of predestination that says God determines in advance who will be saved to go to heaven.

In 1862, because of her poor health, Eddy sought treatment from Phineas P. Quimby, a Portland, Maine, advocate of mind-over-matter healing. Eddy "discovered" Christian Science shortly after her friend Quimby died in 1866. As the story goes, on February 1, 1866, Eddy injured her back when she slipped on a patch of ice. Although she was unable to walk for several days, Eddy, reading the account in the New Testament Gospel of Matthew of one of Jesus's healings, concluded that she had been healed. She got up, dressed and walked out to greet some friends.

The incident set off years of study. In 1870, Eddy taught her first Christian Science class to a small group in Lynn, Massachusetts. Five years later, the first edition of her book *Science and Health,* now know as *Science and Health with Key to the Scriptures,* was published. Four years later, the Church of Christ, Scientist was born. This congregation in Boston is known as the Mother Church. She also founded the Massachusetts Metaphysical College to teach the Christian Science approach to health.

Eddy remained active in Christian Science writing and teaching until her death in 1910.

HOLY TEXTS

Christian Scientists base their beliefs on the Bible and use the King James Version in their studies, but they also give great weight to *Science and Health With Key to the Scriptures,* by church founder Mary Baker Eddy. Considered the textbook of the movement, it includes the church's teachings.

DOCTRINE

God—According to Christian Science teachings, God is Divine Mind with both male and female aspects, the Father-Mother of the universe.

Good Deeds—There are many references to the Golden Rule in the work of Mary Baker Eddy, and the church teaches it should underlie all actions.

Creation—God is the creator of all things and his creation is spiritual in nature.

Humankind—Human beings are created in the image of God, are spiritual in origin and nature, and therefore governed by spiritual laws. But their spiritually perfect identity is crossed with a mortal body.

Angels—The definition of angels in *Science and Health* says angels are "God's thoughts passing to man; spiritual intuitions, pure and perfect; the inspiration of goodness, purity and immortality, counteracting all evil, sensuality and mortality."

Sin—Sin is caused by humans who try to live apart from God.

The Devil—Evil, according to Christian Scientists, is neither created nor empowered by God but its power comes only from the human mind.

Judgment—Church founder Mary Baker Eddy taught that judgment comes daily and hourly, but that no final judgment awaits mortals.

Heaven—Christian Scientists accept heaven as the state of mind where God is supreme and harmony reigns.

Hell—The church regards hell as the state of mind of those who do evil, or separate themselves from God. Eddy taught that sinners create their own hell by doing evil deeds.

Miracles—Christian Scientists believe the miracles of Jesus as described in the New Testament illustrate a divine principle that healing and regeneration can continue through spiritual healing of the mind. They see so-called miracles as natural manifestations of God's law.

Messiah—Christian Scientists believe Jesus was the messiah, and that Christ expresses God's spiritual, eternal nature and that he is therefore always present. They do not teach that Jesus will come again physically.

DOCTRINES SPECIFIC TO CHRISTIAN SCIENTISTS

Christian Scientists believe that physical healing can come through prayer and spiritual communion with God, and they generally reject medical treatment from physicians and hospitals.

Eddy's writings specifically prohibit church members from learning hypnotism.

Members are required to pay a per-capita tax of at least one dollar annually to the Mother Church. Most Christian Scientists are affiliated with both a local congregation and the Mother Church in Boston.

CALENDAR

The Church of Christ, Scientist uses the calendar commonly used in the United States.

RELIGIOUS FESTIVALS AND HOLIDAYS

The only holiday given special treatment within the Christian Science church is Thanksgiving. On that day, Christian Scientists gather in their churches for special readings and testimonials.

Christian Scientists observe communion twice a year, on the second Sunday in January and the second Sunday in July. Unlike most Christian traditions, this is not a sharing of bread and wine. The congregation kneels for silent prayer, then says the Lord's Prayer together.

Visitors are invited to participate fully in communion as they feel comfortable.

ATTITUDE TOWARD OTHER HOLIDAYS

In her *Church Manual,* Mary Baker Eddy specifically says "there shall be no special observances, festivities, nor gifts at the Easter season. . . ."

Christian Scientists vary greatly in their attitudes toward birthdays. Because the church does not take note of time or age, some ignore birthdays altogether, while others have observations they do not specifically call birthday parties.

They celebrate other holidays of the culture in which they live or work.

Christian Scientists should not be included in Easter-related activities.

TITLES

Nurse—Someone trained to provide non-medical care according to Christian Science teachings.

Practitioner—Someone recognized by the church to practice Christian Science healing through prayer.

Reader—A lay person elected to conduct the regular weekly services in a Christian Science church.

Teacher—A practitioner who has been trained by the church to teach Christian Science.

COMMUNITY WORSHIP

Christian Scientists gather for the Sabbath on Sunday mornings for singing, prayer and reading of both the King James Bible and *Science and Health with Key to the Scriptures,* written by Mary Baker Eddy. The church publishes a schedule of twenty-six topics, each of which comes up twice a year in the same order. The order of the service, beginning with a hymn and ending with reading of the "Scientific Statement of Being" from "Science and Health . . ." and I John 3: 1-3 from the New Testament, was laid out by Eddy in her writings. "Organ or piano music of an appropriate character" is a part of services whenever possible, according to Eddy's teachings.

Each service is to be conducted by two readers (in the Mother Church, one must be male and one female). Readers are required to state Mary Baker Eddy's name before presenting any of her writings. During the recitation of the Lord's Prayer, a regular feature of Sunday and communion services, the First Reader responds to each verse with a reading from *Science and Health.*

Church members also meet on Wednesday evenings, as required in the "Church Manual." These meetings also consist of readings from the Bible and "Science and Health . . . ," prayer, hymns and sharing of experiences.

Although some exteriors are elaborate, the main parts of the interiors of most Christian Scientist churches are simply decorated auditoriums without religious art or icons. There will likely be a separate room or rooms for Sunday School, which children are expected to attend until they are twenty. There probably will not be a kitchen or social hall, since Christian Science churches are expected to be devoted entirely to religious study.

Each church sponsors a Reading Room, where Christian Science materials may be bought or borrowed, and an annual lecture to address public topics from a Christian Science point of view is given.

Christian Scientists welcome people of all faiths and denominations to their services. In fact, members are urged to give up seats to any visitors if necessary. Guests should participate as they feel comfortable.

PRIVATE WORSHIP

Each member is expected to pray daily, and to read regularly from the Bible and the work of Mary Baker Eddy.

DRESS

There are no specific dress requirements for Christian Scientists.

DIETARY LAWS

Christian Scientists are expected not to drink alcohol, smoke or take drugs.

Alcohol is an inappropriate gift for Christian Scientists. When entertaining Christian Scientists, alternatives to alcoholic drinks should be offered.

PLACE OF CHILDREN

Children, usually when twelve years old, are regarded as equal members in the church if their applications are approved. They are expected to participate in Sunday School until age twenty. Christian Science Sunday School is serious study, without crafts or games. Even pre-school children are taught the rudiments of the faith.

ROLES OF MEN AND WOMEN

The Christian Science movement was founded by a woman, and so there is no question that women and men can function equally within the Church of Christ, Scientist. Church founder Mary Baker Eddy sometimes referred in her writings to

God as Mother or as Father-Mother. Offices in the church are supposed to be filled without reference to gender. Both men and women serve at all levels of the church.

HOUSEHOLD

There are no specific religious objects for the households of Christian Scientists. Most homes would be marked only by the presence of the written work of Mary Baker Eddy and the absence of medicines.

Non-Christian Scientists should respect Christian Scientist preference for prayer rather than medical treatment whenever possible.

MILESTONES

Birth—Although a birth is regarded as a joyous occasion, there is no infant baptism or other blessing of infants within the Christian Science church.

Gifts and cards are appropriate for new babies and parents.

Marriage—Christian Scientists do not regard a wedding as a ceremony of the religion and, since the church has no clergy, there is no one to perform a ceremony. Christian Scientists who marry have civil ceremonies or ceremonies performed by ministers of other denominations.

Wedding gifts and cards are appropriate.

Death—Christian Scientists usually use the term ''passed on'' to mark the end of a mortal life to show that they believe life goes on immortally.

The church has no funeral ceremony and Christian Scientists do not have funerals in church. Families who choose to have funerals may opt for a funeral home or another kind of public chapel where friends may be asked to give readings from the Bible and from the work of Mary Baker Eddy. Mary Baker Eddy recommended that the bodies of female church members be prepared by other women.

Flowers, cards and gestures of support are appropriate.

CONVERSION

To join The Mother Church or a branch Church of Christ, Scientist, a potential member must subscribe to the teachings of founder Mary Baker Eddy. The church accepts members from other denominations only after they have dissolved all ties with the previous church. Children, at age twelve or after, are allowed to join.

Potential members of the Mother Church must make applications and be sponsored by two members. The church manual states that names must be plainly written, that married women should use their own given names, and that women should sign "Miss" or "Mrs." before their names.

Membership applications are acted upon by the Christian Science Board of Directors at semi-annual meetings.

Members may be excommunicated for severe violations of church teaching.

MAJOR ORGANIZATIONS

First Church of Christ, Scientist
175 Huntington Avenue, A172
Boston, Massachusetts 02115

FURTHER READING

Christian Science—A Sourcebook of Contemporary Materials. Boston: The Christian Science Publishing Society, 1990.

John, Dewitt. *The Christian Science Way of Life.* Boston: The Christian Science Publishing Society, 1962, 1990.

Eddy, Mary Baker. *Church Manual of The First Church of Christ, Scientist in Boston, Massachusetts.* Boston: The First Church of Christ, Scientist, 1895.

Eddy, Mary Baker. *Science and Health with Key to the Scriptures.* Boston, Massachusetts: The First Church of Christ, Scientist, 1934.

Peel, Robert. *Health and Medicine in the Christian Science Tradition.* New York: Crossroad Publishing Company, 1988.

HINDUS

"Truth is One; sages call it by various names."
—The Rig Veda 1:164:46

H INDUISM, like the country India, takes its name from the Sanskrit word Sindhu, for the Indus River. Indian Hindus usually prefer to call their religion by the Sanskrit term for eternal truth, *Sanatana dharma*.

Hindu organizations project that by the year 2001, one sixth of the world population will be Hindus. As of 1993, according to *Hinduism Today* magazine, 816 million Hindus were scattered around the globe, with more than 760 million of them in India.

The Hindu population in the United States increased drastically with changes in immigration laws in the mid-1960s. More than 650,000 Hindus are estimated to live in the United States.

SYMBOL

Om, or *Aum*, is the Sanskrit term that represents ultimate truth for Hindus. This is also the sacred sound chanted by Hindus in meditation.

ORIGINS

Hinduism is one of the world's oldest religions, and cannot be traced back to a single founder. Rather, it evolved over thousands of years in India. Some scholars say modern Hinduism really began to take shape when the light-skinned Aryans invaded northwest India sometime before 1200 B.C.E. and incorporated some of the religious practices of the darker-skinned native Dravidians with their own. The Aryans worshipped a variety of gods who represented the forces of nature. The natives had their own deities, including a mother goddess. The mingling of these two groups and their beliefs gave rise to Hinduism as it is known today.

HOLY TEXTS

The Vedas—Sanskrit for "sacred teaching." The Vedas originally served as priestly manuals and were handed down orally. They were said to have originated with the Rishis, or great seers. The oldest written version dates to about the 14th century.

The Rig Veda—Consists mostly of 1028 hymns and liturgies to 33 gods.

The Yajur Veda—Details the ceremonies for sacrifices.

The Sama Veda—Contains 1,549 verses, mostly from the Rig Veda, set to music for a cantor.

The Atharva Veda—Includes 731 hymns, some of them from the Rig Veda, and is a mixture of prose and verse including incantations, charms and curses.

The Upanishads—The concluding part of the Vedas. These short essays were written around the 6th century B.C.E. and represent commentaries or lessons on the Vedas.

Other holy texts include:

Bhagavadgita—The Sanskrit word for the "Lord's Song." This 700-verse poem is a dialogue between the god Krishna and his disciple the warrior hero Arjuna. This poem is part of a 106,000-verse epic called the Mahabharata.

The Ramayana—This epic poem is literally "the life story of Rama," told in 24,000 couplets.

The Puranas—Literally "ancient narratives." They are written in verse form as a dialogue between teacher and student and contain the stories of Hindu mythology as well as instructions for Hindus in their lives.

There are no special rules for handling the Hindu scriptures. However, some very strict Hindus regard all written material with such great respect that they refuse to step on writing. Non-Hindus should be aware of this in cases where plaques might be imbedded in the floor or newspapers spread over an area.

DIVISIONS

Many Hindus primarily worship one of the three major deities, and are thus identified with Vaishnavism, or Vishnu worship; Shaivism, or Shiva worship; or Shaktism, also called Tantrism, or worship of the goddess Shakti.

In the United States, perhaps the most visible Hindu-related group is the International Society for Krishna Consciousness, or ISKCON, better known as the Hare Krishnas. ISKCON was founded in New York in August 1966 by Indian immigrant Srila Prabhupada, a few days before his seventieth birthday. ISKCON regards Krishna, an incarnation of the Hindu god Vishu, as "the supreme personality of the godhead." Male Hare Krishnas shave their heads, sometimes leaving ponytails growing from the crown, considered a sacred spot.

Internationally, ISKCON has three hundred temples and forty rural communities in seventy-one countries.

DOCTRINE

God—Hindus generally accept that there is one supreme deity, but believe there are many valid paths to the supreme being. Hindus also recognize a range of gods with particular responsibilities and characteristics who are different manifestations of the one supreme being.

Good Deeds—*Karma,* the law of cause and effect, means that each individual determines his own destiny by his thoughts and deeds. Thus, good deeds create good karma, or *punyam,* and ensure good results; bad deeds create bad karma, or *papam,* and ensure bad results.

Creation—There is no beginning or end, but a continuous cycle of creation and dissolution.

Humankind—Every individual carries the essence of divinity, known as the soul or the *atman.* Individuals bear ultimate responsibility for their own destiny, but should recognize their interdependence with the gods.

Angels—Hindus recognize the existence of many divine beings, including the gods, who may serve as protective spirits.

Sin—Everyone sins or commits wrongdoing because of ignorance, and each sin has its price socially and spiritually. But Hindus think of sin as violation of order and not as an offense against a personal moral God. Sin will bring about bad karma or *papam.*

The Devil—Hinduism has no concept of a specific devil, or personification of evil, but sees the world as populated with both good and bad beings.

Judgment—Actions in life determine the path of the soul after death; judgment comes in the form one takes in the next life, until one escapes the cycle of incarnation, death and reincarnation.

Heaven—All souls eventually can find liberation, known as *brahman* or *paramatman,* a pure, indescribable transcendence.

Hell—There is no physical place where evil souls go, although they may suffer between lives for their bad deeds.

Miracles—Hinduism recognizes the possibility of miracles. Hindu mythology is full of stories of miracles.

Messiah—Hindus recognize no messiah per se, but do expect the Kalki, the last incarnation of the god Vishnu, to arrive on a white horse at the end of the Age of Darkness to conquer death.

DOCTRINES SPECIFIC TO HINDUISM

All life forms are regarded as important and of a divine nature. An emphasis on taking care of the environment and respecting the natural world follow from this. In Hinduism, cows especially are revered as symbolic of the natural world because cows give nourishment through their milk.

There are dozens, if not hundreds of gods, goddesses and semi-divine figures in Hinduism. Here's a sampling of some of the best known:

Vishnu—One of the trinity of Hinduism (with Brahma and Shiva), Vishnu is regarded as protector of the universe. He is believed to have come to earth in a variety of forms, or avatars, at different times for different purposes. Among the best known incarnations are Rama and Krisha.

Brahma—The second god in the trinity, he is usually depicted with four faces. He is in charge of creation.

Hanuman—A monkey god known for physical strength and his heroism in service to the god Rama, as told in the Ramayana.

Lakshmi—Goddess of prosperity and wife of Vishnu.

Agni—Fire, worshipped as a god.

Shiva—The Destroyer, the third god in the Hindu trinity, known in the Vedas as Rudra. Shiva is the god of destruction and regeneration.

Shakti—The Supreme Mother and consort of Shiva, Shakti is also personified as Durga, Parvati, Kali and Uma.

Ganesha—An elephant-headed god known as a remover of obstacles.

CALENDAR

The Hindu calendar is lunar-solar. It is divided into twelve lunar months varying in length from twenty-nine to thirty-two days, and each month is divided into a dark and a bright half. An extra month is inserted once every three years to balance the difference between lunar and solar years so that the lunar months roughly correspond to months on the Gregorian calendar. The extra month comes after a month with two new moons and takes the name of the month before it.

The months of the Hindu calendar are:

Chaitra (March–April)   Asvayuja (September–October)
Vaisakha (April–May)   Kartika (October–November)
Jyeshta (May–June)   Margasira (November–December)
Ashadha (June–July)   Pushya (December–January)
Svavana (July–August)   Magha (January–February)
Bhadrapada (August–September)   Phalguna (February–March)

RELIGIOUS FESTIVALS AND HOLIDAYS

As a religion with many deities, Hinduism also has many holidays. Celebrations vary in custom and importance from one area to another. Here are just a few of the most important festivals.

Shivaratri—A winter festival celebrating Lord Shiva with singing, dancing and food.

Ramanavami—A spring festival celebrating the birth of Lord Rama, during which the story of Rama is read all day without ceasing.

Krishna Janmashtami—Krishna's late-summer birthday celebration continues until midnight since it is believed Krishna was born at night; festivities include worship, singing, dancing and feasting.

Deepavali or Diwali—The festival of lights, celebrated in the fall with lamps and fireworks. Friends exchange gifts and sweets during this time.

Sankranthi—A harvest festival when people celebrate the bounty with new clothes and gifts.

Guru Purnima—A summer holiday when one shows gratitude to spiritual teachers.

Raksha Bandham—A summer holiday for sisters. A girl ties a yellow thread around her brother's wrist and the brother gives her a present and promises to protect her.

When in a Hindu home or temple, guests should remove their shoes and show respect for the gods. They are invited to participate in the festivities as they feel comfortable.

ATTITUDE TOWARD OTHER HOLIDAYS

Hindus observe as they wish according to the culture in which they live or work.

TITLES

Acharya—A scholar and authority on religious observance.

Guru—A spiritual teacher or master.

Priest—One who performs rituals and makes sacrifices; there are many different classifications of priest, depending on their particular sect or role in a ceremony.

Swami—Usually a member of an order of Hindu monks.

COMMUNITY WORSHIP

Hindus regard their temples as places where the divine meets the physical universe and where mortals receive special divine assistance. Consecrated statues, or representations of Hindu gods known as *murti,* stand in the inner sancta of temples where they are cared for by priests. In temples with full-time priests, the deities are washed, dressed and decorated daily, then set down to rest at night.

Hindus may visit a temple for private devotion or for a service conducted by a priest. Hindus are expected to have a ritual bath and to dress well, preferably according to Indian tradition, when they go to the temple. Worshippers must remove their shoes before entering the temple, since leather is considered impure. When they arrive, they ring a bell to announce their presence to the deities.

In order to purify himself and the place of worship, a priest goes through several preparatory steps including chanting and meditation. Some worship services are more elaborate than others, but they follow a similar set of sixteen steps, patterned after the customs of showing hospitality to an honored guest:

- Alerting the deity that *puja,* or worship, is about to begin. This is often accompanied by an offering of flowers.
- Offering a seat to the god.
- Pouring water on the feet of the deity to cleanse them.
- Putting water mixed with sandalwood paste into the hands of the god.
- Offering the god water for sipping and purification.
- Bathing the idol with milk, yogurt, melted butter, honey and sugar water, and pure water.
- Offering the idol a set of garments.
- Providing the idol with a sacred thread.
- Offering the god sandalwood paste and scents.
- Offering the god flowers and addressing the god with 108 or 1016 names.
- Offering incense.
- Offering a lamp.
- Offering food and water for a meal, and money.
- Waving lights from burning camphor.
- Greeting the idol by placing hands together in supplication, followed by walking around the deity clockwise, keeping the idol to the right side.
- Offering flowers again.

After all these steps are completed, the priest invites the deity to leave again. For the participation of the congregation, the priest:

- Carries the lamp on a tray into the congregation. Worshipers hold their hands palms down and slightly apart, move them quickly across the flame, then touch their eyes with their fingertips. The ritual is repeated twice more. The worshipers may lay an offering on the tray, or put it in the temple box later.
- Next, the priest pours holy water into the right hands of the worshipers, who drink it.
- At some services, the priest may put sandalwood paste into the right hands of worshipers, who wipe it into the left palm. With the right ring finger, the worshiper puts a small dab of paste in the center of his forehead. The priest will then distribute red powder, which should be applied over the paste on the forehead. The red dot on the forehead shows that the worshiper has attended religious services.

A Hindu with a special request can write out a prayer and give it to a priest, who will burn it in a sacred fire, thus sending it directly to the intended god. A worshiper may also request a short worship done specifically for a special occasion or need.

Visitors should remove their shoes and always sit so that they are lower than the images of the deities. If participating in the service, take all offerings from the priest with the right hand. One should not touch a statue of a deity or sit with one's feet pointing toward the images, the priest or anyone else.

PRIVATE WORSHIP

Most Hindu worship, or *puja,* takes place in the home, often in the kitchen. Hindu families set aside shrines to deities chosen for the household, and senior family members lead worship.

Observant Hindus are expected to perform religious rituals daily. Among them:

• Making an offering to the family deity.
• Studying or chanting a portion of the Vedas.
• Remembering ancestors.
• Making an offering to the spirits in the form of birds or animals.
• Performing an act of kindness or hospitality.

Before participating in *puja,* or worship, family members may ritually purify themselves to prepare for uttering sacred words. This is done by pouring water into the cupped right hand, uttering Vishnu's name and sipping and swallowing the water. The ritual is done identically three times. The fourth time, the worshiper lets the water trickle down into a dish.

After the main worship service, each family member may offer flowers, rice or other offerings to the deity.

If visiting a Hindu home, guests should remove their shoes. During family worship, visitors may participate to the extent they feel comfortable. If entertaining Hindu guests, hosts should offer them the opportunity and facilities to perform daily worship.

DRESS

Hindu practice requires clean and modest dress. Clothing styles vary by region, climate and tradition. Marks on the head and body of Hindus may indicate whether they worship Vishnu or Shiva. Three horizontal marks on the head and/or body indicate worship of Shiva, while vertical marks signify Vishnu worship.

~ress, comfortable for sitting, is recommended for Hindu
Shoes should be easily removable.

DIETARY LAWS

Many Hindus practice vegetarianism and eat no meat or fish. But even Hindus who are not vegetarians will usually eat no beef, or pork, nor anything cooked with beef or pork, since cows are considered sacred and pigs are considered unclean.

There are three categories of food, associated with the three categories of *gunas,* or human qualities:

Tamasic food is considered impure. This category includes beef, pork and veal, meats with preservatives, deep-fried food, hard liquor, food that has been cooked twice or left over and food that has been touched by an animal or another human being. These foods are believed to arouse unwelcome passions such as jealousy and to dull the mind. Some Hindus also avoid red foods.

Rajastic foods include other meats, fish and poultry, strong spices, peppers or onion, and stimulants such as coffee, tea, chocolate and cola. These are believed to cause restlessness, sexual aggression and anger, and thus should be avoided.

Sattvic foods include fruits, vegetables, grains and other foods believed to produce good physical and mental health.

Strict rules govern the kitchens of observant Hindus. Menstruating women do not prepare food or, in some cases, even enter the kitchen. Women bathe before handling food and, just as in the temple, no shoes are allowed in the kitchen. Women use only their right hands to touch food during preparation; likewise, diners use only their right hands to put food in their mouths.

Diners are expected to ritually clean their mouths with water before and after dinner. Some use a lime twig to clean their teeth as well. When drinking during a meal, some Hindus do not touch the rims of their cups with their lips, but pour liquid into their mouths.

In the most traditional households, men eat first and diners sit on the floor, although in many American Hindu households, families eat together around a table.

Some Hindus voluntarily fast as a religious observance on a certain day of the week to honor a specific god or goddess, or as a form of penance.

If invited to a Hindu home for a meal, be prepared to remove your shoes before entering the house. Do not expect to help in the kitchen or to handle food. If entertaining Hindus, avoid serving pork or beef. Since many Hindus are vegetarian, plenty of non-meat dishes should be available unless the host is certain the guest eats meat.

PLACE OF CHILDREN

The importance Hindus place on childhood is obvious in the number of sacraments attached to advancement.

Among them are:

The first outing—The baby's first official trip to a temple or shrine, usually when the child is three or four months old. Mother, baby and other female relatives take offerings, such as flowers, for the deity and say prayers for the health and welfare of the child. That night, the baby is shown the moon.

The first solid food—This ritual is performed by an infant's father in the home or in the temple. The first food, said to help determine a child's destiny, is usually boiled rice with yogurt, clarified butter and honey.

First haircut—Performed on a child one to three years old. The first hair may be kept for an offering.

Ear piercing—May be performed on both boys and girls, in the temple or in the home, on the first birthday. The child then wears gold earrings.

The beginning of education—May be performed in the home or in the temple when the child is three to four years old. To signify readiness to learn, the child draws the first letter of the alphabet in uncooked rice.

Presentation of the sacred thread—Performed by fathers for their sons when the boys are between nine and fifteen years old, in the home or in the temple. Before the ceremony, the boy has a symbolic last meal of childhood with his mother. Then the boy presents offerings to Agni, the god of fire, and his father presents him with a white cord to be worn over his left shoulder and under his right arm. This signifies spiritual adulthood, and the boy may begin studying with a guru.

ROLES OF MEN AND WOMEN

The regard for men over women is exemplified in the Hindu prayers for sons rather than daughters and the fact that women's body functions—menstruation and birth—make them ritually impure. On the other hand, Hindus have female as well as male deities and the woman of the household is charged with seeing that religious rituals are properly observed. She is responsible for the preparation and serving of food, and for arranging the celebration of sacraments for her children. She may also lead family worship in the home along with her husband, but will rarely have a role in public worship.

It is best to not extend a hand for shaking, but wait to see whether one is offered. The most common Hindu greeting involves no touching at all. It is the *namaste,* in which an acquaintance puts the fingertips of both hands together holding the hands in front of the chest or face and nods or bows slightly.

HOUSEHOLD

Hindu homes usually have a shrine to gods or goddesses of particular importance to the family. Orthodox Hindus begin the day by waking and bathing the gods and end the day by putting them down to rest. Families may also have, near the front door, a picture of Ganesha, the god who removes obstacles. Observant Hindus will pay homage to him when entering or leaving the house. Religious symbols may also be mounted above the door to the main family room.

Guests should show respect for Hindu religious symbols. When bringing hospitality gifts to a Hindu home, fruit, wine and candy are appropriate.

MILESTONES

Birth—Even before birth, observant Hindus may bring offerings and say prayers during specific rituals to ensure conception, to protect the fetus and to ask for a son. Shortly after birth, parents may have an astrological chart done for their baby.

Both mother and child are considered ritually impure for ten days after birth, and traditionally only the midwife or physician has contact with them. The naming ceremony, performed when the infant is between eleven and forty days old, is thus an introduction to society as well as a religious ceremony.

In more elaborate ceremonies, both the parents and the baby dress in new clothes. The mother sits on her husband's right and holds the baby on her lap. The baby may have a soot mark on its forehead to turn away envy. The family priest holds a metal plate of rice in front of the family. The father, using something gold, traces the name of the family deity and the proposed name of the child into the grain. He then whispers the baby's new name into its right ear. Names traditionally have spiritual meaning, such as the names of gods or goddesses from mythology. After the ceremony, guests are invited to a reception.

Less elaborate rituals may be conducted by the women of a household. In this case, the new name is announced by the oldest woman.

Gifts for the baby are appropriate and may be given to the parents at the ceremony.

Marriage—Regarded as one of the most important events in a Hindu family, marriage also marks a woman's arrival at adulthood.

Hindus believe love develops after marriage, and so there is no courtship. In India in general, as well as specifically among Hindus, many marriages are arranged by the parents. At one time the couple met for the first time on their wedding day, but now most families discuss the arrangements and introduce the man and woman well ahead of time for the wedding so that if either is dissatisfied, the wedding is called off.

Before a marriage can take place, the family priests must determine whether the couple's astrological charts are compatible. If the horoscopes match, the families set a day for the wedding, taking the star charts into consideration. In India, most weddings take place between December and July, avoiding the monsoon season and the time of major festivals.

A betrothal or "word giving" celebration may be held so that the woman's father may officially promise that his daughter will marry the man. The promise is considered binding, and the two families may exchange gifts to signify the agreement. A few days before the wedding, the two families offer worship to their family deities and pray for health, prosperity and many children for the bridal couple.

Hindu wedding ceremonies vary by culture and social status. The bride usually wears gold jewelry given to her by her parents. Both bride and groom may wear head coverings. The religious service itself may last several hours. It is usually conducted by a priest before a ceremonial fire in a wedding pavilion, built to symbolize the Universe, and may have many steps including:

- Invocation of family deities and introduction of the bride's parents.
- Invocation of Ganesha, the remover of obstacles.
- Preparation by the bride's parents of vessels of purified water to be used during the ceremony.
- Giving the bride away. The bride's father washes the feet of his future son-in-law and requests that he accept his daughter as his wife. The bridegroom agrees to treat the bride as an equal partner and confirms his intention to marry her.
- Wedding. The bride and bridegroom place their right hands on each other's heads, with a symbolic mixture of sweet and bitter substances in their palms, while the priest invokes the gods to provide stability to their relationship.
- Presentation of the symbols. The curtain that has separated the bride and groom is removed and they face each other. The bridegroom ties a necklace of wedding medallions around the bride's neck and a sacred rope around her waist. The couple smears each other's palms with milk, exchanges rings, pours rice on each other's heads, and exchanges garlands. The priest symbolically ties the ends of their garments in a sacred knot. (Instead of rings, some couples tie a yellow thread around each other's wrists, the bride wearing hers on the left arm, the groom on the right.)

- Seven-steps ritual. With his right hand on the bride's right shoulder, the bridegroom speaks a mantra and the bride steps with her right foot onto each of seven piles of rice made by the priest signifying nourishment, strength, prosperity, happiness, children—especially sons—pleasure and friendship. After the seventh step, the couple may take vows of commitment.
- Blessing. The priest recites Hindu scriptures invoking the blessings of all the gods on the newlyweds and their guests. He places sacred rice—which has been touched by everyone—on the couple to represent these blessings.
- Conclusion. The ceremony ends with friends and family bringing sacred lights to the newlyweds and wishing them happiness and prosperity.

A reception following the ceremony may last several hours.

Guests should watch the wedding ceremony respectfully, participating when they are comfortable doing so. Gifts are appropriate.

Death—Hindus believe that the body dies but the soul lives on to return in another body. Since they are not sure when the soul leaves the body, Hindu ritual is designed not to injure the soul.

A dying Hindu should be given water from the Ganges River in India if possible, and encouraged to utter a name of God. After death, the corpse must be bathed and dressed in new clothes and covered with white cloth. Someone must stay with the body until it can be cremated, chanting the names of God or reading the Bhagavadgita to assist the soul on its journey.

Ideally, cremation takes place within twenty-four hours of death.

Traditionally, the body is carried on a stretcher to a funeral ground, escorted by a son who carries a pot of coals to light the fire for cremation. In the United States the body is more likely to be carried by ambulance or hearse to a crematorium. A symbolic offering of food is presented to the deceased before cremation, and relatives may place flowers on the coffin before it moves into the cremation oven. Sacred readings and chants may be done as the coffin moves. Only infants are not cremated, but are buried.

After the funeral, members of the family take ritual baths.

The family mourns for ten to thirty days, during which they are considered ritually unclean. In a *shaddra* ceremony signifying the end of mourning, ten balls of cooked rice are put out for birds, believed to be departed souls. At this time, ideally, the ashes of the deceased should be scattered on flowing water. After this, men may shave their hair and beards. Women can once again participate in food preparation.

At one time, widows were expected to throw themselves on their husbands' funeral pyres in an act of self-cremation called *sati*. There is no basis for this in Hindu scripture, and it is no longer practiced.

Expressions of condolence such as cards or flowers are appropriate. If attending a Hindu funeral, wear white if possible—never black. At the service of cremations, guests are expected to sit reverently and watch, participating wherever they feel comfortable. Visits of condolence should be made to the family before the *shaddra* ceremony. Gifts of fruit are considered appropriate at this time.

CONVERSION

There is no conversion ritual for Hinduism.

MAJOR ORGANIZATIONS

Himalayan Academy
(Publishers of Hinduism Today)
1819 Second Street
Concord, California 94519

Vedanta Society of Southern California
1946 Vedanta Place
Hollywood, California 90068-3996

International Society for Krishna Consciousness
84 Carl Street
San Francisco, California 94117

FURTHER READING

Viswanathan, Ed. *Am I a Hindu?* San Francisco, CA: Halo Books, 1992.
Klostermaier, Klaus K. *A Survey of Hinduism.* Albany, NY: State University of
    New York Press, 1989.
Knipe, David M. *Hinduism.* San Francisco, CA: HarperSan Francisco, 1991.
Kanitkar, V.P. (Hemant), and Cole, W. Owen. *Hinduism, a Teach Yourself Book.*
    Lincolnwood, Il: NTC Publishing Group, 1995.

FOR CHILDREN
Hirst, Jacqueline Suthern. *The Story of the Hindus.* Cambridge, England, and New
    York: Cambridge University Press, 1989.

JAINS

~~

"All things breathing, all things existing . . . should
not be slain or treated with violence . . ."
—*Acaranga Sutra*

THE Jain attitude toward nature, respecting the interdependence of all things living and non-living, is the basis for the science of ecology and the environmental movement. But Jainism itself is not well known outside India. Authorities estimate that two to three million Jains live in India today, and several hundred thousand elsewhere in the world.

SYMBOL

The symbol of Jainism is a complicated design that includes a swastika whose arms represent the four possible states of the soul (divine, human, other life forms, and hell); three dots to indicate right knowledge, faith and conduct; a half-moon as a symbol of the resting place for souls; a raised hand to indicate non-violence; and a wheel to indicate continuity of the religion.

ORIGINS

Jainism takes its name from the word *jinas,* or "conquerors," a title that refers not to military conquest but to victory over the cycles of life.

Jainism claims to date from time immemorial and to be based on twenty-four Tirthankaras, or master teachers (literally "guide to crossing the river"). Historically, Jainism began in northeastern India during the 6th century B.C.E., with a man known as Mahavira, or "Great Hero," who is regarded as the twenty-fourth and last of the master teachers. Jainism grew up around the time Buddhism was beginning and has several similarities with it.

According to Jain teaching, Mahavira was born as Nataputta Vardhammana into a wealthy family in northern India. His parents were followers of Parshva, a spiritual guide of two centuries earlier who is now considered to have been the twenty-third master. One story describes how, as a child, Mahavira calmed a stampeding elephant and rode it back to his father's stables. As a result, he was given his title as "Great Hero."

After his parents died, Mahavira, then thirty, retreated to live as an ascetic—eating little and spending long periods in silence and meditation—for more than twelve years. During this time, he lived off alms people dropped into a cup he held silently, and by eating fruits and berries. He achieved enlightenment, or freedom from the cycles of life, while meditating under a tree. He cast off his clothes, and went on to teach for thirty years before dying at the age of seventy-two. Jains believed he achieved perfection, or nirvana.

His teaching was passed on and spread throughout the north of India.

HOLY TEXTS

There is no bible of Jainism, although some work attributed to Mahavira has been recorded after his death. Jain literature is divided into three main groups:

The Purvas, or old texts (fourteen volumes).
The Angas, or limbs (eleven volumes).
The Angabahya, or subsidiary canon.

The Tattvartha Sutra, written in the 2nd century CE, is a commentary written by monks that summarizes the Jain doctrine.

Much of Jainism is handed down from individual teacher to student.

There are no particular rules for handling Jain scripture.

DIVISIONS

Dating from some two hundred years B.C.E., Jain monks divided into two groups, the *Shwetamber,* or white-clad monks, and the *Digamber,* or sky-clad monks, who live in the nude.

Although the two groups are defined by their positions on clothing, they also disagree on which scriptures to emphasize and on some elements of the life story of Mahavira.

DOCTRINE

God—Jains do not believe in a supreme being.
Good Deeds—Respect for life, and thus respectful treatment of all living

things, is a foremost principle of Jainism; thus Jains value good deeds toward animals and even insects, as well as toward fellow humans.

Creation—There was no creator of the universe; the universe had no beginning and will have no end.

Humankind—The human soul, like the universe, has no beginning and no end. Humans can come to perfection, omniscience and omnipotence; every person may possibly become a god.

Angels—Jainism recognizes no superhuman guardian spirits.

Sin—Like Hinduism, Jainism teaches that good deeds create good karma or good results, and bad deeds create bad karma or bad results. In Jainism, thoughts are as significant as deeds in influencing karma.

The Devil—There is no superhuman evil force, but everyone is capable of doing evil.

Judgment—There is no divine being who passes judgment; one's fate is determined by the balance of good and bad acts.

Heaven—Jainism accepts the idea of seven levels of heaven, but these are temporary stations for the soul between lives. The level of heaven a soul retires to is determined by the thoughts and deeds of the soul in past lives. The ultimate goal of the soul is *moksha,* or liberation.

Hell—Jainism also recognizes seven levels of hell; like heaven, these are temporary stations for the soul between lives. The level of hell is determined by the thoughts and deeds of a soul in past lives.

Miracles—Jains do not accept the idea of a supernatural god's interference in nature, but most Jains believe humans are capable of knowing past, present and future and thus can perform what others might think of as miracles.

Messiah—There is no concept of a supernatural messiah coming to save humankind in Jainism.

DOCTRINES SPECIFIC TO JAINISM

Ahimsa—non-violence. This is the most widely known principle of Jainism. According to Jain doctrine, every being, whether human, animal or plant, has a soul, or *jiva.* Devout Jains refuse to ride in vehicles because they could crush living organisms, use no products that involve animal by-products, and keep no pets.

Parasparopagraho jivanam—interdependence of all life on all other life and other aspects of nature.

Anekantavada—relativity of all aspects or points of view, or acceptance that no one perspective of a situation is completely true.

Jiva—the soul or spirit. In Jainism, all living things, not only humans, have souls. During its time in the world, the soul, or *jiva,* goes through a cycle of death and rebirth through various life forms from bacteria to human beings.

Karma—Jains use the illustration of a ball with a sticky exterior to represent the *jiva,* or pure soul. Good deeds and thoughts and bad deeds and thoughts stick to it as good or bad karma. The amount of good versus bad karma determines the future state of the soul.

Moksha—liberation. The goal is ultimate liberation of the soul by achieving perfect karma. A liberated soul is a *Siddha,* or perfected being.

THE THREE JEWELS

Jainism recognizes three qualities necessary to achieve Moksha, or liberation:

- *Right Faith*—Beliefs in the teachings of Jainism.
- *Right Knowledge*—Understanding of the operation of karma.
- *Right Conduct*—Behavior conforming to the five vows of Jainism.

THE FIVE VOWS

Jain monks and nuns take five vows, which lay people are expected to obey to a lesser degree:

- *Ahimsa*—non-violence. Jain monks and nuns carry brooms or feathers to brush their paths in an attempt to clear it of any insects that might be stepped on inadvertently. Likewise, some of them cover their noses and mouths to prevent accidentally inhaling any tiny insects and thus killing them. Lay-people are expected to not cause any intentional harm.
- *Satya*—truth. Jains are expected to not only avoid lying but to avoid partial truths or misleading statements; however, one should remain silent if the truth would cause injury.
- *Asteya*—honesty. Jains are expected to respect other people's possessions and to avoid stealing. When accepting alms, a monk or nun is expected to take only what is needed.
- *Bramhacharya*—celibacy. Sexual abstinence for Jain monks and nuns includes avoidance of thinking sensual thoughts. Lay Jains should practice monogamy and avoid promiscuity.
- *Aparigraha*—non-possession. Jains are expected to avoid attachment to material things and thus avoid the temptation to sin in order to acquire possessions. Some Jain monks do not even own clothes.

CALENDAR

Some Jains date their calendar from the birth of Mahavira. Many Jains use the same calendar as the Hindus, which is a lunar calendar with an extra month added every three years to synchronize it with the solar calendar.

RELIGIOUS FESTIVALS AND HOLIDAYS

Paryushana Parva—also known as Daslakshini—an eight-to-ten-day festival during the period of the rains in India.

Samvatsari—the last day of the year, observed by worship and prayer. Jains at this time are expected to confess their transgressions against others, and to forgive those who have wronged them.

Mahavir Jayanti—the birthday of Vardhamana Mahavira, the twenty-fourth master teacher. It is celebrated with worship and prayer.

Anyone attending a festival at a Jain temple or home should avoid wearing leather. Leather purses should be set aside. Otherwise, guests should participate to the extent they feel comfortable.

ATTITUDE TOWARD OTHER HOLIDAYS

Jains celebrate as they wish.

TITLES

Sadhu—monks.
Sadvi—nuns.
Shravakas—laypeople who listen to monks' lessons.
Upasakas—laypeople who minister to monks.

COMMUNITY WORSHIP

Although Jainism is built on principles of asceticism, some Jains practice worship in temples that are elaborately decorated on the outside. Inside, the principle features are images of the Tirthankaras, usually either seated in meditation or standing erect. The images may be identical except for a marking at the bottom that indicates which of the twenty-four each image represents. Each temple has at least one image.

The service itself consists of recitation of a prayer, or mantra, expressing salutations to all the Tirthankaras as a group while standing in front of an image. The worshiper then gives the image a symbolic bath and offers it eight substances:

- pure water
- rice
- *chandan* (sandalwood and saffron paste)
- flowers
- coconut
- a lamp
- incense
- dried fruit or nuts

The worshiper then calls out the names of all twenty-four Tirthankaras, and ends by waving lamps over the image.

Other rituals include *Samayika,* or a forty-eight-minute period of prayer, meditation and scripture, and *Pratikraman,* a fifty-minute time of meditation. Both are performed while sitting on woolen mats while fingering a 108-bead *mala,* or rosary.

Many Jains perform temple worship only during festivals or holidays.

Out of respect for Jain's views, non-Jains should not wear or bring leather to a Jain worship service. Guests may participate as they feel comfortable, and should feel free to come and go during the ceremony.

PRIVATE WORSHIP

Some Jains practice daily *puja,* or worship, at home immediately after bathing and before eating in the morning.

If entertaining a Jain houseguest, a host should simply offer an opportunity for privacy.

DRESS

While performing rituals, Jains wear loose cotton clothing. Some monks and nuns wear white; other monks wear nothing, or only loincloths.

Wearing loose, comfortable clothing is a good idea for Jain functions since guests will probably be sitting on the floor if attending a Jain temple.

DIETARY LAWS

Because of their high regard for life, Jains are vegetarians. Since they also revere the life in plants, they eat the least amount needed for sustenance. Many Jains also avoid alcohol and tobacco.

Hosts entertaining Jains should not serve meat.

PLACE OF CHILDREN

There is no coming-of-age ceremony for Jain children, but children are allowed to participate in worship.

ROLES OF MEN AND WOMEN

Jain men and women are considered equal, but are often kept separate. During Jain worship, women usually sit on the right and men on the left as seen when entering the room. Jains frown on physical contact between people of the opposite sex in a social situation because the ideal of the religion is celibacy, and anything that would detract from that is regarded as improper.

Non-Jains should not extend a hand to Jains of the opposite sex, but wait to see whether one is offered. Guests attending a Jain worship service should observe the seating customs and sit with people of their gender.

HOUSEHOLD

Jain households are expected to operate under the principles of Ahimsa, or non-violence, and Aparigrapha, or non-acquisition. Jains are prohibited from practicing certain occupations—such as forestry—that involve the taking of life, including the life of plants.

MILESTONES

Birth—There is no specific Jain ceremony for infants.

Gifts and cards for a new baby are appropriate.

Marriage—Many Jains adapt the Hindu marriage ceremony to their purposes.

Guests should enjoy the ceremony and participate as they feel comfortable. Gifts and cards are appropriate for the bride and groom.

Death—Jains practice cremation, but regard it as a necessary means of disposal of the dead. Jain funerals resemble Hindu funerals.

Flowers, cards and expressions of sympathy are appropriate.

CONVERSION

Conversion to Jainism usually takes place through study under an individual teacher, who determines whether any ceremony is necessary.

MAJOR ORGANIZATIONS

Jain Study Center of North Carolina
401 Farmstead Drive
Cary, North Carolina 27511

FURTHER READING

Tobias, Michael, *Life Force—The World of Jainism.* Berkeley, CA.: Asian Humanities Press, 1991.

JEHOVAH'S WITNESSES

"Ye are my witnesses, saith Jehovah, and
my servant whom I have chosen."
—Isaiah 43:10

Most people know members of this sect from their regular door-to-door visitation, literature in hand, as they try to convert people to their faith. But the Jehovah's Witnesses are a large and fast-growing denomination, with almost a million members in the United States and more than 5.5 million worldwide.

SYMBOL

The watchtower is the symbol generally associated with Jehovah's Witnesses.

ORIGINS

Charles Taze Russell was the prime leader of a Bible class that met in Allegheny City, Pennsylvania, in the 1870s and grew into the Jehovah's Witnesses. Russell was born to Scots-Irish Presbyterian parents in Allegheny, now part of Pittsburgh, on February 16, 1852. As a teenager, he worked with his father's chain of men's clothing stores and joined the Congregational Church, but did not fully accept its doctrines. One day in 1870 he wandered into a small Bible study meeting in a basement near one of the family stores and found enough enthusiasm and inspiration there to begin his own small Bible group.

Russell believed that Jesus would come again but in spiritual, not human, form. He put his views into a pamphlet called "The Object and Manner of the Lord's Return," and published several thousand copies and, in 1876, contributed an article called "Gentile Times: When Do They End?" to a magazine. In this writing, he predicted that in 1914, the "times of the nations" would end and the end of the world as it now exists would begin.

In July 1879, Russell's Bible class published the first issue of a magazine called *Zion's Watch Tower and Herald of Christ's Presence*.

His class formed Zion's Watch Tower Tract Society in 1881, and incorporated in 1884 with Russell as president. Soon, congregations began establishing in other cities. During these days, they were known as Russellites, Millennial Dawn People and International Bible Students. By 1900, the group had established a branch in London.

By the time Russell died in 1916, his followers had bought a building in Brooklyn under the name People's Pulpit Association of New York. In 1931, they took the name Jehovah's Witnesses.

HOLY TEXTS

Jehovah's Witnesses have their own version of the Bible, the New World Translation, which uses the name Jehovah for God throughout. The translation was released in sections between 1950 and 1960.

Jehovah's Witnesses consider the sixty-six books of the Bible to be inspired and historically accurate. They refer to the Jewish Bible or the Old Testament as the Hebrew Scriptures and the Christian New Testament as the Christian Greek Scriptures.

DIVISIONS

There is only one central group of Jehovah's Witnesses, but over the years some disaffected members have left and formed splinter groups. Among them are the Laymen's Home Missionary Movement and the Dawn Bible Students Association.

DOCTRINE

God—Jehovah's Witnesses believe in one true God, whose name, they say, is Jehovah and who has four qualities: justice, power, love and wisdom. They reject the traditional Christian belief in the Trinity, or three-in-one God, that includes Jesus and the Holy Spirit. They deny the deity of Jesus but recognize him as God's creation and first son. Before coming to earth in human form, they believe, Jesus existed in spirit form as the archangel Michael.

Good Deeds—While Jehovah's Witnesses do not believe doing good is necessary for salvation, they say true faith is manifested in positive actions toward others.

Creation—Jehovah created everything, beginning with Jesus Christ, who was formed from nothing.

Humankind—Humans were created by Jehovah in his image and therefore should exercise the attributes of Jehovah: justice, power, love and wisdom. There is no distinction between body and soul and neither is immortal.

Angels—Jehovah and his first creation, Jesus Christ, made a spirit realm that includes millions of angels, also called "sons of God."

Sin—Adam, the first human, was created perfect by Jehovah; Adam died because of disobedience to Jehovah and passed sin to all humankind.

The Devil—Satan is the invisible ruler of the world.

Judgment—Jesus began judging the nations in 1918, and judgment will continue until the Battle of Armageddon. Those who are judged unfit are doomed to eternal death; the others will be resurrected to live either in heaven forever with Jehovah or in the earthly kingdom for 1000 years. A second period of judgment will follow the Battle of Armageddon and those who pass will live in eternal paradise on earth.

Heaven—Only 144,000 people, the "elect," will go to heaven and rule with Christ; other believers will live under a new system on earth in peace and harmony, and those believers who have died will be physically resurrected. Jehovah's Witnesses arrived at the number 144,000 from the Christian New Testament Book of Revelation.

Hell—There is no burning hell, only eternal death.

Miracles—Jehovah's Witnesses believe that by performing the miracles recorded in the Bible, Jehovah was exercising his power to draw attention to Jesus. Although Jehovah may still intervene in people's lives, he no longer performs such signs in such a public way.

Messiah—Jehovah's Witnesses believe Jesus Christ is the messiah who came to earth in human form as chronicled in the Christian New Testament and a second time in invisible spirit form in 1914. According to this teaching, he began the reign of his kingdom in 1918.

DOCTRINES SPECIFIC TO JEHOVAH'S WITNESSES

Among other specific beliefs outlined by Jehovah's Witnesses in their literature are:

Earth itself will never be destroyed, but the present system will end in the battle of Armageddon.

The end of the present system is at hand.

The human soul ceases to exist at death.

Believers should direct prayers to Jehovah through Christ.

True believers should not participate in ecumenical movements.

Believers should not dabble in spiritism.

Worshipers should not use images.

The two positions of Jehovah's Witnesses that probably get the most attention are the refusal to accept blood transfusions and the refusal to salute the flag. According to the Witnesses, accepting blood by mouth or intravenous transmission violates God's law because the Bible commands believers to "abstain from blood," a divine order that cannot be suspended even in an emergency. Witnesses do not pledge allegiance, salute the flag, sing the national anthem or even vote in a government election. They maintain that the early Christians did not involve themselves in political affairs, and that salutes and anthems can be regarded as acts of worship due only to Jehovah. For this reason, Jehovah's Witnesses will also refrain from singing school songs.

CALENDAR

Jehovah's Witnesses adopt the calendar of the culture in which they live, but set their chief religious holiday by the lunar calendar.

RELIGIOUS FESTIVALS AND HOLIDAYS

The only major religious holiday observed by Jehovah's Witnesses is the annual observance of the Lord's Evening Meal, Memorial Supper or Last Supper at the time of the first full moon in spring. Witnesses re-enact the scriptural account of Jesus' serving the bread and wine to his disciples.

Non-Witnesses, and many Witnesses, do not take communion during the Lord's Evening Meal. Traditionally only those Witnesses who are sure they are among the 144,000 to be taken into heaven partake of the bread and wine.

ATTITUDE TOWARD OTHER HOLIDAYS

Birthdays—Jehovah's Witnesses do not celebrate birthdays, because they draw attention to an individual and because they believe early Christians did not celebrate birthdays.

Mother's Day and Father's Day—Jehovah's Witnesses believe these holidays are closely linked to ancient customs of ancestor worship and thus do not take part in them.

Valentine's Day—Jehovah's Witnesses reject the customs associated with Valentine's Day.

Halloween—Jehovah's Witnesses regard Halloween customs as pagan and thus do not participate.

Although they consider themselves Christians, Jehovah's Witnesses do not celebrate Christmas or Easter, saying both are connected with non-Christian customs and worship.

Likewise, they do not acknowledge national holidays such as Independence Day, Memorial Day or Thanksgiving. "Though we respect the authorities in whatever country we may reside, for conscientious reasons we do not give them what we view as worshipful honors,'' says Jehovah's Witness literature.

Jehovah's Witnesses and their children should not be expected to participate in secular or religious holiday observances. They should be offered the opportunity to be excused from situations where others are celebrating. While gifts, cards and parties are not appropriate to acknowledge Witnesses' birthdays or holidays, special treats may be offered at other times for the sake of friendship.

TITLES

There is no clergy among Jehovah's Witnesses. There is, however, a hierarchy of "overseers." The *circuit overseer* is in charge of about twenty congregations; the *district overseer* supervises about a dozen circuits; and the *branch overseer* is head of a committee over an entire country.

Witnesses who carry literature door-to-door or into public areas are called *publishers*. *Elders* are male publishers who have demonstrated by their lives that they have the experience and character to teach others. *Ministerial servants* assist elders and probably will eventually become elders.

While they may serve different places and functions in the organizational hierarchy, all Witnesses address each other only as Brother or Sister.

COMMUNITY WORSHIP

Jehovah Witnesses call their congregational meeting places Kingdom Halls, and they gather there for singing and teaching. They do not, however, conduct a Sabbath worship service since they believe only Jews were expected to set aside the Sabbath. There is no choir and no offering at a Jehovah's Witness meeting. Some sessions do allow question-and-answer periods in which the congregation participates.

Visitors may participate with the congregation.

PRIVATE WORSHIP

Witnesses are encouraged to read the Bible and study Jehovah's Witness literature daily. Many Witness families set aside a time to study a daily scripture lesson—often before, during or after a family meal.

DRESS

At all congregational events and in their door-to-door visiting, Witnesses are expected to dress neatly and modestly. Women are discouraged from wearing conspicuous jewelry, cosmetics or hairstyles.

Women must wear head coverings when praying aloud or conducting a Bible study in the presence of their husbands—even if their husbands are of another faith—to signify their respect of what they see as the Biblical authority that gives men "headship" over women. Men, on the other hand, are expected to pray, teach and prophesy with their heads uncovered.

DIETARY LAWS

Jehovah's Witnesses do not believe they are either commanded to fast or prohibited from fasting. They allow alcohol in moderation, but condemn drunkenness and smoking.

When entertaining Jehovah's Witnesses, no foods are prohibited. Smoking is inappropriate in a Kingdom Hall.

PLACE OF CHILDREN

Parents are expected to teach their children the faith in the home. There is no coming-of-age ceremony among Witnesses, but children are expected to make decisions on their own to become full members of the faith. Generally they will follow a course of study, attending meetings and then going door-to-door to distribute literature as unbaptized publishers. When they are ready, they will request baptism and say a prayer of dedication to Jehovah.

A card or expression of support is appropriate for a child who is becoming a full member of Jehovah's Witnesses.

ROLES OF MEN AND WOMEN

Jehovah's Witnesses' literature says there is no spiritual distinction between men and women; however, the organization teaches that men have "headship" over women, both in the family and in the congregation. While they are regarded as equal in God's sight, men and women have separate roles on earth.

Women are generally not allowed to be in charge of congregations, ask questions challenging men in congregational meetings or address such gatherings. Outside the congregation, however, women may conduct Bible studies. Women also take the message of Jehovah's Witnesses door-to-door and into public arenas.

A female guest should not publicly challenge a man giving a presentation at a Kingdom Hall. After the meeting is over, however, she may approach him privately to raise any questions.

HOUSEHOLD

Jehovah's Witnesses are expected to possess and read the literature of the denomination. Thus, Witnesses' homes will often be full of distinctive small hardbound books and colorful newsletters.

On holidays, Witnesses' houses may be conspicuous for their lack of decoration.

Visitors should not bring holiday gifts or decorations to Witness households.

MILESTONES

Birth—The arrival of a child is considered a family matter and a joyous occasion, but Witnesses have no special religious ceremony for new babies.

Gifts, cards, telephone calls and visits are appropriate for the baby and its parents. Friends may also offer to have a shower for the expectant couple. The anniversaries of the baby's birth should be ignored.

Marriage—Witnesses are encouraged to have weddings that include the congregation. The wedding service is usually conservative and traditional, with scripted pledges between bride and groom. The wedding couple is not permitted to write their own vows. Since there is no clergy among Witnesses, a member of the congregation often registers with the government in order to be permitted to perform the marriage. Only religious music is usually permitted in the service itself. A reception afterward may include food, alcohol and secular music. At the reception, the groom is presumed to be head of the new household, and thus the host.

Witness wedding ceremonies have little congregational participation. Guests are expected to observe and enjoy. Gifts for the bride and groom are appropriate. Guests should drink moderately, if at all, at the reception. Special musical requests from guests may not be honored by a band at the reception, since Witnesses are expected to see that all entertainment is in keeping with their religious principles.

Death—Witness funeral services include some eulogizing of the deceased, but emphasize the lessons of the Bible, including the hope of resurrection. There is no specified length of time for mourning, no prescribed period in which the funeral must be held and no required method of disposal of the body.

Witnesses emphasize visits with the family at the time of death and for days, weeks and months afterwards. Friends and neighbors may prepare food for the bereaved family, or offer to do chores or run errands. Flowers, cards and telephone calls are also appropriate, but flowers should not be arranged in the shape of a cross, a heart or any other symbol that could have religious significance.

CONVERSION

One becomes one of the Jehovah's Witnesses by accepting their teaching and being baptized.

A member can also be expelled or "disfellowshipped" for heresy such as idolatry, or for misconduct such as adultery, homosexuality, greed, lying, drunkenness, murder or causing discord in the congregation.

ORGANIZATIONS

Watchtower Bible and Tract Society of New York, Inc.
25 Columbia Heights
Brooklyn, N. Y. 11201-2483

FURTHER READING

Hoekema, Anthony A. *Jehovah's Witnesses*. Grand Rapids, Mich.: Eerdmans, 1978.

Jehovah's Witnesses in the Twentieth Century. Brooklyn, N.Y.: Watchtower Bible and Tract Society of New York, Inc., 1989.

Reasoning from the Scriptures. Brooklyn, N.Y.: Watchtower Bible and Tract Society of New York, Inc., 1985.

School and Jehovah's Witnesses. Brooklyn, N.Y.: Watchtower Bible and Tract Society of New York, Inc., 1983.

The Secret of Family Happiness. Brooklyn, N.Y.: Watchtower Bible and Tract Society of New York, Inc., 1996.

JEWS

"Hear, O Israel, the Lord is our God, the Lord is One."
—*Deuteronomy 6:4*

As practitioners of the oldest of the world's three great monotheistic religions, today's Jews build on thousands of years of history. The Jewish religion addresses almost every aspect of life, from sex to food to work to charity. In the United States, adherence to these rules varies widely, from Jews who unscrew the light-bulbs in their refrigerators before the Sabbath to avoid inadvertently turning on a light, and thus working, to Jews who ignore even the most basic dietary laws. Since Jewish life is as much about culture as it is about religion, even Jews some-times have trouble sorting out religion from tradition.

According to the American Jewish Yearbook for 1996, there are about thirteen million Jews in the world, with almost six million of them in the United States, more than any other country.

SYMBOL

The six-pointed Star of David, or Magen David, is generally accepted as the symbol of Judaism.

ORIGINS

Jews consider Abraham, a nomadic shepherd who originated in Chaldea about four thousand years ago, as the first Jew. It was Abraham who reportedly first recognized and worshipped the one God, YHWH, or Yahweh.

According to holy writings, the Jewish line comes down from Abraham through his son Isaac—born of his wife Sarah when she was already an old woman—and Isaac's son Jacob. God gave Jacob the new name Israel. Jacob's twelve sons by his wives Rachel and Leah and their maids are regarded as the founders of the twelve tribes of Israel.

Jacob's family ended up in Egypt, where through political turmoil they became slaves. A leader named Moses was chosen by God to lead them out of Egypt about 3,200 years ago. According to Jewish belief, God persuaded the pharoah to allow the Israelites to leave by sending a series of plagues to the country, then aided the Israelites in their escape by a miraculous parting of the Red Sea, which washed back over the Egyptian soldiers following them. Moses himself died before Jews were able to occupy Canaan, the land they believe God had promised them. His successor, Joshua, led their invasion of Canaan.

Frustrated by inter-tribal bickering, the tribes of Israel eventually united under a series of kings—Saul, David and Solomon. David established Jerusalem, still known as the City of David, as the seat of his kingdom and Solomon built a temple there that became the center of religious life.

This time of relative peace was followed by times of division, war, tumult and persecution.

After the reign of Solomon, the kingdom split into the ten tribes of the northern kingdom of Israel and the two tribes of the southern kingdom, known as Judah. When the northern kingdom was defeated by Assyria some two hundred years later, the ten tribes there were exiled or assimilated and are known as the Ten Lost Tribes. The descendants of Abraham became known by the name of the surviving kingdom of Judah and their religion is known as Judaism.

The southern kingdom was conquered by the Babylonians in the first of a series of invasions that eventually saw most Jews killed, captured or exiled from Jerusalem under Roman rule. The Jews scattered and established communities around the Mediterranean Sea.

Jews remained without a homeland until May 14, 1948, when, after the United Nations recommended the establishment of a Jewish state, Israel declared its independence.

HOLY TEXTS

A collection of twenty-four books make up the Hebrew Bible, or Tanach, which takes its name from the arrangement of the three parts—Torah, Neviim and Ketuvim. Christians, who accept the same text as the Old Testament of their Bible, divide it differently into thirty-nine books. Jews do not use the term Old Testament. The term Torah is sometimes used to refer only to one part of the Tenach, and at the same time to the whole Hebrew Bible.

Torah, also known by the Greek name Pentateuch, consists of the five books of Moses. Torah means "teaching," and the Torah teaches Jews about their history and laws and the way to live a proper life. *Genesis* tells the story of the creation and of God's covenant with Abraham. *Exodus* describes the escape of the Israelites, led by Moses, from Egypt. *Leviticus* lays out rules of living and establishes the priesthood. *Numbers* enumerates the Israelites. And *Deuteronomy* recaps the story and reestablishes the laws. On each Jewish Sabbath, a specified portion of the Torah is read in public from special scrolls.

Neviim, or the Prophets, the second section, is made up of eight books: Joshua, Judges, Samuel (I and II), Kings (I and II), Isaiah, Jeremiah, Ezekiel and the Minor Prophets.

Ketuvim, Writings, or the Wisdom Literature, includes eleven books: Psalms, Proverbs, Job, Song of Songs, Ruth, Lamentations, Ecclesiastes, Esther, Daniel, Ezra-Nehemiah and Chronicles (I and II).

The actual scroll on which the books of Moses are written is usually referred to as the Sefer Torah. The materials of the scroll are carefully prescribed. The parchment must be the skin of a kosher animal and the pen must be a quill. Only a specially trained scribe, called a *sofer,* is allowed to write on the scroll and *sofers* are called in to repair damaged scrolls.

Jews revere the physical Torah as well as what it says, and they demonstrate their reverence by kissing it when they come into its presence. If they drop it, they kiss it upon picking it up again. There is also a belief that one who drops the Torah must fast for forty days. Generally, if it is dropped in front of a congregation, those present will split the time among them.

To keep from touching the parchment when they read, Jews use a *yad,* or pointer. They also show their respect for their holy books and other religious items by burying them when they are worn out.

Another piece of primary Jewish literature is the Talmud, which means "study" and consists of commentaries and interpretations of Jewish law as well as parables and proverbs.

In a synagogue, when the Torah is being removed from its cabinet, or ark, the congregation stands out of respect, then is seated again when the Torah is placed on the platform, called the *bimah,* to be read. If a rabbi or anyone else walks around the sanctuary with the Torah raised, the congregation also stands. If the rabbi brings the Torah close to them, Jews in the sanctuary may press the corner of their prayer shawls or prayer books to the Torah, then to their lips.

Non-Jews should stand when the Torah is taken out or when it is walked around the sanctuary.

DIVISIONS

Orthodox—Orthodox Judaism requires strict adherence to the ancient Mosaic laws and customs of the Israelites. Divine law as recorded in the Torah is regarded as the sole guide for life. Strict Orthodox Jews carefully observe dietary laws, Sabbath precepts, and dress customs. They may have large families because of adherence to prohibitions against birth control in keeping with the commandment to "be fruitful and multiply." Men and women are separated during worship, and women cannot lead worship. Some strands of Orthodoxy require total separation from people who do not share similar ideas and practices. Some so-called ultra-Orthodox men wear black hats and long black coats and have untrimmed beards and grow side curls, and their wives wear head coverings. Even Orthodox Jews who do not advocate separation from society may live in distinct communities, necessitated by proximity to a synagogue, since they are prohibited from driving on the Sabbath, and the availability of Jewish schools and shops.

Conservative—As its name indicates, Conservative Judaism claims to attempt to "conserve" Judaism. It is generally known as the middle ground within Judaism, especially in America. Conservative Judaism maintains that Jewish law was not carved in stone, so to speak, for all time, but is intended to adapt to circumstances. The motto of the movement, "tradition and change," describes this attitude that Jews must grapple with ideas and practices. Women in the Conservative movement are given the same educational opportunities as men and are now being allowed to lead worship. But not all Conservative Jews agree with the practice.

Traditional—Some American synagogues that are a part of none of the other organized movements describe themselves as "traditional" and pick up beliefs and practices from each. Traditional Jews fall between Conservative and Orthodox.

Reform—The first Reform synagogue in the United States was founded in Charleston, South Carolina, in 1824, organized by the children and grandchildren of Jewish immigrants who wanted a more American service. The movement caught on well with Jews who were becoming assimilated into American culture. Claiming to be constantly "reforming" Judaism, the Reform movement aims to keep Judaism contemporary. Reform Judaism considers the Torah divinely inspired but not a divine revelation; thus it is instructional but not binding. Reform Jews, therefore, may choose or not choose to maintain many of the historic practices and rituals. Many of Reform Judaism's prayers, hymns and lectures are in English or in the language of the country where worship takes place. Reform Jews often call their synagogues "temples." Reform congregations were the first to allow men and women to sit together and to allow instrumental music in worship since the destruction of the ancient Temple. The Reform movement ordained the first woman rabbi in 1972.

Reconstructionist—Reconstructionist Judaism varies most from other branches in its regard for the deity as a force or power of goodness in the universe, not a supernatural being. Likewise, Reconstructionist Jews do not see the Torah as divine truth but as a humanly produced document. Women in Reconstructionist congregations enjoy the same rights and responsibilities as men.

Jews also differentiate themselves by geographic roots. Cultural differences, traditions and customs are often obvious in Jews whose ancestors settled in different parts of the world after they were dispersed from Israel:

Ashkenazic—From a word meaning "Germany," these are the Jews with roots in Central Europe including Russia. They make up the largest number of Jews in the United States.

Sephardic—From a word meaning "Spain," these Jews have their roots in Spain and Portugal.

Edot HaMizrach—From a term meaning "the eastern community," these are the small number of Jews from Ethiopia, Persia, Yemen and other eastern areas.

DOCTRINE

God—God is the creator of the universe and also a very personal deity who requires his people to live morally and ethically. In the Ten Commandments—which, according to the Torah, were handed down to Moses by God—God tells his people to have no other gods before him. Jews consider his name so holy that some refuse to spell it out fully, writing it instead as G-D.

Good Deeds—Jews believe they are commanded to perform service for others, called *mitzvot*. They consider gifts to the poor to be fulfilling an obligation, and they focus on the concepts of justice and righteousness rather than charity.

Creation—The universe was created from nothing by God.

Humankind—God created humans in his image. But he has given men and women free will and they have responsibility for the consequences of their actions.

Angels—Angels are God's messengers whose visits to Abraham and other patriarchs of the faith are recounted in the Torah.

Sin—Sin is willful disobedience of or rebellion against God and human beings by nature are weak and therefore sin. But people have two natures: the capacity to do good and the capacity to do evil. The two natures are constantly at war. Beginning with the temptation and fall of Adam and Eve, the Torah is full of stories of humans' sinfulness.

The Devil—While there are references to Satan in the Torah, these are frequently considered to be symbolic terms for the forces of evil, not references to a literal devil. In the story of Job in the Wisdom literature, the devil is portrayed as a fallen angel whose role is to confound people and trick God.

Judgment—Judaism teaches that God punishes evil and rewards good, that the soul is immortal and that humans' actions on earth determine their fate after death. But many Jews believe reward and punishment are spiritual, not physical, and represent closeness to or distance from God.

Heaven—A faithful Jew's reward is intimacy with God in the afterlife.

Hell—The Bible refers to *sheol,* a netherworld where souls descend, but many Jews believe that punishment for the soul does not take place in a particular location but is felt through distance from God.

Miracles—God's miracles are recorded throughout Jewish scriptures.

Messiah—A descendant of the House of David, who is yet to come, will establish God's kingdom on earth. In the meantime, Jews must work toward making the world more godly.

DOCTRINES SPECIFIC TO JEWS

THE TEN COMMANDMENTS

A basis for Jewish law is the Ten Commandments, which the Torah says in Exodus 20 were handed down by God to Moses on Mount Sinai. Here's a summary:

- There is only one God and none should be held before him.
- There should be no images or idols for worship.
- God's name should not be taken in vain.
- The Sabbath should be observed.
- The Israelites should honor their parents.
- They should not commit murder.
- They should not commit adultery.
- They should not steal.
- They should not lie against their neighbors.
- They should not covet.

THE THREE PRINCIPLES OF LIFE FROM THE TALMUD
Learning
Service of God
Justice toward one's neighbors

CALENDAR

Jewish time theoretically begins with creation. To determine the Jewish year, one only has to add 3,760 to the commonly used figure (the year 2000, for example, is 5,760) except for the period between Rosh Hashana and January 1, when the difference is 3,761.

Both solar and lunar, the Jewish calendar alternates between months of twenty-nine and thirty days, since it takes 29 1/2 days for the moon to revolve around the earth. But the lunar calendar has only 354 days—not 365, as the solar calendar requires since it takes 365 1/4 days for the earth to travel around the sun. Therefore, in an attempt to synchronize solar and lunar cycles, the Jewish calendar is constructed on a nineteen-year basis with twelve years of twelve months each and seven—the third, sixth, eighth, eleventh, fourteenth, seventeenth and nineteenth—with an extra month called Adar II. Jewish months do not coincide with the Gregorian calendar. The addition of Adar II ensures that they stay within the same season.

The months of the Jewish calendar are:

Tishrei—September/October	Nisan—March/April
Cheshvan—October/November	Tyar—April/May
Kislev—November/December	Sivan—May/June
Tevet—December/January	Tammuz—June/July
Shevat—January/February	Av—July/August
Adar—February/March	Elul—August/September

RELIGIOUS FESTIVALS AND HOLIDAYS

All Jewish days begin at sunset. All holidays occur on the same day of the Jewish calendar but vary in their placement on the secular calendar. Among the major holidays are:

Rosh Hashana—The first day of the month of Tishrei is regarded as the Jewish New Year or "head of the year." It begins a ten-day period of self-examination known as the Days of Awe. According to Jewish tradition, Rosh Hashana marks the anniversary of the creation of the world and the day on which God opens the Book of Life to record one's deeds. Unlike many Jewish holidays, Rosh Hashana is synagogue-centered. The best known symbol of the holiday is the *shofar,* or ram's horn, which is sounded every day except the Sabbaths for a month before the holiday at morning prayers—to call in the new year. Some Jews buy new clothes, get haircuts and symbolically empty their pockets of lint into running water to symbolize the fresh beginning. Another custom calls for tossing bread, symbolic of one's sins, into a moving body of water to be washed away. Round bread, or *challah,* is traditionally served at the Rosh Hashana meal to symbolize the circle of the year. Bread or apple is dipped in honey as a wish for sweetness in the year to come.

Yom Kippur—Considered the holiest day of the year for Jews, Yom Kippur, which comes ten days after Rosh Hashana, is the Day of Atonement. On this day, Jews believe, God once again closes the Book of Life. It is a time when Jews must face themselves, those they have wronged and God to make peace. Jews are expected to fast and pray, forgoing physical pleasure for concentration on spiritual matters. They ask for God's forgiveness, but are also expected to confess and atone for offenses against their fellow mortals. At the synagogue, the rabbi wears white, and Torah scrolls and tables are draped in white, which serves as both a symbol of purity and a reminder of mortality, since it is the color of a shroud. The synagogue service begins with the Kol Nidre, a chanted prayer that includes an acknowledgment of transgressions and a promise of God's forgiveness. The service ends with the chanting of the words "The Lord is God," seven times, followed by a blast of the *shofar* and the vow "Next year in Jerusalem."

Hanukkah—The best known symbol of Hanukkah is the *hanukiah,* a special eight-branched menorah, or candelabrum. (There is a ninth candle in the center, used to light the others.) One additional candle is lighted each night throughout the eight-day Festival of Lights, which celebrates a miracle. Two blessings are recited nightly in the home before the candles are lighted, praising God for his commandments and his wondrous deeds. The festival is based on the story of the Maccabees, a group of Jewish men who defied Syrian conquerors and reclaimed the Temple more than two thousand years ago. According to the legend, the Maccabees rekindled the sacred eternal lamp of the Temple, but had only enough oil to last for one day. Miraculously, the lamp burned for eight days, enough time to purify new oil to burn. During the time that Hanukkah candles burn, families often relax and play games. A popular game is played with a *dreidel,* or small four-sided top with a Hebrew letter on each side. A common food is potato pancakes, or *latkes,* fried in oil. Many families also exchange gifts during Hanukkah, which occurs in late November or in December.

Pesach—Passover, in March or April, commemorates God's efforts to release the Israelites from Egyptian slavery. According to the Book of Exodus, God brought a series of plagues down on the Egyptians. The last one was the death of all firstborn Egyptian children. To mark their houses so that the plague would "pass over" them, the Israelites were told to slaughter a lamb and smear its blood on their doorposts. When the pharaoh consented to their release, the slaves left in such haste that they did not have time for their bread to rise. Thus, during the eight days of Pesach, observant Jews eat nothing with leaven. The unleavened bread consumed during this time is called *matzot.* Before the holiday, Jews clean their house of every crumb that could have the prohibited ingredient. During the first one or two nights of the eight-day commemoration, Jews take part in a special meal called a Seder, during which they retell the story of the escape from slavery. The meal includes symbolic foods: a roasted egg symbolizing an offering and the continuity of life; a green vegetable representing renewal, which is dipped in salt water symbolizing the sweat and tears of the Hebrews; a roasted shank bone to commemorate the lambs sacrificed for the blood marks on the doors; bitter herbs to remind Jews of the sorrow of slavery; and *charoset,* a mixture of apples, nuts and wine, to represent the mortar the slaves used to make bricks for the Egyptians.

Purim—A sort of Jewish April Fool's Day, Halloween and Mardi Gras, Purim takes place on the 14th of Adar in the spring. Jews wear masks and costumes, have parades and carnivals, give treats to friends, eat, drink and practice general silliness. Still, Purim has a serious basis in the story of the Jewish woman Esther, who married King Ahaseurus of Persia in the fifth century B.C.E. without his realizing her Jewish roots. When Haman, one of the king's courtiers, later plots to kill all the Jews, she is able to intercede and save her people. Haman himself is executed instead. The story celebrates escape from destruction and the triumph of courage and justice.

Shavuot—The Festival of Weeks, comes on the sixth day of the Hebrew month of Sivan, recognized as a time for harvest. It celebrates the receiving of the Ten Commandments, and thus the Torah, by Moses on behalf of the Jews. Some Jews stay up all night the night before the holiday to study the Torah. Families often have festival meals to celebrate Shavuot, with wine, candles and dairy products to signify the Torah as "milk and honey" to the Jews.

At Rosh Hashana, it is appropriate for non-Jews to wish Jews a good year or a happy new year. Gifts and cards are appropriate for Jewish friends at Hanukkah. If invited to a Passover seder, a non-Jew should be careful not to take any food that is not permitted during that time. Wine or candy marked specifically "Kosher for Passover" would be best. In some households, the Haggadah, or Passover liturgy, is passed around the table. A non-Jew who wishes may read from it, but should not feel obligated. On other holidays, a non-Jew can simply wish a Jew a good holiday.

ATTITUDE TOWARD OTHER HOLIDAYS

Jews celebrate as they wish, according to the culture.

TITLES

Rabbi—Literally, teacher; head of a Jewish congregation. Addressed as "Rabbi."

Rebbitzen—The rabbi's wife. Addressed as "Mrs."

Cantor—Worship leader for a congregation who chants the prayers and leads responsive parts of liturgies; in some synagogues the cantor also assists with religious education. Addressed as "Cantor."

Shamash—The sexton who supervises the preparation and function of the synagogue. Addressed as "Mr."

Gabbai—Serves as an assistant during worship services, assisting the rabbi as needed. Addressed as "Mr.," "Miss," "Ms.," or "Mrs."

Mohel—A person, usually medically trained, who performs circumcisions. Often a rabbi or a physician. Addressed as "Rabbi" or "Doctor."

Mashgiach—Supervisor of food production to ensure that it meets Jewish dietary requirements. Addressed as "Mr." or, if a rabbi, as "Rabbi."

COMMUNITY WORSHIP

Jewish communal worship takes place in a synagogue, from a Greek word for gathering. It is also called a *shul,* a Yiddish word for school. Synagogues have three essential features: an ark, or cabinet, that stores the scrolls of the Torah; a lectern, from which to read them aloud; and an eternal light placed in front of the ark to represent the menorah that stayed lighted at all times in the ancient Temple in Jerusalem. Other common features include tablets containing the first few words of each of the Ten Commandments, and a menorah, or ritual candelabra. No images of human or divine figures are allowed in a synagogue's artwork.

The holy ark is the focal point of the assembly room and is often elaborately carved or covered with embroidered curtains. The ark is usually in a raised area called a *bimah,* traditionally on the eastern wall of the synagogue so that the congregation is looking toward Israel and Jerusalem.

In many synagogues prayers are conducted daily: in the morning, afternoon and evening. Some prayers require the presence of ten adult Jews (stricter groups still require that they be men) called a *minyan.*

Prayers play an important part of Jewish worship, but Jews do not kneel in their synagogues and homes except, among some congregations, on Yom Kippur and Rosh Hashana. In some synagogues, it is the practice to kneel during portions of the service that refer to the Holy Temple in Jerusalem, where Jews did prostrate themselves as a sign of their devotion. During the High Holy Days, one person may prostrate himself as a symbol.

In Orthodox synagogues, men and women sit in separate areas.

Usually Jews who join synagogues are required to pay a membership fee and yearly dues. Discounts are frequently offered for students, senior citizens and people of low incomes. Tickets may be sold to popular services, such as those for Yom Kippur and Rosh Hashana.

Because many services are long—2 1/2 to 3 1/2 hours—it is acceptable in many synagogues for people to enter and leave while services are in progress. However, no one should leave when the Torah is being read or when the ark is open.

In an Orthodox synagogue, guests should observe the separate seating arrangements for men and women.

DRESS

Probably the piece of clothing most identified with Jews is the *kepah* (Hebrew), or *yarmulke* (Yiddish), a skullcap worn by many Jewish men and a few women. It may be simple or elaborately embroidered or appliquéd. It is both a sign of respect to God and a symbol of Jewish identity.

When actually reciting prayers, observant Jewish men wrap themselves in prayer shawls, called *tallit.* In the Book of Numbers, the Torah instructs the Hebrews to "wear fringes on the corners of your garment, look at them, and remember all of God's commandments, and do them." White or sometimes blue-and-white fringes, called *tzizit,* are on the four corners of the shawl, with knots and threads totalling 613—the number of commandments in the Torah.

For daily prayer, some Jewish men—and a few women—also wear two small boxes attached to leather straps and known as *tefillin,* or *phylacteries.* Four passages from the Torah are inside each box. One box is centered on the forehead, the other goes on the arm. Use of the *tefillin* comes from several passages in the Torah, including Deuteronomy 6:8, which instructs Hebrews to bind God's words as a sign on the hand and a frontlet between the eyes.

If attending synagogue, dress modestly. To attend an Orthodox or Conservative synagogue, it is best if women have their arms covered. Guests should not wear prayer shawls or *tefillin*. Synagogues that expect men to cover their heads usually provide extra yarmulkes. Although married Orthodox women are expected to cover their hair, it is not necessary for visitors to Orthodox synagogues.

DIETARY LAWS

The system of Jewish dietary laws is called *Kashrut*. These laws are contained in the Torah and elaborated upon in the Talmud. Not only are Jews told which species they can eat, they are also instructed on how to prepare their food. Proper food is known as *kosher*; prohibited food is *trafe*.

- In general, all fruits, vegetables, grains, fungi, seeds, roots and nuts are permitted—except during Passover, when stricter rules apply.
- All insects are forbidden, so plant products must be washed carefully to ensure that no small insects are attached.
- Fish with both fins and scales are kosher, but shellfish, shark, sea mammals, frog, turtle and octopus are prohibited.
- Meat is permitted if it comes from an animal that chews a cud and has a split hoof, but only if it is slaughtered according to specific laws that prevent cruelty. All pork is prohibited.
- Certain portions of even kosher meat are prohibited, including the sciatic nerve, suet and blood.
- Dairy products are kosher—but they must be kept separate from meat in order to maintain the biblical prohibition against boiling a kid in its mother's milk. The strictest households have separate sets of cookware, china and utensils for meat and dairy, so that the two are never served on the same plate.
- Birds raised for their meat are kosher if they are prepared under the supervision of a rabbi. Wild birds are prohibited.
- Animal by-products, such as eggs, are permitted if they come from a kosher species.

If preparing a meal for a Jewish friend, it's best to ask whether certain foods are appropriate. If in doubt, entertain the friend at a certified kosher restaurant since even kosher food served on dishes that have not been kept kosher would be deemed unclean. If taking food to a Jewish home and unsure whether the family keeps kosher, it is best to buy prepared food that is certified kosher, or to take a kosher wine.

PLACE OF CHILDREN

The Torah tells Jews in Genesis to "be fruitful and multiply," and strict Orthodox Jews forgo birth control. Throughout the Hebrew Bible, children are regarded as a blessing.

The Bible lays down the law, literally, to children about how they should treat their parents since honoring a father and mother is one of the Ten Commandments. But Jewish law and tradition also outlines parents' obligations to their children, including protecting them, educating them to earn a living, instilling the proper values and preparing them to participate fully in the faith.

According to the Talmud, at age thirteen Jewish children are ready for the "fulfillment of the commandments," although some Jews regard twelve as coming of age for girls. At this age, boys become *bar mitzvah,* or sons of the commandment, and girls are *bat mitzvah,* or daughters of the commandment, fully responsible for keeping the commandments of God and bearing the consequences when they disobey them. In most Jewish families, the coming of age of a child is an occasion for both a moving religious ceremony and a festive celebration. Orthodox Jews observe the ceremonial passage only for boys.

The core of the ceremonial passage to adulthood is being called to the front of the synagogue to read or recite from the Torah during a regular synagogue service. Often, the *bar* or *bat mitzvah* also leads prayers and chants. After the service, or sometimes on the evening before, the *bar* or *bat mitzvah*'s parents traditionally host a celebratory meal or reception.

In some synagogues, teenagers go through an additional confirmation ceremony within three years of becoming *bar* or *bat mitzvah*. Most confirmations are held on Shavuot, celebrating the gift of the Torah from God.

The *bar* or *bat mitzvah* is a celebratory occasion. Etiquette for any other worship service applies during the worship portion of the ceremony—dress conservatively and stand to show respect for the Torah with the rest of the congregation. Gifts are appropriate for the boy or girl coming of age, but should not be brought to the synagogue. They should be sent ahead or taken to the party or reception.

ROLES OF MEN AND WOMEN

Women are highly regarded in the faith, and in fact, historically, it has been the mother—not the father—who determines whether a child is Jewish. Anyone born of a Jewish mother is regarded as Jewish, while a child born of a Jewish father and a non-Jewish mother must convert. Today some of the more liberal branches of Judaism recognize patrilineal as well as matrilineal lineage.

However, there are certain restrictions on women in strict Jewish communities. For instance, women are regarded as unclean during the time of their menstrual cycle, and strict Jews require that they undergo a ritual bath before returning to the marital bed. This requirement has the added result of requiring married women to abstain from sexual intercourse during the time of the month when they are least fertile.

In Orthodox synagogues, men and women are seated separately for worship. But while they have varying roles in public worship, depending on the particular congregation, women play a significant role in worship at home. Women are responsible for the lighting of the Sabbath candles and are charged with the responsibility of keeping the home kosher. The mother is also generally assumed to be in charge of the education of the children.

Men, on the other hand, were traditionally responsible for public worship, studying the Torah and supporting the family and Jewish causes materially. For many years, Torah study was denied to women, but now women's study groups are cropping up.

Generally, a person should not extend a hand to an Orthodox Jew of the opposite sex, but wait to see whether the Orthodox person offers a hand first. In Orthodox synagogues, guests should observe the convention of sitting segregated by gender.

HOUSEHOLD

Observant Jewish homes are easily identified from the front door by the *mezuzah*. Although this word literally means "doorpost," the mezuzah is actually a small container affixed to the doorpost that holds a scroll with handwritten verses from Deuteronomy outlining the major principles of Judaism. As Jews pass through the door, they are supposed to kiss the mezuzah as a reminder of their dedication to God. When Jews move into a new home, they may consecrate it as a Jewish home with a formal ceremony that includes installing the mezuzah. Some Jewish homes have mezuzahs on the doorposts of rooms inside as well.

The highlight of the week in an observant Jewish home is the Sabbath or Shabbat, which begins Friday night at sundown and lasts twenty-four hours. This is a time for a family meal a little more special than those during the rest of the week. The Sabbath officially begins with the lighting of at least two candles, reminding Jews to remember and observe. Traditionally, the woman of the household lights the candles and says the blessing over them. Wine is served, with some poured into a special cup to be blessed by the man of the house or by the family. Bread for the Sabbath is called *chalah,* a twisted egg bread, and it is also blessed with a special prayer. The lengthiest blessing of all comes after the meal and includes a petition that eventually the Sabbath will last forever.

The Sabbath is considered a time of rest and peacefulness. Observant Jews are prohibited from working, spending money, driving, using electricity or even talking on the telephone. Modern technology has made these restrictions less severe by providing timers for lights and answering machines for telephones. It is also considered special for a married couple to make love on the Sabbath.

The Sabbath officially ends when three stars are visible in the night sky on Saturday. At this time, a brief service, Havdalah, may be held that includes blessing wine, spices and light.

It is considered appropriate to bring bread and salt to a Jewish family's new residence. When visiting a Jewish family on the Sabbath, a guest should follow the lead of the family. Strictly observant Jews will not use appliances, including the television and telephone, on the Sabbath. If in doubt, ask the host whether something would interfere with observance.

MILESTONES

Birth—Observant Jewish families circumcise male babies in a ceremony called a *brit milah,* or covenant of circumcision, as described in both Genesis and Leviticus. The rite symbolizes Abraham's relationship with God. Unless the baby's health is in danger, this ceremony takes place on the eighth day after birth, usually in the morning.

Since the circumcision is regarded as a religious obligation, it must be performed by a trained Jew in the presence of family and a *minyan,* or group of ten adult men. (In less strict branches of Judaism, women are counted in the ten.) To prepare the baby, its mother bathes him, sometimes in the company of other women friends and relatives. The child's godparents hand him over to the *mohel,* or ritual circumcisor. After the foreskin is clipped away, the boy's father says a blessing and the child is considered a part of the covenant family. The child is also symbolically placed on a padded chair, the "throne of Elijah," as a reminder of that ancient prophet's call of the Jews to their responsibilities as children of God. The baby is given his Hebrew name, which will be used on religious occasions.

Girls receive their Hebrew names in the synagogue on the Sabbath or at the morning prayers on Monday or Thursday following their birth. On that day, their fathers are called up to read from the Torah. A festive meal is usually served after *brit* and baby-naming ceremonies.

Some Orthodox families have an additional ceremony for their firstborn sons thirty-one days after birth. The first child in a family, especially a son, was obligated by Jewish law to assist the priests at the Temple, but Jews developed a ceremony for buying back the child as described in the Book of Numbers.

Strictly observant Jews traditionally do not invite people to a *brit* or a baby-naming; however, in many families the ceremonies have become occasions for celebration. Gifts and cards are appropriate for the baby.

Marriage—Genesis, the first book of the Hebrew Bible, says God created woman so that man should not be alone. Unlike in some religions, no special significance is given to celibacy in Judaism. In fact, Jews take seriously the commandment to "be fruitful and multiply."

The Jewish wedding traditionally took place in one of three ways, all requiring the presence of two witnesses—by a written commitment, by a gift of something of value or by the acknowledgment of the intent to physically consummate the relationship. Today's Jewish weddings are likely to have components of all three.

The *ketubah* is a marriage contract, signed by two witnesses, that outlines a man and woman's roles and responsibilities in marriage. A husband is obligated to provide for his wife and to consider her sexual satisfaction. A wife is expected to honor her husband.

Unlike some cultures which regard it as unlucky for the groom to see the bride before the ceremony, Jewish husbands-to-be are expected to see their wives on their wedding day symbolically to prevent a deception of the kind endured by Jacob in the Hebrew Bible, who was tricked into marrying the wrong sister.

Couples are traditionally married under a *chupah,* or canopy, symbolizing their new relationship and the new home they intend to establish. At Jewish weddings, parents traditionally escort the bride and the groom into the room, sometimes preceded by bridesmaids and groomsmen. The bride stands on the groom's right side under the canopy.

Although some elements may be added or subtracted, Jewish weddings usually follow a basic format: After opening prayers and greetings, the rabbi usually says a few words and the couple affirms its commitment. The groom places a wedding ring on his bride's finger and she on his in a double-ring ceremony. Seven traditional blessings are chanted. Then the couple shares a cup of wine, symbolic of their shared life. The rabbi pronounces the couple married. And, in perhaps one of the best-known rituals of the Jewish wedding, the groom steps on a glass and breaks it and friends and family yell *"Mazal Tov,"* or best wishes. Several explanations exist for the glass-breaking. One is that the broken glass is a reminder of the destruction of the Temple in Jerusalem and the hardships endured by the Jewish people. Another is that the shattered glass is a symbol of the temporary quality of material goods, or, oppositely, that it signifies the fragility of human relationships. Yet another is that it frightens away demons who would spoil the happiness of the couple. And still another is that it connotes the breaking of the bride's hymen on the wedding night.

Traditionally, immediately after the ceremony the bride and groom spend a few minutes alone before joining the party that fulfills the Talmudic instructions to rejoice. Perhaps the best-known custom at a Jewish wedding reception is the lifting of the bride and groom in chairs while their guests dance around them.

If a Jewish marriage does not work out, Jewish law provides for the possibility of a Jewish decree of divorce, called a *get,* which is historically a male prerogative.

All rules of etiquette for worship apply if a wedding is held in a synagogue. If men are expected to cover their heads during the service, the hosts or synagogue will often provide yarmulkes. Gifts are appropriate but should be sent ahead or taken to the reception.

Death—In Jewish tradition, no one should leave while in the presence of a dying person, a way of showing respect. Once death has been confirmed, the person's eyes and mouth should be closed and he or she should be covered. Other customs include lighting a candle, a symbol of the soul, and opening a window for the soul's escape. Prayers and psalms may be said. And friends and relatives may ask forgiveness of the deceased for any wrongs they have committed. Mirrors in the house are covered. From death to burial, a body must not be left unattended, but Jewish custom discourages gathering around the corpse.

Jewish law generally prohibits autopsies; however, since under a Jewish principle the need to save a life holds precedence over obedience to specific laws, some autopsies may be permitted. Cremation is prohibited. And Jewish law frowns on embalming the dead out of respect for the processes of nature and to diminish disturbance of the body. If there must be a long delay before a funeral can be held, or if embalming is required by civil law, provisions can be made.

The body is washed by Jews, either at a Jewish funeral home or by members of a burial society, as a religious act. Jewish law lays out the order of the bath from head to foot, right side first and then left. Blood lost at the time of death is not washed away since blood is regarded as part of the body. After the cleansing, a specific amount of water—twenty-four quarts—is poured over the body as a symbol of purification.

Once cleansed, the body should be clothed in a plain white shroud. A man should be wrapped in his prayer shawl with the fringes cut, since they are reminders of obligations of the mortal world.

Jews should be buried in wooden caskets, preferably unlined. In some cases, soil from Israel is placed in the coffin. Jewish law requires burial in the earth, and not in a mausoleum, although a structure may be built above the grave.

Mourners—close family members—historically tore a garment to represent their grief. This is often done before the funeral. However, today many families pin on a black ribbon, which is ceremonially torn and worn for several days.

The funeral should take place as quickly after death as possible, although not on the Sabbath or a major holiday. Although there are few requirements for funeral liturgy, certain psalms and prayers (such as the 23rd Psalm) are frequently used.

Only Jews may carry the casket of a Jew to its burial. They should pause several times, usually seven, on the way to the grave as an indication of regret at parting and to give those present time to reflect. At a Jewish burial, family members throw the first shovels of dirt onto the lowered casket, and all those present who wish to may follow suit. Strict observance requires that the shovel not be handed from person to person, but be placed in the ground and retrieved by each succeeding mourner. At the grave, mourners recite a special prayer. Those attending the graveside service form parallel lines for close family members to walk through as they leave as a sign of respect.

When returning home after the funeral, those present wash their hands with a vessel of water symbolizing purification after contact with the dead. The pitcher or cup should be replaced and picked up again by each person, not handed down the line.

Jews are required to mourn for seven relatives: father, mother, brother, sister, son, daughter and spouse. Jewish law and tradition recognizes several degrees and rituals of mourning:

- **Aninut.** The time between death and burial is used to make arrangements and notify friends and family of the death. All obligations, including religious ones, are suspended during this time.
- **Shiva.** This seven-day period is the time for remembrances and condolences. Friends and acquaintances may pay calls on the family. During this time, family members do not conduct business, participate in entertainment, wear new clothes, shave, cut their hair or have sexual intercourse. They sit on low seats, to symbolize submission to God's will. And they recite the mourner's prayer daily. A special candle burns for seven days.
- **Sheloshim.** After shiva and before a month has passed, mourners gradually reassume their ordinary practices.
- **Matzevah Dedication**. The unveiling of the gravestone takes place sometime after the end of shiva, generally about eleven months after death.
- **Avelut.** The year following a death is an extended period of mourning during which children are required to say the mourner's prayer daily for eleven months for their deceased parents.
- **Yahrzeit** is the anniversary of the death of a loved one, observed by lighting a candle.
- **Yizkor** is a special prayer recited at Yom Kippur, Passover, Sukkot and Shavuot by anyone who has lost a parent, spouse, child or sibling.

Flowers should not be sent to a Jewish funeral or house of mourning. A charitable contribution in honor of the deceased is considered appropriate. Jewish law also says mourners should be allowed to grieve, so expressions of condolence are inappropriate until after the funeral.

Visitors to a family sitting shiva should enter without ringing the bell or knocking. Food may be taken, but non-Jews should not take food prepared in a non-kosher kitchen to a family who keeps kosher.

CONVERSION

According to the Talmud, to become a Jew one must know and accept the commandments of the Torah, be immersed in a ritual bath and, if a man, be circumcised.

For actual conversion, the prospective convert must appear before a *bet din,* or court of three rabbis. They inquire about background and knowledge of Judaism, and then attempt to ensure that conversion is by free will and desire, not by pressure. The convert must promise to practice Judaism to the exclusion of all other religions, to obey Jewish law and to raise any children as Jews. The convert must also be ritually cleansed in a *mikvah,* or Jewish ritual bath. Every part of the body must be touched by the water three times, with special blessings recited.

Following the bath, the *bet din* members sign the document signifying conversion. The convert may be given a Hebrew name.

Male converts must also be ritually circumcised. If they have already been circumcised, the ritual is considered fulfilled by drawing a drop of blood from the penis.

MAJOR ORGANIZATIONS

American Jewish Committee
The Jacob Blaustein Building
165 East 56 Street
New York, New York 10022

Jewish Reconstructionist Federation
Church Road and Greenwood Avenue
Wyncote, Pa. 19095

Union of American Hebrew Congregations
838 Fifth Avenue
New York, New York 10021

Union of Orthodox Jewish Congregations of America
333 Seventh Avenue
New York, New York 10001

Union of Sephardic Congregations, Inc.

8 West 70 Street
New York, New York 10023

Union for Traditional Judaism
241 Cedar Lane
Teaneck, N. J. 07666

United Synagogue of Conservative Judaism
155 Fifth Avenue
New York, New York 10010-6802

FURTHER READING

Bennett, Alan D., ed. *Journey Through Judaism*. New York: UAHC Press, 1991.

Biale, Rachel. *Women and Jewish Law*. New York: Pantheon Books, 1995.

Diamant, Anita, and Cooper, Howard. *Living a Jewish Life*. New York: Harper Perennial by HarperCollins, 1991.

Dosick, Rabbi Wayne. *Living Judaism*. San Francisco: HarperSan Francisco, 1995.

Einstein, Stephen J., and Kukoff, Lydia. *Every Person's Guide to Judaism*. New York: UAHC Press, 1989.

Fox, Rabbi Karen L., and Miller, Phyllis Zimbler. *Seasons for Celebration*. New York: Perigee Books, The Putnam Publishing Group, 1992.

Freedman, Rabbi E. B.; Greenberg, Jan; and Katz, Karen A. *What Does Being Jewish Mean?* New York: Prentice Hall Press, 1991.

Isaacs, Rabbi Ronald H. *Becoming Jewish*. New York: The Rabbinical Assembly, 1993.

Kertzer, Rabbi Morris N. *What Is a Jew?*, fourth edition. New York: Macmillan Publishing Company, 1978.

Neusner, Jacob. *An Introduction to Judaism*. Louisville: Westminster/John Knox Press, 1991.

Pilkington, C. M. *Teach Yourself Judaism*. Lincolnwood, Illinois: Teach Yourself Books, NTC Publishing Group, 1995.

Singer, David, ed. *American Jewish Yearbook*. exec. ed. Ruth R. Seldin. New York: The American Jewish Committee, 1996.

Waskow, Arthur. *Down-to-Earth Judaism*. New York: William Morrow and Company, Inc., 1995.

FOR CHILDREN
Wood, Angela. *Judaism,* World Religions Series. New York: Thomas Learning, 1995.

LATTER-DAY SAINTS

"Adam fell that men might be; and men are that they might have joy."
—*The Book of Mormon*

ALSO known as the Mormons, the Church of Jesus Christ of Latter-day Saints is one of the country's fastest-growing religions. Even people who know little or nothing about the faith are familiar with the church's famous choral group, the Mormon Tabernacle Choir, who sing in an auditorium with such magnificent acoustics that those in the back can literally hear a pin drop. Tour leaders demonstrate the phenomenon several times a day.

Latter-day Saints, who founded the state of Utah, are so plentiful there that the anniversary of their arrival is a state holiday. But church members are not confined to Utah by any means. Latter-day Saints number almost 10 million worldwide as of 1997, with more than 4.9 million in the United States and more than 5.1 million abroad.

ORIGINS

The Church of Jesus Christ of Latter-day Saints is an American-based religion founded by Joseph Smith. He was born in Sharon, Vermont, on Dec. 23, 1805, one of eight surviving children of a common laborer. After years of moving around in New England in an attempt to earn a living, the family moved to western New York when he was a child.

Smith claims to have had his first vision when still a young teenager. According to church teachings, the community was in the middle of a religious revival in 1820 and young Joseph was confused by the conflicting claims of various religious groups. As he prayed for guidance in a grove near his home, God and Jesus visited him in a pillar of light and advised him not to join any of the existing sects, but to prove himself worthy of restoring the original church of Jesus Christ.

Three years later—in September 1823—he reported having a vision of an angel named Moroni, "a messenger from the presence of God," who led him to a hill where he was shown gold-like plates engraved with ancient records, and stones that could be used for translating them. Although Smith was allowed to see the plates, he did not claim possession of them until 1827.

The first edition of what Smith said he had found on the tablets was pulled together as the Book of Mormon in 1830, bearing the name of the major original writer believed to be an ancient historian. On April 6 of the same year, Smith and five friends founded the Church of Jesus Christ of Latter-day Saints in a log cabin in Fayette Township, Seneca County, New York. Church members are nicknamed Mormons after the book.

But Smith's new church was not welcome. He and his followers fled harassment, going first to Kirtland, Ohio, where they built the church's first temple in 1836. Driven from Ohio, they next went to Missouri, where soon, according to church records, an order from the governor directed that they be "exterminated or driven from the State." From there, they went to Illinois, where they established the community of Nauvoo in 1839, building homes, cultivating farms, setting up businesses and starting construction of a magnificent temple overlooking the Mississippi River.

Their peaceful existence there did not last long. Among complaints of non-Mormon neighbors was that Smith taught that polygamy was acceptable. Opponents of the church jailed Smith and his associates, and on June 27, 1844, a mob executed them.

Smith was succeeded by Brigham Young. In the winter of 1846, Young led his followers out of Illinois in an exodus that ended 1300 miles away on July 24, 1847, when 148 men, women and children paused overlooking the Great Salt Lake. According to church records, Young uttered the words "This is the right place." Others soon arrived. From its earliest days in its new community, the church sent missionaries abroad and pioneers to the unsettled lands of the West, where they built as many as six hundred settlements.

In 1890, the Mormons ended their acceptance of polygamy, although a few tiny offshoots of the church still continue the practice.

HOLY TEXTS

Latter-day Saints accept the Christian Bible, with thirty-nine books of the Old Testament and twenty-seven books of the New Testament. They also have their own sacred scriptures in the Book of Mormon. Latter-day Saints see the book, which is subtitled "Another Testament of Jesus Christ," as a companion to the Holy Bible. The book consists of fifteen sub-books divided into 239 chapters, with history, prophecy, doctrine and material about the Messiah.

The Book of Mormon is the story of ancient American civilizations that resulted from tribes from Israel who traveled to the continent six hundred years before

Christ and remained in North America for another one thousand years. Christ himself is supposed to have appeared after his resurrection to these groups on the American continent.

Texts other than the Book of Mormon include:

Doctrines and Covenants—Smith's revelations for establishment of the Kingdom of God and the constitution of the church. Smith wrote 133 of its 138 sections; the others were added by later leaders.

Pearl of Great Price—A collection of writings and revelations first published in 1851. It includes autobiographical material by Smith.

DIVISIONS

By far the largest group is this one headquartered in Salt Lake City, **The Church of Jesus Christ of Latter-day Saints**. But at least three other groups also exist, established by people who refused to follow Brigham Young west:

The Reorganized Church of Jesus Christ of Latter Day Saints. It came together under Joseph Smith III, who it claimed was his father's rightful successor. This group, known as the Reorganization, formed in 1860 and has headquarters in Independence, Missouri. The Reorganized Church differs with the Salt Lake City group over several issues of doctrine and practice. It is the second-largest group with more than one thousand churches and 150,000 members in the United States.

The Church of Christ (Temple Lot), a small group which, in 1867, set up headquarters in Independence, Missouri, on the temple lot established by Smith and his followers in 1831.

The Church of Jesus Christ (Bickertonites), organized in Pennsylvania in 1862.

These two smaller groups have fewer than ten thousand members combined.

DOCTRINE

God—The Church of Jesus Christ of Latter-day Saints sees God, Jesus Christ and the Holy Ghost as "the godhead," separate divine entities united in purpose. The Holy Ghost is spirit. God and Jesus Christ have glorified and perfected resurrected bodies of flesh. The Reorganized Church, however, sees God, Jesus Christ and the Holy Spirit as one.

Good Deeds—Service to others is a criterion for judgment. In addition, the Church of Jesus Christ of Latter-day Saints has an extensive aid program for members and a far-reaching disaster-relief program. The denomination operates farms, canneries and sewing factories to produce food and clothing to support these efforts.

Creation—The world is a conscious creation of God, according to Mormon teachings, but church doctrine does not set a time frame for its creation or insist that it was created from nothing.

Humankind—All humans existed as spirits before their earthly conceptions and agreed to come to earth to fulfill a divine plan. Once born, humans lose their memories of their previous existence. They are given a physical body, which they will be divided from at death and rejoin in resurrection. While on earth, humans are tested by temptation.

Angels—The Lord uses angels as messengers. They have human-like form and include the spirits of those not yet born on the earth, those who ascended without earthly death and those awaiting resurrection of the body.

Sin—Human beings will be punished for the sins they commit, but not held accountable for any "original sin" committed by Adam and Eve as described in the Old Testament Book of Genesis.

The Devil—Satan was a child of God who rebelled and who tries to keep humans from following God's wishes.

Judgment—Everyone will be resurrected, righteous and unrighteous. People are judged by what they have thought, done and desired, both before birth and after death. In the afterlife, they will be assigned to specific levels of salvation. Only those who have committed the unpardonable sin of blasphemy against the Holy Spirit, once they have received the Holy Spirit, are eternally damned.

Heaven—The faithful can eventually achieve the status of gods and goddesses. To get to this highest level, Mormons must know the right signs, rituals and passwords. Mormons are taught these in special Temple ceremonies.

Heaven is not a single paradise, but a series of kingdoms, each of which may have more than one level:

- Telestial—the lowest kingdom.This is the place for unrepentant sinners who have spent time in punishment; at the end of the millennium, having served their sentence, they are brought out of spiritual prison and put into this kingdom.
- Terrestrial—the middle kingdom. Good people who fail to live up completely to the faith are assigned to this kingdom.
- Celestial—the highest kingdom. The highest level of the highest kingdom is the presence of God.

Hell—There are three types of hell: a personal hell caused by disobedience; a temporary state of punishment while awaiting resurrection; and permanent punishment because of the unpardonable sin of blasphemy against the Holy Spirit. People can escape the first state by repenting; they will be released from the second state at resurrection. Only the third state is permanent.

Miracles—Latter-day Saints believe miracles are events that happen through divine intervention, but that one has to have faith to experience a miracle.

Messiah—Jesus Christ is the messiah and will come again at the end of mortal time.

DOCTRINES SPECIFIC TO MORMONS

A unique belief of the Church of Jesus Christ of Latter-day Saints is that the dead can be baptized by proxy through the living. Church members believe no other religion's baptisms are valid, so Mormons have relatives who have died baptized into their faith. Reasoning among Latter-day Saints is that people may decide after death to be a part of the church. Since the church regards baptism as essential, baptism by proxy is the only way the converted dead can fulfill their obligation.

Because of the concern for the spiritual life of the dead, genealogy plays a great role in Mormonism, and a computer system allows researchers to tie into the world's largest genealogical research facility at church headquarters in Salt Lake City.

The Reorganized Church does not share the practice of baptisms for the dead. Although the church believes that people who have not accepted the faith in life will have an opportunity after death, they do not believe baptism is necessary for this to take place.

The Church of Jesus Christ of Latter-day Saints also believes that divine revelation for the direction of the entire church comes to the president of the church from God. Presidents are viewed as prophets as Moses, Abraham and other biblical figures are.

Although it is not required, young adults are encouraged to give time to missionary endeavors. About a third of all men aged nineteen to twenty-one, and an increasing number of women, make this commitment. The missionaries are assigned in pairs to specific assignments and the service is temporary.

**THE THIRTEEN ARTICLES OF FAITH OF THE
CHURCH OF JESUS CHRIST OF LATTER-DAY SAINTS**

The following articles were compiled by church founder Joseph Smith in 1842:

1. We believe in God, the Eternal Father, and in His son, Jesus Christ, and in the Holy Ghost.
2. We believe that men will be punished for their own sins, and not for Adam's transgression.
3. We believe that through the Atonement of Christ, all mankind may be saved, by obedience to the law and ordinances of the Gospel.
4. We believe that the first principles and ordinances of the Gospel are: first, faith in the Lord Jesus Christ; second, repentance; third, baptism by immersion for the remission of sins; fourth, laying on of hands for the gift of the Holy Ghost.

5. We believe that a man must be called of God, by prophecy, and by the laying on of hands by those who are in authority, to preach the Gospel and administer in the ordinances thereof.
6. We believe in the same organization that existed in the Primitive Church, viz., apostles, prophets, pastors, teachers, evangelists, etc.
7. We believe in the gift of tongues, prophecy, revelation, visions, healings, interpretation of tongues, etc.
8. We believe the Bible to be the word of God as far as it is translated correctly; we also believe the Book of Mormon to be the word of God.
9. We believe all that God has revealed, all that He does now reveal, and we believe that He will yet reveal many great and important things pertaining to the Kingdom of God.
10. We believe in the literal gathering of Israel and in the restoration of the Ten Tribes; that Zion will be built upon this (the American) continent; that Christ will reign personally upon the earth; and, that the earth will be renewed and receive its paradisiacal glory.
11. We claim the privilege of worshiping Almighty God according to the dictates of our own conscience, and allow all men the same privilege, let them worship how, where, or what they may.
12. We believe in being subject to kings, presidents, rulers and magistrates, in obeying, honoring and sustaining the law.
13. We believe in being honest, true, chaste, benevolent, virtuous, and in doing good to all men; indeed, we may say that we follow the admonition of Paul—we believe all things, we hope all things, we have endured many things and we hope to be able to endure all things. If there is anything virtuous, lovely, or of good report or praiseworthy, we seek after these things.

CALENDAR

Mormons use the calendar commonly used in the West.

RELIGIOUS FESTIVALS AND HOLIDAYS

Christmas—Mormons celebrate Jesus's birth on Dec. 25 according to the traditions of the culture they live in. In Salt Lake City, Temple Square glows with thousands of lights and people visit for nightly concerts.

Easter—Mormons also celebrate Easter with traditional songs, services and festivities.

Gifts and cards are appropriate for Christmas and Easter.

Headquarters of the Church of Jesus Christ of Latter-day Saints in Salt Lake City are closed on July 24, a state holiday in Utah, to commemorate the arrival of the Mormons there in 1847. Churches in other parts of the country may mark the day in some way with a special gathering or service.

ATTITUDE TOWARD OTHER HOLIDAYS

Latter-day Saints celebrate as they wish according to the culture in which they live or work.

TITLES

The Church of Jesus Christ of Latter-day Saints has no professional clergy, but it has a clearly delineated hierarchy. Only the General Authorities are full-time paid church workers.

The General Authorities consist of:

The First Presidency—the President of the Church and his two counselors, chosen for life. The president is regarded as a prophet who receives revelation from God to lead the church. Addressed as "President" with his last name.

The Quorum of Twelve Apostles—chosen for life. Along with the First Presidency, these men make up the top administration of the church. The Apostle who has served the longest succeeds the president when he dies. Addressed as "Elder" with their last names.

The Quorums of the Seventy—These men are responsible for carrying out the church policies and serving as leaders in specific geographic areas. Addressed as "Elder" or "Brother."

The Presiding Bishopric—The bishop and two counselors are responsible for overseeing the church's finances and supervise the ministry for young men and women under eighteen years old. Addressed as "Bishop" with last name. The Church of Jesus Christ of Latter-day Saints is organized into wards, or local congregations, each of which has a bishop and two counselors; several wards make up a stake, overseen by a president and two counselors; and several stakes make up an area, also overseen by a president and two counselors.

The Church of Jesus Christ of Latter-day Saints and the Reorganized church recognize two types of priesthood with three levels in each. These are not considered clerical, however, but are open to any qualified male of the church:

Melchizedek Priesthood—
- *Elders*—ordained at eighteen or adult converts. Addressed as "Elder."
- *Seventies*—serve as General Authorities and may be designated presidents of

geographic areas. Addressed as ''Elder'' unless serving as President or in an office with another title.
• *High Priests*—includes bishops, stake presidents, high councils or general authorities. Addressed according to office.

Aaronic Priesthood—
• *Deacons*—ordained at twelve and over—can distribute the sacrament and help with duties around the church.
• *Teachers*—ordained at fourteen and older—can instruct others and prepare the sacrament.
• *Priests*—ordained at sixteen and over—can baptize, administer the sacrament and ordain priests, teachers and deacons.

Unlike the larger Church of Jesus Christ of Latter-day Saints, the Reorganized Church ordains both men and women.

The most common forms of address among Mormons are "Brother" and "Sister," but these are not used for unbaptized children or non-members. Because of the implied relationship within the church, non-members should not call Mormons "Brother" or "Sister."

COMMUNITY WORSHIP

The most sacred ceremonies of the Church of Jesus Christ of Latter-day Saints are performed in regional temples, and only church members certified by their congregational leaders to lead moral lives, be honest in their business dealings and be faithful in their tithes to the church can enter the innermost temple sanctum. These certifications are called ''recommends.'' They are renewed each year, and many Mormons fail to get them.

No regular worship services are held at the temples, but take place in local chapels. Members hold services in these chapels to hear spiritual talks and have the sacrament—the preferred term among Latter-day Saints for the elements representing the body and blood of Jesus Christ. Mormons use bread and water—not juice or wine.

Mormons consider Sunday the Sabbath. Services are known as sacrament meetings. They follow a prescribed form of congregational song, invocation, song, prayer, blessing of sacrament, serving of sacrament, speakers, song and benediction. Families may spend the rest of the day visiting the sick, engaging in wholesome entertainment or enjoying the outdoors. They are encouraged not to participate in any activity that might require anyone else to work on the Sabbath—dining out, playing golf, etc.

Since the church has no professional priesthood, any person, male or female, young or old, may be asked to pray or speak before the congregation. On the first Sundays of the month, speaking is replaced by testimony. Church members take turns making statements of faith or relating experiences that have happened. Also at the First Sunday services, the church blesses any newborn babies that have been brought for the occasion. Members are expected to fast for two meals on the First Sunday and break the fast with the sacrament.

Besides regular worship services, Mormons sometimes have "firesides," much more informal gatherings of singing and speaking that may be held in the meeting house or in someone's home.

The Church of Jesus Christ of Latter-day Saints invites anyone present to partake of the sacrament, which is offered in individual pieces of bread and cups of water. Guests should participate in that and other parts of worship as they feel comfortable. While temples of the Church of Jesus Christ of Latter-day Saints are closed except to specially credentialed members, the temple of the Reorganized Church in Independence, Missouri, is open to everyone.

PRIVATE WORSHIP

The Church of Jesus Christ of Latter-day Saints expects religion to be taught in the home. The church urges its families to set aside nights for family members to read scriptures, talk and pray or enjoy a family outing together. These are called Family Home Evenings. Congregations do not plan any church activities on Monday evenings to allow families this time, but some families may choose to observe another evening. Church members are expected to pray and read scriptures daily from the time they are able to read.

Friends, coworkers and acquaintances of Latter-day Saints should try to include the entire family in any event on a family's designated night, or attempt to reschedule any conflicting activity.

DRESS

After entering a temple of the Church of Jesus Christ of Latter-day Saints, church members must dress completely in white.

People who have been admitted to the temple are given a special form of underwear, generally referred to as their "garments," which they are expected to wear next to their skin for the rest of their lives. The modest garments represent the clothing Adam and Even donned after they succumbed to temptation in the Garden of Eden in the Genesis account of creation.

For Sunday church services, women are encouraged to wear dresses and male adults usually wear jackets and ties.

DIETARY LAWS

Latter-day Saints are expected to abstain from alcohol, tobacco, coffee and tea. They are also expected to eat little meat.

Beverages other than coffee, tea and alcohol should be provided when entertaining a Latter-day Saint. Alcohol, coffee and tea are also inappropriate gifts to Mormons.

PLACE OF CHILDREN

Children are considered very important within the Church of Jesus Christ of Latter-day Saints. The church provides programs for children from age three to eleven.

Children usually are baptized and join the church at eight, which is considered the age of accountability. After age twelve, boys can "receive the priesthood." Special organizations are also provided for girls after age twelve.

ROLES OF MEN AND WOMEN

Because the church has no professional clergy, all the roles in the local congregation are filled by members. The local bishop "calls" men and women to fill specific functions. Either men or women may be called upon to address the congregation, but only men are ordained to the priesthood.

Latter-day Saints teach that the father and mother are a team at the head of the family.

HOUSEHOLD

Many Latter-day Saints have a picture of Jesus in their homes. The other distinguishing characteristic of a Latter-day Saint household is the absence of coffee, tea or alcohol.

MILESTONES

Birth—Whenever parents are ready, they bring their infants to be blessed and given a name before the congregation. This name will go on the records of the church. The blessings usually take place on the first Sunday of the month during the regular worship service. At the designated time, a male member of the priesthood—usually the baby's father—brings the child forward. Other members of the priesthood who have been invited to participate form a circle with him. The father then offers a personal blessing and says the baby's name.

If invited to a baby-blessing, guests should participate in the service to the extent they are comfortable. Cards and gifts are appropriate for a new baby.

Marriage—The Church of Jesus Christ of Latter-day Saints puts great stock in marriage and teaches that a husband and wife who have had their relationship "sealed" by the church can be married throughout eternity. Because sealings can take place only in a temple, many Mormon weddings occur there; civil marriages may be sealed at a temple later. Mormons may also seal the marriages of their dead ancestors in the temple by proxy.

For a sealing, the couple meets with family and friends in a designated area of the temple. An official greets the assembly and offers words of advice. The couple kneels facing each other across an altar in the center of the area, while mirrors on opposite walls reflect their images infinitely. After words from the official explaining the sealing, the couple kisses. They may also exchange rings.

The Reorganized Church has no special service to seal marriage for eternity.

Since non-members of the Church of Jesus Christ of Latter-day Saints are never admitted into the inner rooms of a temple that has been consecrated, no non-members will be invited to a sealing. Many Mormon couples have receptions afterwards that include non-Mormon family and friends. Cards and gifts are always appropriate for the bride and groom.

Death—A Latter-day Saint's funeral usually follows a format similar to that of a weekly worship service, but will include eulogies. Most Mormons will have a viewing of the body at the funeral home, traditionally on the evening before the funeral, and a brief viewing in the church before the service. Under some circumstances, however, the family may prefer to have a closed casket. The casket is closed during the funeral.

Cards, flowers and memorial gifts are appropriate.

CONVERSION

Latter-day Saints do not take church affiliation lightly. Anyone who expresses interest in joining is known as an investigator. Before being baptized, a candidate must be interviewed by a local member of the priesthood and prove to be familiar with the teachings of the church. Since Mormons do not recognize the baptisms of any other churches, all candidates must be baptized.

Baptism is by immersion at a local meetinghouse or nearby body of water, historically on a Saturday night before the first Sunday of the month, although it can be at another time. Several people may be baptized at once. Since the candidate for baptism has answered questions before a member of the priesthood, these are not repeated at the time of baptism. The service begins and ends with a prayer. With each person baptized, the officiating bishop or other official says a prescribed prayer and baptizes the candidate in the name of the Father, the Son and the Holy Ghost.

At the next First Sunday church service, a confirmation follows when a member of the Melchizedek priesthood lays hands on the newly baptized member and bestows the gift of the Holy Spirit.

MAJOR ORGANIZATIONS

The Church of Jesus Christ of Latter-day Saints
15 East South Temple St., 2nd floor
Salt Lake City, Utah 84150

Reorganized Church of Jesus Christ of Latter Day Saints
The Auditorium
P. O. Box 1059
Independence, Missouri 64051

FURTHER READING

Arrington, Leonard J., and Britton, Davis. *The Mormon Experience.* New York: Vintage Books, 1980.

Ballard, M. Russell. *Our Search for Happiness—An Invitation to Understand the Church of Jesus Christ of Latter-day Saints.* Salt Lake City: Deseret Book Company, 1993.

Britton, Davis. *Historical Dictionary of Mormonism.* Metuchen, N.J., and London: The Scarecrow Press Inc., 1994.

Ludlow, Daniel H., ed. *Encyclopedia of Mormonism.* five vols. New York: Macmillan Publishing Company, 1992.

Naythons, Matthew. *The Mission—Inside the Church of Jesus Christ of Latter-day Saints.* Waltham, MA: Epicenter Communications, Warner Books, 1995.

Shipps, Jan. *Mormonism—The Story of a New Religious Tradition.* Urbana, Ill. and Chicago: University of Illinois Press, 1987.

MUSLIMS

"There is no god but Allah; Muhammad is his messenger."
—Islamic confession of faith

MUHAMMAD Ali. The Ayatollah Khomeni. Kareem Abdul-Jabar. Saddam Hussein. Television portrayals of Muslim figures seem to be confined to international enemies in flowing headdresses and African-American athletes in silk shorts. But while Arab leaders and American sports figures garner attention, millions of Muslims live out their faith quietly. They conduct their lives by its clock and calendar and eat, dress and socialize by its rules. Followers of Islam say theirs is a religion with very practical application. It encourages responsibility, accountability and fidelity.

Islamic organizations estimate that a billion people—one of every five on earth—are considered Muslim. The religion is present on every continent of the world (except, maybe, Antarctica). Islam is the dominant faith in northern Africa, the Middle East, Afghanistan, Pakistan, Bangladesh, parts of India and Indonesia, and the southern republics of the former Soviet Union. In the United States, millions of citizens describe themselves as Muslim. Islam is often described as the country's fastest-growing religion, expected to pass Judaism to become the second largest faith after Christianity in the early years of the 21st century.

SYMBOL

The crescent beside the star, which appears on the flags of several countries, is the symbol of Islam.

ORIGINS

Islam claims roots going back to Ibrahim (Abraham) of the Hebrew Bible through his son Ismail (Ishmael). The Book of Genesis tells the story of Ibrahim and his wife Sarai, who lived to old age without children. To make God's promise of descendants come true, Sarai urged Ibrahim to take her slave girl, Hajar (Hagar), as a wife. Hajar gave birth to Ismail, but Sarai soon banished the slave and her son. Sarai, despite her advanced age, later bore Isaac, through whom the Jewish line claims to have descended.

Historically, however, Islam is the newest of the world's three great monotheistic religions. Its founder was Hadhrat Muhammad, who was born in Saudi Arabia about 570 and died in 632. Muhammad was a merchant's son from Makkah, or Mecca, whose name in Arabic means "glorified." Muhammad claimed that when he was about forty he was visited by a figure identified as the angel Gabriel, who showed him words on a roll of cloth and told him to recite them. Although he was illiterate, Muhammad was able to understand the words. Some two years later, he again received messages from God, which continued throughout his life.

Muhammad gained quite a following, and leaders of Makkah became frustrated with his growing influence and developed a plot to assassinate him. Muhammad fled to a nearby town that became known as Madinat al-Nabi, or the town of the prophet, shortened to Madinah, or Medina. There, he became the ruler of the city.

In 628, responding to a dream, Muhammad and his followers set out to visit Makkah. They negotiated a treaty promising peace for ten years, and were allowed to return again the next year. But the truce did not hold, and in 630, Muhammad took over his home city. He visited the Ka'bah shrine, believed to have been built by Ishmael to honor the one God, and cleansed it of the idols of polytheism, but ultimately returned to Madinah.

Muhammad died in 632. So many followers of Islam have named their children in honor of the prophet that more people in the world bear the name Muhammad than any other. Whenever devout Muslims refer to the prophet himself, they follow his name with the phrase "peace and blessings of God be upon him," sometimes abbreviated in writing as "p.b.u.h."

HOLY TEXTS

Qur'an—The words Muhammad said he received from God became known as the Qur'an (sometimes called the Koran in America). Qur'an means "recitation." The holy book itself names the religion Islam, which means "surrender," referring to giving up one's will to the will of Allah, the one God. The Qur'an also dictates that followers of Islam will be known as Muslims. Muslims resent being referred to as "Muhammadans," saying they worship Allah, or God, not the prophet.

Muslims believe the Qur'an does not contradict the scriptures of Jews or Christians, but completes them. They regard the Qur'an in its Arabic form as divine dictation, a literal, word-for-word script of what Allah told Muhammad. Therefore, only the Arabic version is regarded as the true Qur'an. All translations are considered semblances produced only for convenience.

Even the physical book of the Qur'an is revered. Muslims do not handle it when they are ritually unclean—women who are menstruating, for example, would not touch it—and they sometimes kiss it before traveling. It is stored in a special room used only for prayer, or placed high enough that nothing can be above it. Recitation of the Qur'an should not be interrupted for any reason, even a threat to the safety of the one reciting, except to correct a mistake in the words of the recitation.

While in the presence of the Qur'an, Mulsims are expected to behave with respect and dignity. When its words are being spoken, they should remain silent and not eat or drink. Non-Muslims should also behave respectfully.

DIVISIONS

Sunni Muslims—Although there are many non-Sunni sects, about 90 percent of Muslims are considered Sunni Muslims, derived from the word *sunnah,* which literally means ''path'' and refers to the prophet Muhammad's practices. Among Sunnis, there are differing schools of thought with varying interpretations of Islamic law, but all are considered orthodox.

Shi'ites—The next largest group of Muslims are the Shi'ites, who are almost entirely in Iran, Persia and parts of Iraq. They originally split from the Sunni in a disagreement over Muhammad's successor. While Sunnis accepted the leaders chosen to follow Muhammad and regarded them only as examples of piety, Shi'ites believe the leadership of the Muslims comes only through descendants of Muhammad's first cousin and son-in-law, Ali. According to Shi'ites, these descendants were sinless and infallible. They await the return of Ali's final childless male descendant, who disappeared in 878, to bring in an idyllic age before the end of the world.

African American Muslims—In the United States, the Nation of Islam led by Minister Louis Farrakhan is a visible presence. Founded in Detroit by an immigrant from Arabia named Wallace Fard, the Nation of Islam gained converts and attracted controversy among black Americans under Elijah (Poole) Muhammad, a native of Sandersville, Georgia, who preached black self-confidence and racial separatism. Malcolm X, the former Malcolm Little, was his close aide for a decade before breaking with the movement, taking a religious pilgrimage, and rejecting the teaching of racial separation. After Elijah Muhammad's death in 1975, his son Wallace, now known as Warith Deen Muhammad, took the reins of the movement. Warith soon turned his followers to orthodox Islam and most became mainstream Sunni Muslims. In response, Farrakhan formed a new Nation of Islam and continued preaching separatism.

Sufis—Mysticism practiced by Muslims is called Sufism, believed to come from the word for wool because of the simple garments worn by the Sufis. Desiring closeness to Allah, Sufis renounce wealth and devote themselves to religious study and meditation. They sometimes use techniques such as prayer beads, breath control and dance, and believe in spiritual guides.

DOCTRINE

God—The one true God, called Allah, is the God of the Bible, the creator and controller of the universe. Allah is all-knowing and all-powerful. He is called Lord but not Father because of its human connotations. The Muslims' Allah never came to earth incarnate; therefore Jesus is considered a prophet with no claims on divinity.

Good Deeds—Allah measures followers not only by their faith but by their deeds. It is the duty of humans to bring about Allah's will on earth through good works.

Creation—Nature is subservient to men and women, who have mastery over even the sun, moon and stars. But creation should be treated with respect.

Humankind—People are not born into sin, but are blessed with "perfections" including an innate ability to sense the divine. All people are created equal by Allah, but exercise free will to determine their fate.

Angels—Angels are created from light and serve Allah as messengers and as escorts for the dead. Each human is assigned two recorder angels to keep up with deeds and actions. The Qur'an also refers to *jinn,* or invisible spirits which, like humans, have free will.

Sin—Adam and Eve sinned, and people sin, but there is no inherited responsibility or "original sin." There was no need for Allah to become incarnate and ransom himself for the sins of humans.

The Devil—Iblis or Shaitan was an angel cast out by Allah for opposing the creation of Adam. Iblis tempted Adam and Eve in the Garden of Eden and leads people's hearts away from Allah.

Judgment—After a tumultuous event that shakes the earth and makes it give up its dead, Allah will examine the book of destiny to determine who has lived according to his will and who has not.

Heaven—The just will ascend to a paradise of gardens where rivers flow with milk and honey.

Hell—Unbelievers descend to Gehenna for fiery torment. For believers, however, there is hope for redemption even from hell.

Miracles—Mulims generally believe Allah has performed miracles in the past and still does. Muhammad regarded the Qur'an as God's greatest miracle.

Messiah—There is no Muslim idea of a messiah coming to earth to rule and to judge, but Sunni Muslims believe a figure called a *mahdi* will come at the end of time.

DOCTRINES SPECIFIC TO ISLAM

THE FIVE PILLARS

Followers of Islam have five religious obligations:

Shahadah—Confession of Faith. The "witness" of the Muslim is that there is no God but Allah and that Muhammad is his messenger. A faithful Muslim repeats the phrase as many as thirty times a day in prayer.

Salah—Prayer. Muslims are required to perform ritual worship or prayer five times a day—dawn (Fajr), noon (Zuhr), afternoon (Asr), evening (Maghrib) and night (Isha). They may pray alone or with others. Parts of the prayer are prescribed, but there are places in the order for personal invocations. A worshiper prepares for prayer by ritual bathing of the face first, including the mouth, followed by the hands and arms to the elbows. The right hand then washes the top of the head. Next, the feet are cleansed to the ankles. Garments must also be clean. To ensure that the place where he is praying is clean, a Muslim kneels on a prayer rug. To pray, a Muslim touches his forehead to the ground facing Makkah.

Zakah—Almsgiving. Because everything belongs to Allah, Muslims are expected to give 2.5 percent of their wealth to the poor. This principle is to help spread the wealth, prevent the rich from hoarding wealth and establish a sense of community and mutual responsibility. Muslims are also expected to contribute voluntarily to good causes whenever possible.

Siyam—Fasting. Annually, all adult Muslims of good health are expected to fast from sunrise to sunset during the month of Ramadan. Specific hours of the fast are determined by the ability to distinguish a white thread from a black thread in natural light. Followers are to abstain from food, drink and sexual relations during those times. Children, the elderly, the sick, pregnant women, nursing mothers and soldiers in battle are exempt from the requirement. Everyone who misses the opportunity to fast during Ramadan because of a temporary condition is expected to make up for it later or donate the cost of the meals that were eaten during fast time to the poor. The fast is intended to remind Muslims of their dependence on Allah and to make them sympathetic to the poor and hungry.

Hajj—Pilgrimage. Every Muslim who is physically and financially able is required to make at least one pilgrimage to Makkah (Mecca) as an adult during the twelfth month of the Islamic calendar. Only Muslims are admitted to the city, and the annual Hajj assemblage is believed to be the largest on earth. The rites of Hajj honor Allah, commemorate the ordeal of Hajar and Ismail when they were exiled and bring all Muslims from all nations together on equal footing.

Because observant Muslims must pray five times daily, it is important that they be given the opportunity to escape to a quiet place at the appropriate time. At the home of a Muslim or in a place where Muslims are gathered at prayer time, the non-Muslim should quietly stay out of the way. If hosting a Muslim at prayer time, offer water for the ritual bath and a place to pray where there are no pictures or images. If pictures are on the walls or furniture, turn the image down or away until after the prayer if possible. If the Muslim does not have a prayer rug handy, offer a clean, plain towel or sheet.

During Ramadan, Muslims appreciate expressions of support. A card or note is always appropriate, as is an invitation to a late evening meal after the day's fasting time is over. For many Muslims, the evening meal during Ramadan is festive.

An expression of goodwill is also appropriate for a Muslim making a pilgrimage.

CALENDAR

The Muslim calendar begins in the year Muhammad migrated to Madina, 622 C.E. The calendar is lunar and consists of twelve months, each twenty-nine days, twelve hours and forty-four minutes long for a year that is 354 or 355 days long depending on how the minutes fall. A day begins at sunset.

The months of the Muslim calendar are:

Muharram	Rajab
Safar	Shaban
Rabi al-Awwal	Ramadan
Rabi al-Thani	Shawwal
Jumada al-Ula	Dhul Qadah
Jumada al-Akhirah	Dhul Hijjah

RELIGIOUS FESTIVALS AND HOLIDAYS

The festivals of Islam are scheduled according to the lunar calendar and therefore may fall during different seasons in different years.

Muslims celebrate two major religious festivals: Eid al-Fitr, festival of bread-breaking; and Eid Adha, the festival of the sacrifice. Many Muslims take several days off work to celebrate the holidays.

Eid al-Fitr—Comes on the first day of Shawwal when the sliver of a new moon is sighted marking a new month and the end of the month-long Ramadan fast. Many families clean and decorate their homes, exchange gifts and cards and donate food and money to the poor. Children traditionally have new clothes for the occasion whenever possible. Some Muslim communities have large gatherings and exchange hearty congratulations for completing the fast.

Eid al-Adha—Takes place on the tenth day of Dhul Hijjah, the twelfth month, at the end of the time when pilgrims are in Saudi Arabia for Hajj. All Muslims, whether on pilgrimage or not, sacrifice animals and share them with the poor. Many Muslims also give gifts and buy new clothes, especially for their children.

Cards and simple gifts are in good taste. If invited to a celebration of either Eid, a non-Muslim may offer to bring food to share, expecting the meat to be provided according to Muslim dietary laws.

ATTITUDE TOWARD OTHER HOLIDAYS

Birthdays—Muslims believe their birth, life and death come from Allah and thus are nothing for which to receive congratulation. However, some families do celebrate birthdays.

Mother's Day and Father's Day—These holidays are regarded by many Muslims as Western commercial innovations and therefore are not celebrated, although Muslims are taught to hold parents in high regard.

Valentine's Day—Because Islam has strict prescriptions for male-female relationships, most Muslims do not celebrate this holiday.

Halloween—Because of an association with paganism, many Muslim children do not participate in Halloween festivities.

Muslims should be excused from any holiday-related activity. Muslim children may be invited to birthday parties and other special events through their parents, who can determine whether to accept or decline.

TITLES

Imam—prayer leader. There are no ordained clergy in Islam. The primary prayer leader is usually referred to as imam, although any male Muslim may lead in prayer. Great Muslim leaders of the past are also referred to as Imam.

Shaykh or **Shaikh**—an honorific title for those with extensive knowledge of Islam or the spiritual master in Sufism.

Ayatullah or **Ayatollah**—literally ''sign of God,'' a Shi'ite title for honored religious leaders.

COMMUNITY WORSHIP

Community worship for Muslims takes place in a mosque or *masjid,* the preferred term which literally means a place of prostration. There is no Muslim Sabbath, but Friday afternoon's prayer is usually communal.

A *masjid* usually has a dome, a frequent feature of Middle East architecture, and a minaret, or tower, where a caller stands to summon the faithful to prayer. Often, through the benefits of modern technology, today's calls come over a public address system.

The prayer room of a *masjid* is carpeted and strikingly bare, since Muslims stand, kneel and bow to pray. At prayer, Muslims face the wall toward Mecca, known as the *qibla* wall. Sometimes there is a *minbar,* or pulpit, from which the prayer leader will give a sermon.

When "in ranks" to pray, Muslims line up with toes and shoulders even with the person next to them. Men take their places in the front of the room, women in the back.

Muslims and visitors are expected to remove their shoes to enter the prayer area. Because of the closeness of the company at prayer, heavy perfumes and spicy meals beforehand may be discouraged although not forbidden. T-shirts with images of people or animals should not be worn as these images are considered distractions or even idolatrous.

PRIVATE WORSHIP

The required five daily prayers are the main component of a Muslim's private worship.

Non-Muslims should respect the privacy of Muslims when they pray.

DRESS

Islamic clothing varies greatly from culture to culture, but in general clothing is to be modest and loose. Most Muslim women still adhere to the custom of covering their hair and wearing clothing that reveals only the face, hands and feet. Some sects and cultures require women to cover everything but their eyes, reserving the view of their bodies only for their husbands. Any clothing that is too tight, too thin or too revealing is considered improper. Men must be covered from the navel to the knees during prayer, and are prohibited from wearing silk.

Although certainly not expected to abide by Muslim customs, non-Muslims attending Muslim events should dress modestly. In a *masjid,* women should wear something that covers their knees. Men should wear long pants.

DIETARY LAWS

Food that is proper for Muslims is considered *halal*. That which is not per-mitted is *haram*. Any minute portion of a forbidden ingredient in any form is considered contaminating. Muslims are prohibited from consuming:

- Pork
- Blood
- Alcohol
- Animals that have died on their own, been killed by other animals or been improperly slaughtered. Muslims believe animals should be killed by slashing the throat and bleeding, and that all slaughter should be done in the name of Allah.

Since food is provided by Allah, each meal should begin with a prayer of thanksgiving and faithful Muslims are taught not to overeat or waste food.

When sharing food with Muslims or providing for a community meal where Muslims are among the crowd, non-Muslims should be conscious of the prohibitions.

PLACE OF CHILDREN

Children are highly prized in Islam, and a great emphasis is put on family responsibility. From the beginning, children are considered a part of the community. They are taught prayers and recitations from the Qur'an very early. At about age seven, parents are expected to enforce the requirement to pray in the home, and by puberty children are required to make daily prayers. At puberty, children are also expected to begin meeting the full requirement of the Ramadan fast, although younger children may symbolically refrain from some foods.

ROLES OF MEN AND WOMEN

Relationships between men and women are taken very seriously by obedient Muslims. Therefore, casual exchanges of hugs and kisses—or even handshakes—between people of different genders are usually considered inappropriate. Muslim men often hug other men and women embrace other women, however.

Men and women are regarded as equal under the Qur'an, but with different roles. The man is seen as responsible for providing for the family, while the woman is obligated to care for it.

From its beginning more than 1,400 years ago, Islamic society gave women civil rights such as the right to inherit or accumulate wealth and earnings, retain their maiden names, initiate divorce and approve arranged marriages. Some cultures where Islam is predominant have adopted abusive practices toward women in the name of religion; however, these are not accepted by a vast majority of Muslims.

When greeting a Muslim of the opposite sex, it is best to speak cor-
dially and wait to see whether a hand is offered.

HOUSEHOLD

Since practicing Muslims are likely to pray at home, many families keep a
clean area with no exposed photographs or images where they can kneel. The space
may have a rug or people may use individual mats.

MILESTONES

Birth—The first word a Muslim baby hears should be "Allah." The father
should whisper the call to prayer in the baby's right ear and the command to
worship in its left ear. Usually within seven days, Muslims hold an *aqiqa,* or
naming and welcoming ceremony, to introduce the baby to the community. The
baby is also offered something sweet to eat. In Muhammad's time, this was usually
a date that had been chewed. Now, it's more likely to be honey, apple sauce or
banana touched to the infant's lips. The calls to prayer and worship are whispered
once again, and the baby is passed around so that each family member or guest
can whisper a prayer in its ear. This is to signify that the baby is a part of the
community and that all present are responsible for its well-being. Sometimes a boy
is circumcised at the time of the ceremony, but this procedure may be done at any
time.

Traditionally fathers slaughter two animals to celebrate the birth of a boy and
one to celebrate the birth of a girl, and give food and money to the poor and needy.

Cards and gifts for Muslim babies are appropriate. When invited to
a ceremony for a new baby, if a non-Muslim feels obligated to pray,
a simple wish that the child be blessed will suffice.

Marriage—Muslims do not regard marriage as a sacrament, but do see it as
a solemn covenant. Muslim men may marry Christian or Jewish women, since they
also believe in one God, but Muslim women are expected to marry Muslims because it is presumed that children will adopt the religion of their fathers. In some
Islamic cultures, men are allowed to have up to four wives—but only with the
permission of the first wife. Divorce is discouraged although not forbidden outright.

Since many Muslim marriages are arranged by parents, courtship often involves a few supervised visits, after which either partner may reject the arrangement. Islamic custom requires that a man provide a dowry for his wife, which
usually consists of jewelry and personal gifts.

An Islamic wedding may be simple or may conform to the culture in which
it takes place. The actual marriage ceremony may be held in a *masjid,* a home or

elsewhere, and consists of an announcement of the dowry, the exchange of vows and the signing of the marriage contract before witnesses. Other arrangements may vary according to the *masjid* or the couple involved. Immediately after or within a few days of the wedding, the family of the bride is expected to hold a wedding banquet, or *walimah.*

Cards and gifts for Muslim weddings are appropriate. Rules of the *masjid* should be observed for the ceremony. Shoes should be removed, and men and women should take their places in separate sections.

Death—Muslims regard death as just another stage of life. If possible, a dying Muslim should be positioned to face Mecca. Ideally, his last words will be the affirmation of faith: "There is no god but Allah and Muhammad is his messenger."

Embalming is discouraged, cremation is not permitted and autopsies are not allowed unless legally mandatory. After death, the body is washed with scented water by members of the family, shrouded in white and taken to the *masjid,* where the community gathers to perform a special prayer. Another prayer may be said for those left behind.

In death as in life, the Muslim should face Mecca. At the graveside, the imam says a prayer and sprinkles dirt onto the body. Guests may do the same thing, also saying a prayer.

Flowers for the family when Muslims die are appropriate. Food may also be offered to a grieving family, but care should be given to abide by Muslim dietary laws. Fruit, salads, breads and cakes are suitable. If a non-Muslim feels it is necessary to pray at a graveside, a simple blessing will suffice.

CONVERSION

To become a Muslim, a convert utters, "I testify that there is no God but Allah and Muhammad is his messenger." This is usually done in front of witnesses.

MAJOR ORGANIZATIONS

Islamic Society of North America
P.O. Box 38
Plainfield, IN. 46168

Ministry of Imam W. Deen Muhammad
266 Madison
Calumet City, IL. 60409

Islamic Circle of North America
166-26 89th Ave.
Jamaica, NY. 11432

Islamic Resource Institute
P.O. Box 20186
Fountain Valley, CA. 92728-0186

FURTHER READING

Al Faruqi, Ismai'il R., Ph.D. *Islam.* Beltsville: Amana Publishers, 1994.

Denny, Frederick Mathewson. *An Introduction to Islam.* Englewood Cliffs, N.J.: Macmillan Publishing Co., 1994.

Farah, Caesar E., Ph.D. *Islam.* Hauppauge, N.Y.: Barron's Educational Series, Inc., 1994.

Maqsood, Ruqaiyyah. *Islam—A Teach Yourself Book.* Lincolnwood, Ill.: NTC Publishing Group, 1994.

Matar, N. I. *Islam for Beginners* New York: Writers and Readers Publishing, Incorporated, 1992.

Netton, Ian Richard. *A Popular Dictionary of Islam.* London: Curzon Press, 1992.

Parents' Manual. Prepared by The Women's Committee, The National Muslim Students' Association of the United States and Canada. World Community of Islam in the West, 1976.

Sardar, Ziauddin, and Malik, Zafar Abbas. *Introducing Muhammad* New York: Totem Books, 1994.

FOR CHILDREN
Gordon, Matthew S. *World Religion Series.* New York: Facts on File, 1991.

Al Hoad, Abdul Latif. *Islam—Religions of the World.* New York: The Bookwright Press, 1987.

SHINTOISTS

*"Let us be grateful for kami's grace and ancestors' benevolence,
and with bright and sincere heart, perform religious services."*
—*from* The General Principles of Shinto Life, 1956

Perhaps no other religion is as totally associated with a single country or ethnic group as Shinto with Japan and the Japanese people. Its practices and traditions are so intertwined with Japanese culture—from the emperor's coronation ceremony to sumo wrestling—that, in many cases, it is impossible to discern what is Shinto and what is secular.

Since more than nine out of ten Japanese people visit Shinto shrines on occasion, a vast majority of today's more than 100 million Japanese people practice Shinto in at least some minimal way. But Shinto is a very inclusionary religion, and its practioners see no reason not to combine Shinto with Buddhism or Christianity.

As Japan continues its development as one of the world's leading industrial nations, its culture is losing some of its distinctiveness. But elements of Shinto remain and are transported around the world as Japanese businesses are established in other countries. In the United States, Shinto shrines are rare, but Shinto's effects are obvious whenever a Japanese-American bows or claps to invoke blessings.

SYMBOL

The mirror is a common symbol of Shinto, representing purity.

ORIGINS

Shinto cannot be traced to a specific date or founder. Its name, adapted from Chinese words, means "way of the *kami,*" sometimes translated "way of the gods," referring to the sacred spirits that exist both in the celestial realm and in nature and human beings.

Traditionally, the Japanese had revered nature, had seen *kami* or sacredness in rocks and mountains and animals. Rituals for the benefit of agriculture, fishing and other daily activities were a part of ordinary life. But it was not until the 6th century, when Buddhism was gaining popularity in Japan, and even being adopted by the Imperial Court, that these beliefs and practices were given the name Shinto to distinguish them from other religions. With the return of ruling authority from the military establishment to the Imperial family in the so-called Meini Restoration of 1867, Shinto became the official religion of Japan.

There really aren't denominations within Shintoism. Most Shintoists practice Jinja Shinto. However there are several religious organizations that grew out of Shinto tradition.

According to Shinto mythology, the imperial line of Japan is directly and divinely descended from the Sun Goddess. Ceremonial rituals around the transfer of imperial power traditionally include the new ruler's consumption of a sacred meal of seaweed and rice wine, and his performance of sacred rites that transform him into a goddess. After spiritual intercourse with himself as a female deity, he emerges as emperor.

After Japan's defeat in World War II, Emperor Hirohito renounced his claims to divinity. His son, Emperor Akihito, was the first of Japan's emperors to be installed as a primarily symbolic figure.

Shinto worship and rituals were required in the schools of Japan until after World War II.

HOLY TEXTS

There are no specific Shinto scriptures with sacred implications. Some historical accounts, however, are considered a valuable part of the Shinto record. The *Kojiki,* or "Record of Ancient Matters," and the *Nihongi,* or "Chronicles of Japan," are considered the most important. Both were written in the early 700s as records of the imperial family and give insight into Shinto rituals and practices.

DIVISIONS

Jinja Shinto—Shrine Shinto. Shinto is practiced at the thousands of shrines throughout Japan. In 1946, after the abolition of Shinto as a state religion of Japan, the organization called Jinja Honcho, or Association of Shinto Shrines, was formed to oversee shrine worship. The organization compiled *The General Principles of Shinto Life,* which outline some basic expectations of practitioners of the faith such as generosity, helpfulness and patriotism. The Association also appoints priests.

Sect—This is a government classification created to recognize more than a dozen Japanese religious organizations that grew—some more directly than others—out of Shinto tradition. They range from faith-healing groups to mountain-worshipers. Unlike the Shinto religion itself, most of these sects are traced to a particular founder.

Folk—Assorted practices and rituals of Japanese life are roughly grouped into the category of folk Shinto.

DOCTRINE

God—Most practitioners of Shinto see many gods, or many facets of god as qualities of nature.

Good Deeds—Shinto recognizes moral relativism, ascribing good and evil to actions according to the situation. In general, people are expected to be generous and to avoid conflict.

Creation—The world was brought into existence by *kami,* or spirits, and through their relationships, but the spirits were born and will die themselves.

Humankind—There is no notion of original sin in Shinto; human beings are considered basically good and, since they are descended from the spirits, are imbued with the sacred.

Angels—While there is no specific concept of angels in Shinto, the *kami,* or divinities, fulfill some of the same roles, such as protecting people.

Sin—Shinto assumes the goodness of humankind and does not consider the human race sinful by nature; it does, however, recognize *tsumi,* translated as "sickness" or "error," which can cause impurity.

The Devil—Since Shinto regards life as good, there is no mythical figure of evil, but there are temptations from the world of darkness that can be removed by purification.

Judgment—Since Shinto claims the existence of neither an eternal paradise nor eternal damnation for the soul, there is no need for a final judgment.

Heaven—Shinto historically includes a term for a heavenly world—*takama no hara*—where the deities live, but it is not tied to a view of salvation.

Hell—The historic Shinto idea of where spirits go after death is a dank netherworld, but carries no implication of punishment.

Miracles—There is no teaching of divinely performed miracles.

Messiah—There is no messiah, past or future, in Shinto teaching.

DOCTRINES SPECIFIC TO SHINTO

Since Shinto emphasizes purification, ceremonies of dedication and purification are performed before constructing or opening businesses or homes, or before driving new vehicles.

Because Shinto believes *kami,* or sacred spirits, exist in nature, tree worship is generally accepted. Many shrines are surrounded by trees. The sakaki tree is considered sacred, and worshipers often attach petitions to the *kami* to tree branches. Mountains are also considered especially sacred in Shinto—perhaps not surprising since they make up so much of the Japanese landscape.

CALENDAR

Japan, and thus Shinto, now follows the Western calendar.

RELIGIOUS FESTIVALS AND HOLIDAYS

Oshogatsu—New Year. To prepare for the beginning of a year, families follow the Shinto practice of cleaning the house and yard, paying all bills and decorating their entryways with bamboo, evergreens and rice straw. People take several days off work to visit with family and friends and to pay respects to their elders. A stew of vegetables and pounded rice is traditional. Families also pay their first visit of the year to a public shrine. Families in mourning do not celebrate the New Year.

Setsubun-sai—Beginning of Spring. Marks the discarding of bad luck and the bringing on of good fortune. The high priest of a shrine fires an arrow to break the bad luck. Worshipers gather beans, which are thrown at them, for good luck.

Bon Festival—Feast of Lights. Celebrated in June, July or August, this festival, though Buddhist in origin, has been adapted in Japan to encompass Shinto ideas. It celebrates the time when the spirits of dead ancestors, highly regarded in Shinto, visit their earthly homes. Families provide welcoming fires and offerings and take advantage of the opportunity to consult the spirits of the dead about important family matters such as possible marriages. In towns, the dead spirits may be invited to participate in street dances or other festivities.

Shichigosan no hi—Seven-five-three Day. Celebrated for about two weeks around November 15, the official holiday, this festival is a joyous occasion for parents. Three- and five-year-old boys and three- and seven-year-old girls are dressed in their best clothes and taken to Shinto shrines, where proud fathers and mothers thank the spirits for letting their children achieve those ages.

Non-Shintoists are welcome to attend and participate in holiday festivities. Greeting cards are appropriate for the New Year and Bon Festival.

ATTITUDE TOWARD OTHER HOLIDAYS

Birthdays—Children's third, fifth and seventh birthdays are celebrated as milestones with parties followed by visits to shrines. Guests bring envelopes with money to help pay for the festivities.

Other holidays—Shintoists participate as they wish.

TITLES

Guji—the chief priest of a shrine.

Shinshoku—a more general term for priest. Shinto priests are usually men with other jobs who have taken on the responsibility of maintaining the shrines and conducting purification ceremonies.

Miko—shrine maiden. Young, unmarried women who perform sacred dances at a shrine and who conduct or assist in shrine rituals.

COMMUNITY WORSHIP

Practitioners of Shinto worship the *kami,* or sacred spirits, at shrines. Shrines are regarded both as homes for the spirits and places to venerate them. A shrine is often set in a pastoral area near a specific tree or rock that is itself considered an object of worship.

The main element of Shinto worship is purification. Upon entering a shrine, worshipers are expected to remove their shoes and wash out their mouths and rinse their hands. People who are ill, wounded or in mourning are considered ceremonially unclean, and thus ineligible to enter the shrine, as are menstruating women.

At regular times throughout the year, Shinto practitioners are also expected to make offerings at a shrine. A priest presides over the offering ceremony. After ritual purification, the priest bows and the worshipers prostrate themselves before the doors of an inner sanctum, which houses a symbol of the *kami.* Food offerings are placed before the *kami* and the priest recites a prayer after each offering. Individual worshipers may be given an opportunity to present symbolic offerings— usually *sakaki* twigs—which they place on a table before the *kami* after bowing and clapping. Music is usually played throughout the ceremony, and the priest or the shrine maidens may perform sacred dances, always facing the sacred doors with their backs to the congregation. When all the offerings have been presented, the priest removes them. All the worshipers prostrate themselves again, and the priest closes the door to the inner sanctuary. These community rituals are often followed by feasts of food and rice wine.

Another elaborate ritual is the *yutate,* or hot water ceremony. In a roped-off area of the shrine, a shrine maiden dressed completely in white sprinkles salt around a cauldron of water, then dips out a bowl of the water for a priest to take into the inner sanctum in a symbolic offering that makes all the water sacred. The maiden then stirs the cauldron vigorously enough to spray water onto those nearby, symbolically spraying them with the spirit of the *kami.* In some shrines, those present drink the water in the cauldron.

In further exercise of the water-purification rites, some Shinto practitioners stand naked beneath waterfalls or at the mouth of a river and wash the body, beginning with the mouth and face. Ablution in the ocean is considered especially purifying because of the salt in the water.

Shintoists go to shrines for special occasions, and the shrines welcome anyone. Normally, guests would not enter the building except for an occasion such as a baby-blessing or a wedding. Visitors should remove their shoes and may go through the purification ritual.

PRIVATE WORSHIP

Many homes have *kamidana,* or models of shrines, usually attached at a high place on the wall in the main room of the house, holding tablets or papers bearing the names of *kami,* or spirits. Many also include a mirror. Some families pray daily and make daily offerings before them.

Before prayers, family members must bathe, or at least wash their hands and rinse out their mouths. They then place an offering—commonly rice, salt, fish, wine or vegetables—before the symbolic shrine. Before praying, a worshiper bows three times to the spirits, and afterward bows again and claps twice. The food offerings may be eaten later.

If visiting a strict household and participating in prayer, guests should wash beforehand.

DRESS

Japanese people who wear American dress for business and relaxation may don traditional clothes for important religious ceremonies. This includes kimonos for women and *hakamas,* skirt-like garments, for men.

During rituals and while attending to shrine duties, priests wear vestments which can range from the plain and drab to the colorful and elaborate, but these are seldom worn outside the shrine. Inside the shrine, the priest is shoeless in special white socks. If a priest wears vestments outside, he puts on special lacquered wooden shoes. Shrine maidens also have distinctive dress—red pant-skirts and white kimonos, worn with white socks. They carry cypress fans.

Japanese people traditionally do not wear shoes in their houses, so they do not have to remove them for private prayer there.

Guests should remove their shoes in most Japanese households and before entering Shinto temples.

DIETARY LAWS

Certain foods are considered special by Shinto practitioners: rice is often offered to the *kami*; saki, or rice wine, is considered sacred in ritual use; and salt is sometimes used as a purification agent.

PLACE OF CHILDREN

Religious celebrations surrounding the achievement of certain birthdays and the devotion of several major religious festivals to children illustrate the high regard of Shinto practitioners for their descendants.

After their first visit to a shrine, usually about a month after birth, children are considered to be under the care of the spirits. Children come of age when they dress in ceremonial kimonos and celebrate their adulthood by visiting a shrine and holding a celebration on January 15 after their twentieth birthday.

ROLES OF MEN AND WOMEN

In the Japanese home, it is often the woman who is responsible for ensuring that ritual cleaning takes place and that offerings are provided daily for the *kami*. Traditionally, the husband or father has the best seat and should be served first at a meal. This custom is no longer universally observed.

Some women serve as Shinto priests. Women also serve as shrine dancers who perform sacred dances and assist the priests or worshipers in some ceremonies.

Very traditional men will expect to be shown a certain degree of reverence. Shaking hands is not a Japanese custom, although many Japanese people in the West will not be offended by an outstretched hand. Japanese people greet each other with a slight bow of the head. Non-Shintoists should bow back when greeted in that way.

HOUSEHOLD

Japanese traditions, and thus Shintoists, are very particular about certain customs. People wear slippers in the house, leaving their shoes outside. A separate set of slippers is usually provided for wear in the bathroom. Many Shintoists also wash themselves off before getting into a bathtub. Bath water may be saved and used for more than one person.

Guests in a Shintoist or traditional Japanese household should follow the family customs, changing shoes for slippers at the door, and slippers for other slippers to enter the bathroom. If staying overnight in a Shintoist or Japanese home, guests should ascertain what is expected of them when bathing.

MILESTONES

Birth—If a woman does not become pregnant as quickly as she hopes, she and her husband might visit a shrine and leave a petition for the local *kami*, or sacred spirit. Babies are traditionally named officially on the seventh day after birth. Families usually put the name on a sheet of paper and display it in the house. About a month after babies are born, in a ritual called *miyamairi*, their mothers take them to the local Shinto shrine to present them to the *kami,* or spirits. A priest chants prayers and performs a purification ceremony for the infant.

Gifts or cards are appropriate for new babies and their parents. Usually only parents and grandparents attend the shrine ceremony.

Marriage—The Shinto wedding is essentially a ceremony of purification frequently performed at a shrine, or a temporary shrine erected in a hotel. The bride's white clothes include a large headdress to hide the horns of envy. The couple sits before the priest, pledges vows to the sun goddess and sips saki, or rice wine, from a cup three times. The priest waves a wand of paper streamers over the couple for purification, the couple exchanges symbolic cups and they and their friends drink sake. Some superstitions surround Shinto weddings. No one should ever speak the word for "cut," for instance.

Few non-family members attend Shinto weddings. A reception or party afterward may include a larger number of people. Gifts and cards are appropriate for the bride and groom. Relatives and close friends usually give money. Normally friends would not give breakable things unless they are requested through a bridal registry. Also one would not give any black or black-and-white items unless they are requested, since black and black and white together are considered funeral colors. White alone is fine.

Death—Shinto regards death as a curse, but reveres dead ancestors as *kami,* or sacred spirits. Thus most Japanese believe that a funeral service is not just a memorial event for the dead, but prepares them for the spirit world. The corpse traditionally is placed in a coffin with its face covered by a white cloth, to be guarded by family members until taken for burial or cremation the next day. At the burial or placement of the ashes, family members may sip saki and undergo the traditional purification ceremony. Families perform memorial rites before the portable shrine daily for one hundred days. Then, at several times during the year, usually around the spring and fall equinoxes, Japanese honor their dead. Anniversaries of a relative's death may also be observed by having a priest conduct special prayers.

Flowers should be white or very light colors. Bright colors are considered inappropriate for rituals having to do with death. Friends may bring food to the family in mourning—usually fruits and vegetables, no meats. Funerals are often held in the family home or in a Shinto shrine. Neighbors and friends may visit the family in mourning.

CONVERSION

Classic Shinto is a Japanese religion. Few outsiders practice it and no attempt is made to convert anyone to it. Some modern Shinto-based sects, however, may proselytize.

MAJOR ORGANIZATIONS

Local Japanese consulates or chambers of commerce.

International Shinto Foundation
New York Center
777 United Nations Plaza
Suite WCRP-9A
New York, New York 10017

FURTHER READING

Earhart, H. Byron. *Religions of Japan*. New York: Harper & Row, 1984.

Ono, Dr. Sokyo. *Shinto: The Kami Way*. Japan: Bridgeway Press, 1962.

Picken, Stuart D. B. *Essentials of Shinto—An Analytical Guide to Principal Teachings*. Westport, Conn.: Greenwood Press, 1994.

Picken, Stuart D. B. *Shinto—Japan's Spiritual Roots*. Tokyo, New York and San Francisco: Kodansha International Ltd., 1980.

Reader, Ian. *Religion in Contemporary Japan*. Honolulu: University of Hawaii Press, 1991.

Tamura, Noriyoshi, and Reid, David. *Religion in Japanese Culture—Where Living Traditions Meet a Changing World*. New York: Kodansha International, 1996.

SIKHS

*"Everyone repeats the name of God but no one is
capable of reaching the depths of his mystery."*
—*Guru Nanak*

SIKH boys in the United States are usually noticed first because of the topknot of
hair on their heads, and their fathers because of the turbans they wear. These are
not mere fashion statements, but important practices of Sikhism.

Sikhism is among the newest and smallest of the Eastern religions. Of the
approximately twenty million Sikhs in the world today, nine tenths still live in
India. Like people of other faiths, however, they are migrating to America, setting
up homes here and becoming part of the religious fabric of the United States.

SYMBOL

The symbol of Sikhism is the *Khanda,* an upright sword with two concave
edges, its blade enclosed in a circle that symbolizes perfection, and its handle
crossed by two single-edged curved swords, or *kirpans,* symbolizing the balance
between physical and spiritual responsibility.

ORIGINS

A spiritual teacher named Guru Nanak is the founder of Sikhism. He was born
in the Punjab region of northern India in 1469, at a time when Muslims had begun
to settle among the Hindus there. Reports say that when he was about ten and his
family was ready for him to receive the sacred thread worn by Hindu men, Nanak
refused. A thread would get dirty or worn, he said. As a young man, he is said to
have announced, "There is no Hindu or no Muslim . . . God is neither Hindu nor
Muslim, and the path I shall follow is God's."

Nanak spent the next several years traveling, teaching and visiting holy sites of both Hindus and Muslims. He rejected the class divisions of Hinduism and maintained that all people are equal in the sight of the divine. He also rejected much of religious ritual. When he was about fifty, he settled down in a new town called Kartarpur.

In 1539, he designated his successor, and a few days later quietly died. His Muslim followers wanted to bury him, while his Hindu followers thought he should be cremated. Sikhism teaches that they covered him with a sheet, and when it was later turned back, the body was no longer there.

Nanak was the first of ten Sikh gurus, or spiritual teachers, who led the religion until 1708, when Guru Gobind Singh died. Instead of designating a successor, Gobind Singh said that Sikhs should now depend on the religion's holy book as the primary teacher.

The Khalsa, or Sikh fellowship, originated with the last Sikh Guru, Guru Gobind Singh, at an assembly in the town of Anandpur in 1699. According to Sikh teaching, the guru asked his followers who would be willing to die for him. Five people came forward in succession; the guru took them away and returned to the assembly with a bloody sword. He did not kill them, but initiated them into the brotherhood of Sikhs, then invited others to join them. Thousands did.

HOLY TEXT

The *Guru Granth Sahib,* the holy text of Sikhism, has been regarded as the religion's primary spiritual teacher since the death of the tenth guru in 1708. It is given the title "guru" to show that it is regarded with the same reverence accorded the religion's human spiritual leaders. The word "sahib" likewise is a title of respect. The *Guru Granth Sahib* grew out of the *Adi Granth,* or first book of Sikhism, which was collected by the fifth guru and includes some Islamic and Hindu texts as well as Sikh writings. Some later material was added before Guru Gobind Singh, the last leader of the Sikhs, consecrated it.

Sikhs believe the *Guru Granth Sahib* is the holy and inspired word of God. They show respect by prostrating themselves when they enter its presence and by keeping it in a special place in the worship hall shaded by a canopy, wrapped in special cloths and resting on cushions. Many Sikh ceremonies, such as baby-namings and weddings, are considered legitimate only if they take place in its presence.

Worshipers must never wear shoes in its presence or sit with their feet pointed toward it or turn their backs on it. They should cover their heads in its presence. The book may be literally put to bed at night and raised up in the morning.

Sikh families with their own copies of the *Guru Granth Sahib* may open it randomly each morning and focus on a particular verse, believed to be the *Guru*'s wisdom for the day.

Out of respect for worshipers, non-Sikh visitors should remove their shoes in the presence of the *Guru Granth Sahib,* should cover their heads and should be careful not to turn their backs on it.

DOCTRINE

God—The one God is the supreme guru.

Good Deeds—Performance of selfless deeds is one way of achieving unity with God.

Creation—The one God is the creator of the universe. He first formed himself into Nam, the Divine Name, and then formed the world.

Humankind—Humans can choose between good and evil, but humans are handicapped by *haumai,* or self-centeredness, and must work toward unity with God, which is the goal of human life. Human life itself is one step for the soul, which has already been incarnated in other forms of life.

Angels—While not recognizing angels per se, Sikhism does accept that messengers of God escort souls to judgment and read out their tally sheets after death.

Sin—Humans, out of weakness, are tempted to evil and need religious faith to overcome the temptation. Sin prevents unity with God. But Sikhism rejects the idea of original sin.

The Devil—There is no personification of evil in the form of Satan, but evil is the temptation to selfishness that draws humans away from God.

Judgment—God judges people according to their deeds and thoughts, but offers grace to those who repent of their sins.

Heaven—The presence of God, or unity with God, is considered to be heaven.

Hell—Hell is considered symbolic; an evil person is condemned to repeat the cycle of birth and death into a lower form until redeemed,

Miracles—Miracles occur and are not violations of the laws of nature, but are merely beyond human understanding.

Messiah—There is no belief in a messiah in Sikhism.

DOCTRINES SPECIFIC TO SIKHISM

FIVE PRINCIPLES OF FAITH

- Equality of all human beings
- Worship of Nam, or God
- Dignity of work
- Charity for the poor
- Service to others

THE FIVE VIRTUES

- Self-control
- Truth
- Patience
- Faith
- Compassion

THE FIVE VICES
- Lust
- Anger
- Greed
- Materialism
- Conceit

THE FIVE STAGES OF SPIRITUAL DEVELOPMENT
- Dharam Khand—Duty— accepting the balance between deeds and consequences
- Gyan Khand—Knowledge— awareness of God
- Karan Khand—Effort— conscious attempt to follow the Guru
- Saram Khand—Grace—rule by God's will
- Sach Khand—Truth—unity with God

CALENDAR

Except for Vaisakhi, Sikh holidays are calculated by the lunar calendar.

RELIGIOUS FESTIVALS AND HOLIDAYS

Other Sikh festivals are held on the same day as Hindu celebrations but have special significance to Sikhs:

Vaisakhi—A three-to-five day festival of eating, drinking and dancing that celebrates the formation of the Khalsa. New members are accepted at this time. It is a time for visiting the temple and holding rallies. The celebration may also include carrying the scripture, the *Guru Granth Sahib,* around the community in a festive parade.

Diwali—Based on the lunar calendar, this Hindu festival comes in the fall. Sikhs see it as a celebration of the release from prison of the sixth guru, Guru Hargobind. He had been imprisoned with fifty-two Hindus. Although the emperor was ready to release the guru, he refused to leave without his fellow prisoners. The emperor's response was to say the guru could take with him everyone who could pass through a narrow gate holding onto his cloak. The story says the guru had long tassels attached to the cloak, and everyone was released. Sikhs celebrate the occasion with lights and fireworks.

Visitors are welcome to enjoy the festivities. In the temple, visitors should follow the rules for being in the presence of the Sikh holy book.

ATTITUDE TOWARD OTHER HOLIDAYS

Sikhs celebrate as they wish.

TITLES

There is no Sikh clergy, but people fulfill certain functions:

Granthi—caretaker of the Guru Granth Sahib and officiator at ceremonies—addressed as "Granthi Sahib."
Giani—a person of spiritual knowledge and/or knowledge of the Sikh scriptures—no particular form of address.
Sant—a spiritual guide or teacher—no particular form of address.

COMMUNITY WORSHIP

The Sikh place of worship is called a *gurdwara,* or "door of the guru." Its main sections are a room for worship, a room where the *Guru Granth Sahib* is kept when not being displayed for worship and a room where community meals are served.

Sikhs remove their shoes and cover their heads to enter the worship areas of the gurdwara because it contains the holy book. As they enter the presence of the *Guru Granth Sahib,* they kneel and bow, touching their heads to the floor, before taking their places in front of it. Men and women sit separately on the floor.

Worship services may last several hours, but people may enter and leave during worship. Much of the service is devoted to chanting verses from the *Guru Granth Sahib* and explaining them. The service leader may do most of the reading, occasionally fanning the scripture with a special fan of yak hair. Some hymns are sung by the entire congregation. Music, performed on traditional Indian instruments, may also be a part of Sikh worship.

At some point in the service, the worship leader will probably open the *Guru Granth Sahib* at random and read a passage, believed to have been fated for special meaning for the congregation at that time. Then the *Ardas,* a traditional Sikh prayer, is recited as everyone rises.

As they bow to the *Guru Granth Sahib* during the *Ardas,* or at the end of a service, everyone is given a taste of a paste of flour, sugar and butter called *karah parshad.* This is stirred with a *kirpan,* or sword, and is usually given to five members of the Khalsa before it is distributed.

A post-service vegetarian community meal is considered a part of Sikh worship, dating back to the founder of Sikhism who, in a radical departure from tradition, fed people of different castes together.

Visitors are expected to remove their shoes and cover their heads in the presence of *Guru Granth Sahib*. Guests are not expected to bow to the scripture, but should show proper respect. Non-Sikhs are expected to accept and eat a portion of the sweet paste. If invited to a post-service meal, a guest should accept if possible since Sikhs may interpret a refusal as a rejection of the principal of the equality of all humankind. There should be no alcohol or tobacco.

PRIVATE WORSHIP

An observant Sikh recites a prayer before any enterprise, usually in the form of hymns or verses of the *Guru Granth Sahib*. Sikhs are expected to start and end their days with thoughts of God. There are prescribed Sikh morning prayers called *Bani* and evening prayers called *Rahiras* and *Kirtan Sohila*.

Sikhs can say their prayers anywhere. If a Sikh is praying, others should be respectful and not interrupt.

DRESS

Men and women who are members of the Khalsa, or brotherhood of Sikhs, wear five signs of their faith:

- *Kesh,* or uncut hair, to represent holiness
- *Kanga,* a comb, holding the topknot of twisted hair and used to comb the hair at least twice a day as a symbol of order
- *Kara,* a steel wristband, a complete circle to signify the unity of the Sikh brotherhood
- *Kirpan,* a sword, symbolizing the warrior aspect of the Sikh in defense of the truth
- *Kaccha,* short gathered underpants, worn initially to ensure comfortable movement while dressed in a *dhoti,* or long piece of wrapped cloth

Many Sikh men wear turbans and all Sikhs cover their heads in the presence of the scripture.

While there is no dress code for Sikh worship, non-Skihs should have a handkerchief or scarf to cover their heads. In a sign of respect, they should dress modestly, making sure their clothes will be comfortable for sitting and kneeling on the floor.

DIETARY LAWS

Sikhs are not supposed to eat meat prepared according to either Jewish or Muslim religious law. They are supposed to forgo alcohol and tobacco. A healthy diet and moderate habits are considered superior to periodic fasting. Overindulgence in food and drink is considered sinful.

Anyone entertaining Sikhs or taking food to a Sikh function should make sure it is not prepared according to Muslim or Jewish law. Alcohol and tobacco are inappropriate gifts for Sikhs.

PLACE OF CHILDREN

From birth, a child is considered part of the religious community. Even when they are infants, children may wear a *kara,* or steel bracelet, which will be replaced as it becomes too small. Children likewise do not get haircuts, but let their hair grow uncut as part of the Khalsa tradition.

ROLES OF MEN AND WOMEN

The *Guru Granth Sahib,* the Sikh scripture, describes God as both Father and Mother. All roles in Sikh worship are open to women and women can be full members of the Khalsa. Women are charged with helping their children to learn about the religion and unlike several major religions, women are not considered unclean either during their menstrual cycle or after childbirth.

However, in much of Punjabi culture, women are considered subordinate to first their fathers and later their husbands. In traditional Sikh homes, men may still eat first.

In much of Sikh society, body contact is considered inappropriate between men and women who are not related. Therefore, when meeting a Sikh of the opposite sex, it is best to wait to see whether a hand is offered. Sikhs usually greet others with folded hands. A slight bow or nod of the head is always appropriate.

HOUSEHOLD

There are no specific religious objects or icons in a Sikh household except that Sikh families who have a copy of the *Guru Granth Sahib* might show it great respect.

If in the presence of *Guru Granth Sahib* at a Sikh home, a visitor should show respect and follow the lead of the host.

MILESTONES

Birth—A few days after birth, parents take a baby to the gurdwara for a regular worship service. They also take a square of cotton or silk fabric to be used as a cover for the *Guru Granth Sahib.* During the *Ardas,* the congregation gives thanks for the baby's family. After the prayer, the *granthi,* or the person presiding over the ceremony, randomly opens the scripture and reads from it. The first letter of the verse that is read becomes the first initial of the child's name. The parents choose a name that begins with that letter. All Sikh boys have the last name Singh, or lion. All Sikh girls have the last name Kaur, or princess.

At the end of the ceremony, the child is given a few drops of water, sweetened with sugar, and the mother also drinks sweetened water; the congregation receives *karah parsad,* or a sweetened flour paste. Sometimes there is also a congregational meal.

Guests should participate in a baby-naming ceremony as they feel comfortable. Gifts and cards are appropriate for babies.

Marriage—Sikh marriages are frequently arranged by the families, and Sikh women are supposed to marry only Sikhs. A Sikh marriage is regarded as forming a bond between the families of the bride and groom as well as the couple.

An engagement ceremony often precedes the wedding. Men from the bride's family and the groom's family exchange gifts, often cloth for turbans. The bride's hands are dyed red, which is thought to make them beautiful. After this, the engagement is regarded as sealed and unbreakable.

Wedding ceremonies themselves are simple and brief. They must be performed in the presence of the scripture, the *Guru Granth Sahib.* The groom arrives first, usually wearing a red or pink turban and scarf, and takes his place in front of the scripture. The bride then comes in, frequently escorted by a female relative. She traditionally wears red.

The man or woman presiding over the ceremony reads a passage of scripture and makes some remarks about the duty of a married couple to each other. The couple acknowledges their pledges to each other—he to honor and protect his wife, she to support her husband—by bowing before the *Guru Granth Sahib.* When the vows have been made, the bride takes the end of the groom's scarf in her hand.

Then the person officiating over the wedding reads the *lavan,* a four-stanza hymn written by the fourth guru, Guru Ram Das. Each verse of the *lavan* describes one of four steps of love, which apply to both man and woman and God and humankind: duty and devotion to the True Guru; unselfishness; detachment from the material world; and, true unity. After each verse, the couple takes a clockwise walk around the *Guru Granth Sahib,* the bridegroom walking in front of the bride. During the last walk, the guests may throw flower petals at the couple. Once this is completed, the couple is considered to be husband and wife. The officiator says a prayer that includes a request for blessings on the couple. Everyone present may be given a symbolic sweet.

Receptions may follow Sikh weddings. In very traditional families, men and women may still eat and dance separately, but in Western countries many receptions are now completely mixed. After the reception, the wife traditionally returns to her family home and the groom and his friends follow. Good-natured harassment of the groom while he waits for the bride to come out is considered a part of the tradition. As she leaves her home, the bride may be given rice to throw over her shoulder.

Money is the customary Sikh wedding gift.

Death—If it is known that a Sikh is dying, his or her family will gather around to recite scripture and offer prayers. The family also usually prefers to prepare the body for disposal themselves, bathing it and dressing it in clean clothes. A Sikh who is a member of the Khalsa is adorned with the five symbols.

Sikh funeral services focus on the expectation of eternal life, and excessive display of grief is considered inappropriate. Many Sikhs are cremated, but because the first guru, Guru Nanak, made it clear that he did not care whether his own body was buried or cremated, Sikh families may follow the custom of the country in which they live. Autopsies are frowned upon, however, as a violation of the dignity of the body.

After the funeral, close family members return home and may start a complete reading of the scripture. On the tenth day, the family may hold another ceremony of scripture and prayer. If the deceased person is the head of a household, another ceremony may follow, acknowledging a new family leader with a ceremonial turban.

Flowers and cards are appropriate. Food taken to the family is appreciated, but should follow Sikh dietary laws.

CONVERSION

From the time of the first guru, baptism was signified by drinking water into which the guru's toe had been dipped. This changed in 1699 with the establishment of the Khalsa (in Punjab, "pure") by Guru Gobind Rai. It is said in the midst of persecution, the guru asked those who were willing to die for their faith to step forward. Five men volunteered, and the guru took each one away and returned with a bloody sword. The crowd thought he had killed them, but he soon returned with all five men. He offered them sweetened water, stirred with a sword, as a symbol of their brotherhood. In honor of their willingness to be martyrs, the guru gave the men a new last name, Singh, or "lion," and recommended that they wear five symbols to show that they were Sikhs: uncut hair, a comb, a wrist bracelet, a sword, and special underpants.

Today people joining the Khalsa must be old enough to understand the significance of their action. They pledge abstinence from alcohol, tobacco and promiscuity. Five men and women who are already members of the Khalsa, representing the original five initiates, must be present as a new person is brought in. The initiation ceremony is known as taking the *amrit,* or sugar water. The person officiating over the ceremony opens the scripture, the *Guru Granth Sahib,* at random and reads a passage, followed by a prayer. Khalsa members then pour water into a steel bowl, adding sugar and stirring with a sword while singing prescribed hymns. When the solution is deemed ready, it is poured into the hands of the initiates, who take five sips of it. It is then sprinkled on their eyes and hair five times, with statements of praise of the Khalsa and God. If the initiate is a convert to Sikhism, he or she is awarded a Sikh name. The service concludes with the consumption of symbolic sweet paste from a common bowl.

MAJOR ORGANIZATIONS

Sikh Dharma
1620 Preuss Road
Los Angeles, California 90035

FURTHER READING

Cole, W. Owen. *Sikhism, a Teach Yourself Book.* Lincolnwood, Ill.: NTC Publishing Group, 1994.

Singh, Daljit and Smith, Angela. *The Sikh World.* Morristown, N.J.: Smith Burdett Company, 1985.

Sikh Religion. Detroit: Sikh Missionary Center, 1990.

TAOISTS

*"Leave all things to take their natural course and
do not interfere. . . . What is contrary to the Tao soon perishes."*
—*Tao Te Ching*

Taoism, or Daoism, is both a religion and a philosophy with Chinese roots thousands of years old. Its name comes from the Chinese word for "the way." Because its practices and beliefs are so interwoven with Chinese culture, many people who accept some of its teachings do not necessarily identify themselves as Taoists. In fact, the Chinese language has developed a word for religion only within the last century.

Only in recent decades has Taoism begun getting attention in the West. But the growing popularity of its teachings in America can be measured by the number of translations of its texts available at bookstores. Even Winnie the Pooh and Piglet are featured in books on Taoism.

SYMBOL

The interlocking Yin and Yang, representing the two opposing forces in the universe, is the symbol of Taoism.

HISTORY

Taoism is said to have evolved in China over centuries, beginning as early as the third millennium B.C.E. in the early days of the Chinese Empire, boosted by the work of Huang Ti, the so-called Yellow Emperor, who is said to have learned the secret of life from a hermit. But an archivist who lived about 600 B.C.E. and who was given the title Lao Tzu, or Old Master, is considered its greatest sage. According to one of the earliest biographical accounts, his family name was Li and his given name Erh, although there is little evidence of his identity, or even of his existence.

Lao Tzu is said to have left the royal court out of disgust with the decadence and deterioration of the dynasty. As he headed west in a cart drawn by two black oxen, Yin Shi, who guarded the Han-ku Pass through which he had to go, asked him to write down his thoughts. The result was the Tao Te Ching. Lao Tzu then rode away. He was later deified. More than a century later, an admirer of his work, Chuang Tzu—about whom also little is known—applied the teachings of Tao to practical everyday matters. His work bears his name.

Early Taoists were reportedly wandering hermits, but their lifestyle eventually evolved into communes where residents sold herbs and acted as priests to nearby communities. Thus, pure Taoism absorbed some aspects of Chinese folk religion with its rites and deities, and Chinese folk religion began to take on aspects of Taoism.

With the rise of Buddhism in China around the beginning of the Common Era, Taoism adopted more of the accoutrements of organized religion. Taoists developed more elaborate rituals and built temples and shrines. One of the people most responsible for the ritualization of Taoism was Chang Tao Ling, who came from a family of Taoist alchemists. He was born in 34 A.D. As the story goes, the spirit of Lao Tzu told Chang Tao Ling to put forth a religion based on Taoist principles to counter the growing influence of Buddhism. The movement that was founded as a result was known as Tien Shi, or Way of the Celestial Masters. It had rituals, gods, and the equivalent of priests and parishes. When Chang Tao Ling died, leadership of the movement passed on to his son and grandson.

In the 300s, Yang Hsi further developed the religious Taoist ritual with his Highest Purity movement in southern China, following his own series of visions. The Complete Reality Movement in the Sung Dynasty from the 900s to the 1200s emphasized the merging of the physical and the spiritual. Among its contributions to Taoist tradition is the exercise known as t'ai chi ch'uan.

Over the following centuries, Buddhism, Confucianism and Taoism continued to become intertwined. When Christianity came to China via missionaries, some Christian practice was mixed in. While religious practices are mingled, Taoist rites, literature and philosophy retain some distinction.

HOLY TEXTS

The main text of Taoism is the Tao Te Ching, translated "The Way and Its Power," a poetic work attributed to Lao Tzu. The Tao Te Ching is an instruction book for a ruler, but its teachings can be interpreted for individuals, society and the universe.

A second important text is the Chuang-tzu, which bears the name of its purported primary author. The Chuang-tzu consists of various literary forms with the overall themes of rejecting the quest for goods and power in favor of unity with the natural world.

DIVISIONS

Philosophical Taoism—*tao chia*. Known in China as School Taoism, this is basically an outlook that places great emphasis on an unaggressive, non-competitive way of life.

Religious Taoism—*tao chiao*. The religious form of Taoism is highly ritualistic and fragmented. Some sects emphasize diet, others magic, others meditation. Many people practice Taoism without considering themselves a part of any sect.

DOCTRINE

God—Tao is both creator and creation, the life force.

Good Deeds—Serving others with patience and tolerance is the correct way to live; unselfishness makes others unselfish and leads to a more peaceful world.

Creation—Everything—divine, human and nature—is fundamentally one.

Humankind—Human beings have the power to upset natural harmony by trying to manipulate nature and the world to suit their own purpose. Each human is a microcosm of the universe, with the same forces at work and the same need for balance.

Angels—Spirits, including the Eight Immortals who have achieved liberated existence through exemplary lives, assist people in need; a guardian spirit also protects children, even before they are born.

Sin—Sin is seen as movement away from the Tao.

The Devil—Taoists recognize the existence of evil spirits or *kuei* in the form of natural disasters or spirits who died violently or were not honored as ancestors by their descendants.

Judgment—In traditional Taoism, gods are constantly making an accounting of people's good and bad deeds; their reward and punishment can increase or reduce their life span, or can be meted out to future generations. Therefore, when good people die young, they are assumed to be bearing the sins of their ancestors. This theory is called *ch'eng fu*, or the transmission of burdens. Some folk forms of Chinese religion called popular Taoism hold that a deity called Yen Lo Wang sentences offenders to be frozen or burned—but all punishment is temporary.

Heaven—Lao Tzu did not teach the concept of an afterlife in paradise, but Taoist teaching gives people the hope of reaching immortality, or *xian*. Some Taoists have formulated elaborate expectations of paradise on mystical mountains or supernatural islands with specific geographic locations

Hell—There is no widespread Taoist teaching about hell, but some Taoist stories tell of a netherworld where people must pay for their wrongdoing. Paper money burned at Chinese funerals is symbolic of efforts by the living to do enough good to free their ancestors' souls from hell.

Miracles—Taoism teaches that everything in nature is in balance. Therefore there is no such thing as a supernatural occurrence.

Messiah—There is no concept of a messiah in Taoism.

DOCTRINES SPECIFIC TO TAOISM

Taoism places a strong emphasis on balance, as exemplified by the symbol of the yin and yang. Taoism teaches that everything has an opposite, and that the poles depend on each other. The yin represents earth, and the female force; the yang represents heaven and the male force. The channels between heaven and earth are discernible to those in touch with Tao.

As a religion, Taoism places an unusual emphasis on the search for health and physical immortality, encouraging a healthy diet and regular exercise. Over the years, the search for immortality led in a variety of directions from alchemy to sexual techniques believed to prolong and preserve life.

Asceticism, in the form of a simple life and restraint of appetites, is a principle of Taoism. Taoists espouse what is sometimes called *wuwei,* or "non-doing," a form of mental openness and physical inaction that allows the Tao to take its course. Taoism values the practice—or the non-practice—of "non-doing" as a form of meditation that encourages identity with the Tao.

Practitioners of Taoist folk religion recognize many deities, among them the **Kitchen God,** who oversees households.

Traditional Taoist religion has a trinity of major deities:

Heavenly Elder of the Primal Origin—Yu Huang Shang Ti—the Jade Emperor—is identified with the present.

Lord of the Sacred Jewels—Ling Pao Chun—embodies yin and yang and is identified with the past.

Very Noble Lord of the Tao—T'ai Shang Lao Chun—the deified Lao Tzu—represents Taoist doctrine and is identified with the future.

Taoism also recognizes the Eight Immortals, those who have attained a liberated existence by fully using their minds and ridding themselves of inappropriate desires. Here are the Immortals and the symbols with which they are frequently identified:

Lu Tung-pin—a sword—a bearded figure who tames evil spirits.

Chung Li Ch'uan—a fan—a large-bellied former general in the Han dynasty who calms stormy seas and is associated with immortality.

Change Kuo Lao—a bamboo musical instrument—a long-bearded old man with a white mule who is consulted by families who want sons.

Lan Ts'ai Ho—a flower basket—appears as a rosy-cheeked youth who has the gods' favor.

Han Hsiang-tzu—a flute—occasionally pictured as a child, the muse of musicians.

T'ieh-Kuai Li—a crutch—appears as a lame beggar who looks out for the poor.

Ts'ao Ku Chiu—a tablet—a dignified bearded figure dressed in official garb who is known as a judge.

Ho Hsien-ku—a lotus—the only woman of the group, an avowed virgin.

Images of the deities are common in homes, and even in restaurants and other businesses. They should be treated with respect. Some Chinese may bow to the images, but non-Taoists would not be expected to do this.

CALENDAR

The Chinese record time from the year 2637 B.C.E., and arrange their calendars around a sixty-year cycle, calculated by combining the ten Heavenly Stems with the twelve Earthly Branches:

The Heavenly Stems	The Earthly Branches	
Metal—yin	Rat	Horse
Metal—yang	Ox	Goat
Wood—yin	Tiger	Monkey
Wood—yang	Rabbit	Rooster
Fire—yin	Dragon	Dog
Fire—yang	Snake	Pig
Earth—yin		
Earth—yang		
Water—yin		
Water—yang		

Each of the Heavenly Stems is associated with a color, so a year is identified by a color and an animal. The cycle repeats every sixty years.

Taoism is organized according to the lunar calendar.

RELIGIOUS FESTIVALS AND HOLIDAYS

Taoist festivals follow the agricultural year and except for the fall harvest festival, occur in the yang, or odd-numbered, months.

New Year's Day—first month, first day. The beginning of the Chinese year and the rebirth of yang, this is the best known and most widely celebrated of Chinese holidays. In temples, Taoists welcome the three major deities with rich food. In the Chinese home, families have huge multi-course meals in honor of the ancestors. People, especially children, wear new clothes and exchange gifts. Costumes, dancing and fireworks are part of the celebration. This usually falls in January or February. The celebration continues for two weeks.

Festival of Lanterns—first month, fifteenth day. Known to Westerners as

Chinese Valentine's Day, this festival on the first full moon of the year marks the end of all Chinese New Year celebrations. Lanterns decorate homes and temples, and in some places there are lantern processions and dragon dances.

Ching Ming Festival—also known as the Lustration festival—begins the third month, third day and does not end until the fourth month. During this period, families clean ancestors' graves and cover them with tiles. They bring offerings of wine for the ancestors' spirits and burn incense. To celebrate the accomplishments, families traditionally have a picnic.

Summer festival—fifth month, fifth day. Some Taoists mark the beginning of summer by driving away the spirits of disease. Boat races are common in honor of an exiled poet who committed suicide by jumping in a river. Friends jumped in their boats to rush to the scene, and threw dumplings to the fish to keep them from eating his body. Yang is considered at its peak at this time.

Seven Sisters Day—seventh month, the seventh day. A day for young lovers, this commemorates a legend of the youngest daughter of the Heavenly Emperor who had six sisters. Because she neglected her duties after she was allowed to marry, her divine father permitted her to visit her husband only once a year, on this day. Religious rites and needlecraft competition are ways the day is celebrated.

Harvest festival—eighth month, eighth day. Celebrated by dining under the full moon and giving thanks for the harvest.

ATTITUDE TOWARD OTHER HOLIDAYS

Birthdays—A child's first birthday is a joyous occasion celebrated by a neighborhood party and marked by the baby's first bite of solid food. Taoists may celebrate other birthdays according to the customs of the culture in which they live. In a Chinese person's life, the most significant birthday is the sixtieth, which marks the completion of a Sexagenary Cycle.

Other Holidays—Taoists celebrate as they wish according to the culture.

TITLES

Priest—One who conducts temple rites.

Taoist—A form of monk, believed to be able to cure people.

COMMUNITY WORSHIP

The *chiao* or offering is the basic Taoist ritual. Only a select group of community leaders are actually inside the temple with the priests performing the rites. In the case of a holiday or major community event, a festival is going on outside for everyone else while the priests conduct the worship.

To prepare themselves for the ritual, the priests heat oil while they chant prayers. A priest in a red headdress throws alcohol on the oil to create flames so that everything to be used in the rituals can be passed over the fire.

When the *chiao* begins, priests call on the three major deities to be a part of the rituals. Priests also place a yellow banner outside with red lettering inviting the gods. At noon, each priest sings and dances for the gods and places a gift, such as fruit or a flower, on the altar. Later rites may include darkening the temple and lighting candles one by one.

As the banner of invitation to the gods is taken down after the *chiao,* the priests leave the temple chanting to find a feast laid out for them. They invite any lost souls to the table, then pass incense over the food and give it to the crowd. A bonfire ends the event.

Other specific observances may be carried out for special occasions from temple dedications to healing services. Candles, incense and offerings are often a part of temple rites.

Guests may participate in festivals as they wish, but should not attempt to enter the temple. They will be welcome to watch the rites from a distance.

PRIVATE WORSHIP

Taoists, like other Chinese families, consider ancestors very important. Many homes have ancestor tablets, and family members may stop before the tablets to ask their ancestors' blessings or to make an offering of incense to a particular deity. Incense and candles are often part of the home ancestor rituals.

When visiting a Chinese home, guests should show respect to the ancestor tablets.

DRESS

There is no distinctive dress for Taoists, but some may wear traditional Chinese garb for special occasions.

DIETARY LAWS

Different sects of Taoism emphasize different techniques. The overall attitude of Taoism to food and drink is balance. Over the years, Taoists have found medicinal purposes for many natural substances.

If entertaining a person who practices Tao, it is best to ascertain whether there are any particular dietary requirements. If that is not possible, offer a variety of foods.

PLACE OF CHILDREN

The child is seen as close to the Way, and children are celebrated for their role in perpetuating the family. A spirit called a *chuang mu* is believed to guard growing children. Parents make an offering of rice to this spirit when the child is sick.

Children are expected to learn the Tao Te Ching and are allowed to participate in Taoist rituals. There are no specific rites for coming of age.

ROLES OF MEN AND WOMEN

There are no particular distinctions between men and women in Taoism. Both men and women can be Taoist priests, although male priests are much more common.

HOUSEHOLD

Many Taoist families, like other Chinese families, have an ancestor altar or room in their homes. The home may also have a kitchen god whose image observes the movements of the household.

When visiting a Taoist home, show respect for the ancestor altar or room.

MILESTONES

Birth—Taoists believe that children are protected, even in the womb, by a guardian spirit called Tai Shen. Pregnant women make offerings on behalf of their unborn children and may ask priests to perform special rituals. After the baby is born, the mother makes offerings of thanks.

The family celebrates the baby's health at four months after birth with a party. Cakes are made with peaches as an offering, then eaten by children at the celebration. Guests customarily bring the baby gifts of clothes.

Guests may be given rice fried in oil for prosperity and an egg dyed red to represent the blessing of a new life. Guests at the party celebrating a baby may be expected to make a donation. This money is traditionally in a red envelope. Other gifts and cards are also appropriate for new babies.

Marriage—Traditionally, Taoist priests examine the birthdays of a prospective bridal couple for approval, and may also be consulted to set the date of the wedding. The bride and her family must tell the family ancestors of the upcoming nuptials.

The bride arrives first at the wedding and is given a wine cup. She bows once for each of the four seasons and stages of life. Both the celebrant and her parents remind her of her duty to be a good wife, daughter-in-law and mother. After silently acknowledging the instruction, she is draped in a veil. In the meantime, the groom is being reminded of his obligations as a husband at the shrine of his ancestors. When he arrives at the bride's side, she removes her veil.

The wedding itself consists of simply sharing a cup of wine and signing a certificate of marriage. Most weddings are celebrated with banquets. The day after the wedding, the wife goes to her husband's family home to acknowledge his ancestors and take her place as a part of his family.

Money, given in a red envelope, is a traditional gift. Other gifts for the bride and groom are also appropriate.

Death—In Taoism, life and death are regarded as different poles of a pair, balancing each other as day and night. Death is neither to be desired nor feared. According to Taoist teachings, when humans die they go "back into the great loom" from which all creatures emanate. However, the soul, or *shen,* remains near the body until burial.

Correct ritual can help to avoid divine retribution, so Taoists spend a great deal of energy and money assuring that their dead are properly buried. A special group of priests, who wear symbolic black headgear, oversee the funeral rituals. The household ancestors' altar is draped in white, and when the corpse is ready for burial, children of the family—who are presumed to give no thought to monetary value—are instructed to fetch some of the person's personal treasures for burial in the coffin. The dead person's favorite foods are also put inside. The family may also place papers with special prayers in the coffin. As the priest prays, these are removed and burned as offerings. At the end of the service, the coffin is sealed and the family has a banquet. Funeral services, which include music, can last for several days.

A Taoist specialist may be asked to determine the most auspicious date of burial according to the calendar. When the time for burial comes, chanting and singing Taoist priests precede the coffin to the graveyard.

Money is traditionally given to the family in a white envelope, except when the deceased person is older than eighty. Then the envelope is red to represent the blessing of longevity. Flowers, cards and food for the family are also appropriate responses.

CONVERSION

There is no official conversion process for Taoism. Traditionally, people begin to study either independently or under a teacher, and adopt the philosophy. Some Taoist religious sects, however, may have membership rituals.

MAJOR ORGANIZATIONS

Union of Tao and Man
117 Stonehaven Way
Los Angeles, California 90049

FURTHER READING

Blofeld, John. *Taoism—The Road to Immortality*. Boston: Shambhala, 1978.
Fischer-Schreiber, Ingrid. *The Shambhala Dictionary of Taoism*. Boston: Shambhala, 1996.
Hoff, Benjamin. *The Tao of Pooh*. New York: Penguin Books U.S.A. Inc. 1983.
Kaltenmark, Max. *Lao Tzu and Taoism*. trans. Roger Greaves. Stanford, CA.: Stanford University Press, 1969.

FOR CHILDREN

Hartz, Paula R. *Taoism—World Religions*. New York: Facts on File, 1993.

ZOROASTRIANS

"Good thoughts, good words, good deeds."
—Zoroastrian Path to the Infinite Light

ZOROASTRIANS, are small in number but generally highly educated. Reference works estimate that there are fewer than 100,000 Zoroastrians in all of India. Despite near extinction at times, Zoroastrians continue to practice their faith and, as they move throughout the world, more cultures are becoming aware of this form of monotheism. The numbers of Zoroastrians worldwide is believed to be about 200,000.

SYMBOL

Fire is the symbol of Zoroastrianism, representing the glorious spirit of God.

ORIGINS

Zoroaster is the Greek name for Zarathushtra, a Persian prophet who may have been the first monotheist. Although tradition teaches that Zoroaster lived around 600 B.C., scholars have dated his life at closer to 1000 to 1500 B.C. in what is now Iran. Little is known about the life of Zoroaster. Zoroastrian teaching says he may have been the son of a priest who left home against his parents' wishes in search of truth when he was about twenty years old. Within a decade, he is said to have begun to have visions. At thirty, he saw Ahura Mazda, the "Lord of Wisdom," or the one true God.

When Zoroaster began to teach that some of the religious traditions of his time, such as pantheistic beliefs and animal sacrifice, were unacceptable, he was forced into exile. He found refuge at the court of King Vishtaspa, who ruled in part of modern-day Afghanistan, and converted the king to his monotheistic beliefs. Zoroaster is believed to have died when he was in his seventies.

When Muslims conquered Persia in the 7th century A.D., Zoroastrianism almost became extinct. A few pockets of practitioners remained to carry on the faith. But its followers have spread it into other areas, including the United States.

HOLY TEXTS

As in many traditions, Zoroastrian teachings were handed down for many years orally before being compiled in writing. The main Zoroastrian scriptures are the *Gathas,* seventeen hymns totaling only about six thousand words, believed to have been composed by Zoroaster. The *Gathas* were incorporated into a larger body of work known as the *Yanna,* which includes other hymns and prayers. Most of the original *Avesta* was destroyed during the Muslim conquest of Persia.

DIVISIONS

Separate sects of Zoroastrianism have formed over disagreements about calendars. Their names are:

Kadimi—or "Ancient"—accepts the historic calendar.
Shenshahi—or "Imperial"—uses a modified version of the old calendar.
Fasli—or "Seasonal"—uses the present seasonal calendar of Iran.

DOCTRINE

God—There is one God, Ahura Mazda.
Good Deeds—A major premise of the faith is the obligation to do good deeds; humans will be rewarded in the present and future life in heaven.
Creation—Ahura Mazda made the world in six stages: land, water, earth, plants, animals, humans.
Humankind—Humans are higher than the animals and have the capacity to choose good or evil.
Angels—Divine beings called Yazutas preside over the elements and do the will of Ahura Mazda; scriptures mention some forty spirits by name, but their numbers are believed to be many more.
Sin—The forces of evil, led by Angra Mainya, lure humans toward evil; those who do evil will be punished.
The Devil—Angra Mainya is an evil or destructive spirit that will ultimately be defeated.
Judgment—Everyone is judged at the dawn of the day after death on the basis of performance in life.
Heaven—Those who consistently choose good over evil in thought, word and deed will be allowed to "cross the bridge" into heaven.

Hell—Those whose evil deeds outweigh the good will fall into hell; but punishment is not final and when the messiah comes, even those in hell will be redeemed.

Miracles—Pure Zoroastrianism does not accept the idea of miracles, but believes everything can be explained by the laws of the universe.

Messiah—Later, Zoroastrian scriptures tell that a savior born of the seed of the prophet and a virgin will fight a final battle with evil and bring about the perfection of the world.

DOCTRINES SPECIFIC TO ZOROASTRIANS

DEITIES

Zoroastrians recognize six divine aspects of Ahura Mazda, known as the Amesha Spentas or the Immortals. Humans are expected to carry out these attributes in their daily lives. Each divinity is also tied to a particular creation:

Vohu Manah—good motivations—animals
Asha Vahishta—righteousness—fire
Khshathra Vairya—proper exercise of power—sky
Aramaiti—right-mindedness—earth
Haurvatat—integrity—water
Ameretat—immortality—plants

The religion also recognizes Spenta Mainyu, or the Holy Spirit of Azura Mazda.

An evil power, Angra Mainyu, works against Ahura Mazda. And to counterbalance the six aspects of the divinity, there are also six archdemons in Zoroastrianism who work to disrupt the plan of Ahura Mazda on behalf of Ahriman:

Aka Manah—evil thoughts
Indra—turning away from the faith
Saura—anarchy
Naonghaithya—disobedience
Taurvi—imperfection
Zairich—mortality

CALENDAR

Rather than breaking the calendar into weeks, Zoroastrians have a solar calendar of twelve months with thirty days each and five days added at the end of the year. Each of the thirty days has a name.

The months of the Zoroastrian calendar are:

Farvardin (March/April)
Ardibehesht (April/May)
Khordad (May/June)
Tir (June/July)
Amardad (July/August)
Shahrevar (August/September)

Mihr (September/October)
Aban (October/November)
Adar (November/December)
Dai (December/January)
Bahman (January/February)
Spendarmad (February/March)

Various attempts to stabilize the Zoroastrian calendar to coincide with the seasons of the year have resulted in several different calendars. Each of the three major calendars coincides slightly differently with the Gregorian calendar.

RELIGIOUS FESTIVALS AND HOLIDAYS

Gahambars—Six seasonal festivals, each lasting for five days, occur throughout the year:

• Maidhyozarema Payangh—Midspring—11–15 of second month
• Maidhyoishema Vastro–dataenya—Midsummer—11–15 of fourth month
• Paitish–hahya Hahya—Harvest Time—26–30 of sixth month
• Ayathrema—Homecoming of the Herds—26–30 of eighth month
• Maidhyairya—Midwinter—16–20 of tenth month
• Hamaspathmaedaya—Equal Day and Night—last five intercalary days, a time when holy work is performed

Hamaspthmaedaya, All Souls—also known as Farvadigan in Iran. The last five days of the year this time, commemorates holy beings of the past, present and future with lamps, flowers and other memorials.
Naoroz—New Day. The largest of the festivals, this day celebrates both the new year and the eventual triumph of good over evil.
Khordadsal Festival—celebrated on Farvardin 6. Marks the birthday of Zoroaster with a feast following a day of prayer at the temple.

Twelve of the names of the thirty days of the month are also the names of months; each time the name of the day matches the name of the month in which it occurs, the day becomes a festival day.

ATTITUDE TOWARD OTHER HOLIDAYS

Zoroastrians celebrate as they wish.

TITLES

Priests—Only the descendants of priests can be priests. Priests tend the sacred fire in the fire temples, and only priests can perform initiation and wedding ceremonies. Priests still observe old rituals for disposing of their own hair and nails, considered impure once they are separated from the body. Priests also wear white masks to prevent the release of saliva during religious ceremonies.

There are several degrees of the priesthood:

- *Ervad*—one who has qualified to conduct common services
- *Mobed*—one who can perform any ceremony
- *Dastur*—the head of a group of priests

All priests are addressed as "Mr."

COMMUNITY WORSHIP

The first, eighth, fifteenth, and twenty-third days of each month are considered sacred to Ahura Mazda and thus function as kind of a Zoroastrian Sabbath. Zoroastrians conduct their community worship in a fire temple, where priests tend an eternal flame. Sandalwood offerings are brought to the fire. Two priests perform the lengthy Yasna, or sacrifice ceremony, each morning, honoring Ahura Mazda.

Non-Zoroastrians are not permitted to enter the fire temple by most Indian groups. Some Iranian groups allow visitors in the company of a Zoroastrian. Guests are expected to sit and listen quietly.

PERSONAL WORSHIP

Observant Zoroastrians pray five times daily—around sunrise, noon, sunset, midnight and dawn—standing and facing a source of light. During prayers, the worshiper unties and reties the *kusti,* or sacred cord around the waist.

Before at least one prayer daily, the worshiper performs a ritual bath, praising Ahura Mazda, washing the exposed parts of the body and unfastening and re-knotting the sacred cord. The observant are also expected to go through this ritual when they get up in the morning, before each meal, and each time they relieve themselves. Before other prayers, many Zoroastrians only wash their faces and hands.

Respect the rituals and give anyone privacy who seems to be praying.

DRESS

Zoroastrians are expected to cover their heads at prayer times and in temples where a sacred fire is lit. In addition, two items of clothing are symbolic of the faith: The *sudra* is a white undershirt with a pocket for storing good deeds. The *kusti* is a sacred cord braided from six strands, each with twelve white woolen threads, with tassels left on the end. The cord is lapped three times around the waist over the shirt and is untied and retied each morning and before prayers and meals. It is also removed for bathing.

***

Out of respect, guests in the presence of the sacred fire should cover their heads.

***

DIETARY LAWS

Old laws categorizing foods into categories of more and less desirable have largely been abandoned. Fasting is discouraged. Among very observant Zoroastrians, food, utensils and dishes are supposed to be prevented from coming into contact with hair, nails, saliva, blood or other body products that have been removed from the body. If food comes in contact with any of these substances, it must be thrown out.

***

Anyone entertaining Zoroastrians or preparing food for them should abide by their dietary laws.

***

PLACE OF CHILDREN

Children are considered very important to Zoroastrians as the means of perpetuating the faith. The child's transition into adulthood is symbolized in the Naozot, or initiation ceremony, with presentation of the sacred white undershirt and woolen cord that identify followers of the faith. After receiving these articles, the child is considered responsible for practicing the faith and distinguishing right from wrong. The ceremony takes place sometime between the ages of seven and fifteen, depending on the customs of the area, and is often held in the family home. The child takes a symbolic bath, then joins the family, friends and priests who have assembled. Facing east toward the presiding priest, the child is wrapped in a white cloth.

The priest sits on the floor. Nearby are trays containing: new clothes for the child, including undershirt and cord; rice; flowers; a candle or lamp; an urn with a sandalwood fire; a mixture of pomegranate, raisins, almonds, grains, rice and coconut. The priest prays, with the child reciting certain parts; then they stand and the priest presents the child with the shirt. The child confesses faith in Ahura Mazda and in Zoroastrianism as "the good, true and perfect religion." While invoking blessings, the priest then passes items from the tray over the child's head, and sprinkles the fruits, grains and flowers on the new initiate. Next, the priest wraps the cord around the child's waist while the child recites more prayers and confessions of faith. At the end of the service, the priest marks the child's forehead with red. If the initiate is a boy, the mark is long and vertical. Girls are marked with a circle.

The service is usually followed by a feast. The child wears new clothes and is showered with gifts.

Friends are frequently invited to initiation ceremonies. Guests should sit and observe, since no congregational involvment is required. Gifts or cards are appropriate.

ROLES OF MEN AND WOMEN

Men and women are considered equal in Zoroastrianism and both can become religious leaders and perform religious rituals—except that in some very traditional groups, the priests are all men. Both boys and girls are initiated into adulthood and the religion. Some aspects of Ahura Mazda, the deity, have feminine identities. Women, however, are considered impure while menstruating or shortly after they have given birth and are not allowed to enter the fire temple during that time.

Zoroastrian men and women should be treated equally. Since non-Zoroastrians are seldom admitted to the fire temple, non-Zoroastrian women should not have to worry about being considered impure.

HOUSEHOLD

Zoroastrians hold high standards of purity and are expected to avoid all forms of pollution. Observant households keep a fire or a light burning. Priests always have a hearth fire.

When visiting a Zoroastrian home, guests should abide by the cleanliness standards of the household—and not turn out the designated light.

MILESTONES

Birth—Some Zoroastrian families maintain a fire or lamp as the time for birth nears. Some light lamps to mark particular points during the pregnancy. And some observe the custom of keeping a lamp in the room with the mother and child for a set time after birth. Most often, the tradition is to maintain the lamp for three days, but some families keep it for ten or even forty days.

A woman is traditionally considered impure for forty days after giving birth, and receives her food on special dishes. At the end of this period, she takes a ritual bath to prepare to rejoin her husband and society.

Cards, gifts and flowers for the baby and mother are appropriate.

Marriage—Marriage is revered in Zoroastrianism and celibacy is discouraged, even for priests. A Zoroastrian wedding is a religious ceremony and Zoroastrians are discouraged from marrying outside the faith. Although Zoroastrians may observe some marriage customs of the country in which they live, the ceremony must be performed by a priest. Both the bride and the groom take a symbolic bath of purification before the wedding, which is usually performed in the evening and in the presence of fire. The service itself includes blessings, vows, admonitions and a statement by the priest. The couple agrees three times to enter the marriage until the end of their lives, and witnesses attest to their approval. Throughout the ceremony, the priest tosses rice on the couple as a symbol of joy and prosperity. The religious ceremony is usually followed by a reception or feast.

Guests should enjoy the wedding festivities. Gifts and cards are appropriate.

Death—To keep the elements of fire, water and earth pure, Zoroastrians ideally do not cremate, submerge or bury their dead. The traditional practice—frequently impossible to carry out in the Western world or in cities—is to place the corpse on stones in a designated area to be destroyed by the elements and/or by vultures.

After death, the deceased person is bathed and dressed in clean clothes. The sacred cord of the religion is tied around the body, which is placed in a front room, preferably on an impermeable surface with hands folded across the chest. Since the corpse is considered impure, professional corpse-bearers draw three circles around the body to mark it apart from the living.

According to Zoroastrian tradition, what then follows is a unique ceremony: A dog with a spot above each eye, making it appear to have four eyes, is brought into the area with the body. Theoretically, if the person is truly dead, the dog will stare at it, and if the person has any life left, the dog will bark. An urn of burning sandalwood is set up near the body. Two priests sit near it reciting prayers. The body should be taken away within twenty-four hours. Two white-clad corpse-bearers recite a statement of their intentions, under the authority of Ahura Mazda. More prayers follow, and relatives and friends pay last respects, bowing before the corpse. The corpse-bearers then cover the face of the body and bear it away, with family and friends following several feet behind. At the traditional "Tower of Silence," or *dakhma,* the body would be left to natural processes. Later, the bones of the skeleton would be collected and dropped into a pit.

Zoroastrians believe the soul remains in the body for three days after death, and on the fourth day is judged. If the good outweighs the bad, the soul "crosses the bridge" to paradise. If not, the bridge becomes a blade and the soul falls into hell to await the final battle between good and evil forces. If good and bad have balanced, the soul remains in limbo. Anticipating and celebrating this passage, relatives recite special prayers on the third and fourth days after death, seeking the mercy of Ahura Mazda on the soul of the departed. Other religious ceremonies are performed on the tenth, thirtieth and anniversary days.

In the United States and in Iran, most Zoroastrians are cremated or buried, but some families, in India, still observe the traditional customs.

Unless the family is very strict, friends are welcome to attend funeral and memorial ceremonies. Gifts, cards and flowers are appropriate.

CONVERSION

In groups that allow conversion of non Zoroastrians, new initiates into Zoro-astrianism go through the same ceremony as young people coming of age and are given a white shirt and girdle. Some groups don't accept converts.

MAJOR ORGANIZATIONS

Federation of Zoroastrian Associations of North America
5750 Jackson Street
Hinsdale, Illinois 90521

Iranian Zoroastrian Association
249 Weyman Avenue
New Rochelle, New York 10805

Persian Zoroastrian Organization
2160 Green Street
San Francisco, California 94123

Zarathushtrian Assembly
1814 Bayless Street
Anaheim, California 92802

FURTHER READING

Bharucha, Ervad Sheriarji Dadabhai, *Zoroastrian Religion and Customs*. Bombay: D. B. Taraporevala Sons & Co. Private Ltd., 1979.

Masani, Sir Rustom. *The Religion of the Good Life—Zoroastrianism*. London: George Allen and Unwin Ltd, 1954.

Mehr, Farhang. *The Zoroastrian Tradition*. Rockport, Mass.: Element Inc., 1991.

Nigosian, S. A. *The Zoroastrian Faith—Tradition & Modern Research*. Montreal: McGill-Queen's University Press, 1993.

CHRISTIANS

"For God so loved the world that he gave his only Son. . . ."
—John 3:16

ONE out of three people in the world is Christian, or at least identifies with some branch of the Christian faith. Since its foundation two thousand years ago, the Christian faith has defined the calendar for most of the world. Its reach around the globe means its nearly 2 billion practitioners are on every continent.

Within the world's largest faith family, there are many feuds. Over the centuries this has resulted in a plethora of branches on the family tree, from the Orthodox and Catholic Christians who claim to date back to Christ's disciples to the Pentecostals of turn-of-the century America. Each branch has its own twigs as well.

This second part of this book attempts to diagram the major branches and twigs and to give some understanding of how they fit together and how they differ. An overview describes the general areas of agreement; separate sections follow outlining the history, practices and beliefs that are distinctive for each branch.

Etiquette tips are offered when needed. Otherwise, visitors should follow the lead of hosts or congregation members and participate wherever they feel it is appropriate.

SYMBOL

The symbol of Christianity is the empty cross or the crucifix, an image of the cross with a crucified Jesus.

ORIGINS

Christianity traces its roots back to the followers of Jesus, a Jew who was born in Palestine during the reign of Emperor Augustus in Rome. The common calendar dates from the time of Jesus' birth. Thus the year 2000 is presumed to be two millennia after his birth. But most scholars agree his actual birth probably occurred a few years earlier. According to the Christian scriptures, Jesus' mother was a virgin named Mary who traveled with her fiancé Joseph from their home in Nazareth to Bethlehem for a census. When they could find no room in an inn, Jesus was born in a stable. There are only scattered incidents in the scriptures describing his childhood, and none from his early adult life.

At about age thirty, he gathered twelve disciples and traveled around Galilee, teaching, preaching and ministering. Jesus often talked in stories, or parables, which illustrated the truths he was trying to get across. He preached compassion for the sick, poor and imprisoned. New Testament accounts describe miracles he performed, including raising people from the dead.

His public ministry in Palestine lasted only about three years before he was arrested and brought before Roman authorities in Jerusalem because of his teachings. He was sentenced to die, beaten and hung on a cross. According to Christian scripture, three days later, some of his followers approached his tomb and found no corpse there. He soon appeared to them and lived among them before ascending into heaven without further mortal death.

His followers established what became the Christian church. Christians teach that Jesus was both human and divine—God come down to earth in human form, to act as an example for everyone who must live on earth.

The beginnings of the church are detailed in the New Testament Book of Acts, which begins with a description of Jesus' ascension and goes on to describe how Jesus' apostles gathered ten days later, were overcome by a divine spirit, began performing miracles and went out to spread the faith. The occasion is known as Pentecost.

A Jew named Paul, who had persecuted Christians, became one of their most vocal proponents after a dramatic conversion experience. Paul made four long preaching and teaching journeys, taking Christianity along major trade routes throughout Asia Minor and eventually to Europe. His letters to the churches he established became a main part of the Christian New Testament.

The religion continued to spread, becoming more organized and more formal. Within three hundred years of Jesus' death, it had become a legal religion of the Roman Empire under Emperor Constantine. In 325, Constantine called church leaders to the Council of Nicea, the first of a series of gatherings that established the basic beliefs of Christianity.

With growth came divisions and developments of different styles of worship, until today, different sects of the world's largest religion may be hardly identifiable as part of the same belief system. They are united, however, in their faith in Jesus Christ.

HOLY TEXTS

The Christian Bible is made up of the Hebrew Bible, or Old Testament, and the New Testament. In addition, the Catholic, Greek and Russian Orthodox Bibles contain other writings known to them as the Deuterocanon and to other Christians as the Apocrypha.

The New Testament tells the story of Jesus Christ's birth, baptism, ministry, death and resurrection, and the origin of the Christian Church. The final book of the New Testament, Revelation, describes a vision of the final conflict between good and evil and the eventual triumph of God.

DIVISIONS

There are many divisions of Christianity. Some of the major groups or denominations are described elsewhere in this volume.

DOCTRINE

God—Most Christians believe in a triune God, or the trinity. God is creator; Jesus lived on earth as a man, died and was resurrected; the Holy Spirit is the unseen power of God that moves in people's hearts.

Good Deeds—Jesus told his followers to love their neighbors and to serve others.

Creation—Christians accept the Hebrew Bible's account of creation of the world by God, although some take the story literally while others view it metaphorically.

Humankind—Humans were made by God in God's image, but are tempted to sin and can never achieve perfection.

Angels—The Christian Bible contains numerous accounts of visitation by angels serving as messengers of God; some Christians also accept the idea of guardian angels who protect people.

Sin—Succumbing to sin is a part of the human condition, but Jesus' death and resurrection ensured anyone who follows him of ultimate forgiveness.

The Devil—Satan, as the literal embodiment of opposition to God or as a symbol for evil, is in a struggle with God and goodness for the souls of humans.

Judgment—Traditional Christian teaching says that God will eventually decide whether people spend eternity in paradise or pain; some Christians think the judgment comes upon each person's death, while others believe God will call up the souls of all the dead at some final collective judgment.

Heaven—People who believe in Jesus as messiah and attempt to pattern their lives after his teachings will spend eternity in God's presence.

Hell—Those who reject Jesus as the messiah or sin without repentance will be doomed to eternal damnation.

Miracles—The Christian Bible contains numerous accounts of miracles performed by Jesus and his followers; many Christians believe God still performs miracles in people's lives.

Messiah—Christians regard Jesus as the Messiah who came to save mankind; most Christians believe Jesus will return to earth, lead a final battle against evil and ultimately triumph.

DOCTRINES SPECIFIC TO CHRISTIANITY

Although there are numerous Christian denominations and sects with different specific beliefs, all share a common faith in Jesus Christ as the son of God and savior whose birth, death and resurrection made it possible for humans to hope for eternal life with God.

The basic beliefs are stated in the Nicene Creed, recited regularly by many Christians and accepted as doctrine by many other groups:

We believe in one God,
the Father, the Almighty,
maker of heaven and earth,
of all that is seen and unseen.
We believe in one Lord, Jesus Christ,
the only Son of God,
eternally begotten of the Father,
God from God, light from light,
true God from true God,
begotten, not made, one in Being with the Father.
Through him all things were made.
For us men and for our salvation he came down from heaven;
by the power of the Holy Spirit
he was born of the Virgin Mary, and became man.
For our sake he was crucified under Pontius Pilate;
he suffered, died, and was buried.
On the third day he rose again in fulfillment of the Scriptures:
he ascended into heaven
and is seated at the right hand of the Father.
He will come again in glory to judge the living and the dead,
and his kingdom will have no end.
We believe in the Holy Spirit, the Lord, the giver of life,
who proceeds from the Father and the Son.
With the Father and the Son he is worshiped and glorified.
He has spoken through the prophets.
We believe in one holy catholic and apostolic Church.
We acknowledge one baptism for the forgiveness of sins.
We look for the resurrection of the dead, and the life of the world to
come.

Many other creeds have been written since the Nicene in the fourth century, but most are based on it.

CALENDAR

Most Christian groups, except for some branches of the Catholic and Orthodox churches, use the Gregorian Calendar.

RELIGIOUS FESTIVALS AND HOLIDAYS

There are many Christian holidays, some celebrated by some groups and not by others. The generally accepted structure of the Christian year follows this pattern:

Advent—The season leading up to Christmas is known as Advent. In many churches, a candle is lighted each Sunday for four Sundays before Christmas and on Christmas Eve night to signify preparation for the coming of Christ. Advent is also a time of Christmas pageants, music, parties and special programs in many churches.

Christmas—Dec. 25 and the days until Jan. 6 are officially the Christmas season in a most Christian churches. Special music and Bible readings at this time focus on the coming of Jesus.

Epiphany—Jan. 6 is known as the Epiphany, celebrating the coming of the wise men, or kings, from the East to worship the baby Jesus.

Ash Wednesday—This marks the beginning of Lent, or the season leading up to Easter. In some churches, people have ash marks put on their foreheads. The ashes remind Christians of their need of repentance.

Lent—The forty days—excluding Sundays—of penance before Easter; usually observed by forgoing some pleasure, such as fasting from a favorite food.

Palm Sunday—The Sunday before Easter, celebrating Jesus's triumphal entry into Jerusalem when he was hailed by people waving palm branches; celebrated with special music. Some churches hand out palm branches or have reenactments.

Maundy Thursday—The Thursday before Easter marks Jesus' last supper with his disciples; many churches have communion services.

Good Friday—Friday before Easter. Commemorates Jesus' crucifixion.

Easter—Celebrates Jesus' resurrection. In most churches this is the holiest day of the Christian year and is celebrated with church services, the wearing of fine clothes and triumphant music.

Pentecost—The seventh Sunday after Easter, when the Holy Spirit is said to have descended onto Jesus' disciples.

ATTITUDES TOWARD OTHER HOLIDAYS

Unless otherwise noted, members of Christian denominations celebrate secular and patriotic holidays as they wish.

TITLES

Offices and titles vary by denomination.

COMMUNITY WORSHIP

Most—but not all—Christians celebrate the Sabbath, or the Lord's Day, on Sunday. Exceptions include some groups with Seventh-day in their names who observe Sabbath from sundown Friday to sundown Saturday. Unless otherwise noted, denominations observe Sunday as their holy day.

Worship form ranges from the highly liturgical and formulated to the spontaneous, depending on the denomination.

PRIVATE WORSHIP

In many Christian homes, families pray together before each meal thanking God in the name of Jesus for the food. Family and private times of devotion are common but not required. Unless noted, Christian denominations ask only that their members read the Bible and pray regularly.

DRESS

Some Christian groups have dress restrictions or particular garb for particular officeholders, while others do not. Few Christian groups have any kind of dress requirement for members, however. Unless noted, denominations have no dress restrictions for worshipers.

DIETARY LAWS

Some Christian groups forbid the consumption of stimulants or alcohol. Others emphasize a healthy diet. Unless noted, denominations make no restrictions.

PLACE OF CHILDREN

The New Testament includes an account of Jesus' perturbation when his disciples tried to prevent children from approaching him. He told the men to let the children come to him, and said everyone should aspire to child-like faith and innocence.

Most Christian organizations hold children in high regard. Many churches offer Sunday School, children's sermons, youth programs, children's choirs, summer camps and other activities designed to keep children participating in the church. Some Christian groups have special coming-of-age ceremonies for children, while others do not. Most Christian groups expect children to make their own commitment to the faith at a time when they realize the significance of the commitment.

ROLES OF MEN AND WOMEN

Christian groups vary significantly in their attitude toward women in office. In some churches, women are welcomed fully in every role of church hierarchy, while others forbid women to hold church office that places them in authority over men.

HOUSEHOLD

There are no required religious objects in Christian households, but some have crosses or depictions of Jesus Christ. Unless noted, there are no special household features in a denomination.

MILESTONES

Birth—Christian customs surrounding birth vary. Some Christian groups have baptism or dedication services for infants, while others do not.

Except as noted, cards, gifts, and flowers are appropriate for new babies and their parents, and guests can participate in congregational portions of ceremonies as they feel comfortable.

Marriage—In general, Christians see marriage as a covenant between a man and a woman, and between the couple and God. Some groups consider marriage a sacrament; others do not.

Except as noted, cards and gifts are appropriate for wedding couples, and guests can participate in congregational portions of ceremonies as they feel comfortable.

Death—The form of Christian funeral services varies somewhat, but most Christians see death as an entry into a better world for believers. Funerals and memorial services celebrate a believer's life, offer comfort to those who are left behind and give testimony about the faith to those who do not share it.

Except as noted, cards, flowers, telephone calls, visits and food for the bereaved family are appropriate at the time of death, and guests can participate in congregational portions of ceremonies as they feel comfortable.

CONVERSION

To become a Christian, a person must express belief in Jesus as the divine son of God sent to earth in human form to die and be resurrected in order to offer eternal life to those who believe in him. This is generally followed by baptism by sprinkling or pouring water onto the head of the person being baptized or by completely immersing the person in water unless the person was previously baptized.

ADVENTISTS

ORIGINS

ADVENTISTS take their name from their eagerness for Jesus' imminent return to the world—the Second Advent. Their concern about unbelievers gives many Adventists missionary zeal to bring as many people as possible into the fold.

Adventism today traces its roots to an American movement called the Millerites. William Miller, who was born in New York, converted to Christianity at a revival in 1816 and joined a Baptist church. After several years of earnest Bible study, Miller became convinced that based on calculations from the prophecies in the Book of Daniel, Jesus would come to earth again between March 21, 1843, and March 21, 1844. Miller began preaching about his calculations and gained followers. After March 21, 1844, had passed with no literally earth-shattering events, a Miller associate, Samuel Snow, recalculated and determined that Jesus would return on Yom Kippur, the Jewish Day of Atonement, which, in 1844, would be October 22. According to some accounts, so sure were some of Miller's followers that Jesus would come to take them to heaven that they disposed of their property and met in fields to wait.

As one Adventist publication puts it, "The day came, but the Lord did not." October 22, 1844, came to be known as the Great Disappointment. Many of Miller's followers gave up the faith. Others believed they had not been in error about the date of October 22, but had misinterpreted what would occur. They decided that on that date in heaven, the final era of preparation for the return of Jesus had begun.

Several groups which differed in some of their doctrinal interpretations evolved. The largest Adventist body is the Seventh-day Adventist Church, co-founded by Ellen White, her husband, James, and Joseph Bates. A follower of Miller, after the Great Disappointment Ellen White had a vision in which she saw Adventists on the path to heaven. She concluded that Jesus had begun the process leading to his return on October 22, but the preparation was not visible on earth. As Adventists heard her message, some became convinced that she was a true prophet.

When Ellen White began prophesying, a few Adventists had already adopted Saturday worship. White intensified the practice by emphasizing the need to observe the Ten Commandments, including the admonition to keep the Sabbath. She also took up the temperance cause, writing about the need for healthful living, vegetarianism and abstention from alcohol, tobacco, coffee, and tea after an 1863 vision. John Harvey Kellogg, an Adventist physician, developed his corn flakes as a health food for his patients, but eventually broke with the church.

The group officially took the name Seventh-day Adventist Church in 1860. A conference of Seventh-day Adventist churches was organized in Michigan in 1861, followed by a General Conference in 1863. Church headquarters was moved to Washington, D.C., in 1903.

In 1858, a group of Saturday-worshipping Adventists who rejected the visions of Ellen White broke off to form the Church of God (Seventh Day).

In 1860, the Advent Christian Church was organized as a Sunday-worshiping Adventist group.

DIVISIONS

Seventh-day Adventist Church—The largest group many times over, the Seventh-day Adventist Church is an international organization with adult membership of more than 800,000 in the United States and more than nine million worldwide. The church is known for its Saturday worship.

Advent Christian Church—Founded in 1860 out of the Miller movement, this church has about 27,000 members and worships on Sunday.

Church of God General Conference—This group predates Miller, but much of its doctrine parallels the Millerite churches. About one hundred churches claim about five thousand members, and hold worship services on Sunday.

The Church of God (Seventh Day)—Although members of this branch of Adventism grew out of the Millerites and agree with the Seventh-day Adventists that the Sabbath should be kept on Saturday, they disagree about the validity of the visions of Ellen White, a leader in the Adventist movement.

Christadelphians—The Christadelphians began about the time Miller expected the world to end, but were founded separately by John Thomas, a doctor who had survived a stormy voyage from England. Christadelphians share the emphasis on the immediate return of Jesus. A small congregation-based group, the Christadelphians keep no denominational membership statistics. Worship services are on Sunday.

DOCTRINES SPECIFIC TO ADVENTISM

Creation—God created the world in six days and rested on the seventh, marking it as a Sabbath.

Judgment—Seventh-day Adventists teach that upon his return to earth, Jesus will raise the righteous dead and take them to heaven with him for a thousand years. The righteous living will instantaneously become immortal, and the wicked living will die when they witness him. Satan will be left on earth alone. When the thousand-year period is up, God will bring the New Jerusalem from heaven to earth. The wicked dead, who have been asleep since Jesus' return, will be raised. Satan will engage God in a final battle and meet defeat. God will pass a final judgment, forcing Satan and the wicked forces to face the consequences of their rebellion, and condemning them to total destruction.

Seventh-day Adventists believe that since his ascension into heaven, Jesus has been ministering in heaven on behalf of humans. The final phase of this ministry, during which the records in heaven are being examined to see who lives eternally with God and who is damned, began in 1844, according to Adventist teachings. This "Investigative Judgment" leads up to Jesus' return. They also believe that people who once accepted Jesus but fell away from the faith are no longer guaranteed eternal life.

Some other Adventist groups teach that Jesus will begin his reign on earth immediately upon his second coming, and that the thousand years will be a period of transition for the earth.

Heaven—Adventists believe Jesus is in heaven until his return to earth, but the ultimate and eternal habitation of the righteous will be a new earth or New Jerusalem after the world is purged of evil by God.

Hell—Most Adventists believe the wicked will be condemned by God at final judgment, not to spend eternity in torment but to be annihilated.

Adventists see themselves as a "remnant" attempting to purify Christianity from pagan and secular influences in the last earthly days. In their Confession of Faith, the Seventh-day Adventists promise to keep the Sabbath, tithe, pray and study daily, eat and drink healthfully, dress modestly, participate only in proper entertainment, worship regularly and participate in communion services.

Adventists groups not based on Miller's teachings do not accept the significance of 1844. Some groups do not share the emphasis on diet and clothing of the Seventh-day Adventists.

TITLES

Minister—Usually addressed as "Elder," "Pastor," or if he or she has a doctorate, as "Doctor."

Congregational Elder—Lay leaders who are responsible for acting in the minister's absence and seeing that the congregation's spiritual needs are met; they serve as members on a church's governing board. No special form of address.

Deacon—A male lay leader responsible for the upkeep of the church facilities; also usually serves as a member of the church's governing board. No special form of address.

Deaconess—A female lay leader whose duties include preparing the elements of communion and taking care of the women during foot-washing ceremonies. No special form of address.

COMMUNITY WORSHIP

The largest group of Adventists, the Seventh-day Adventists, takes its name from the observation of the Sabbath from sunset Friday to sunset Saturday, the seventh day. They strictly observe the commandment to rest on the Sabbath by attempting to keep it free of worldly concerns, spending time with family and friends and engaging in wholesome entertainment, study and worship. Some families clean their house before the Sabbath each week. Traditionally, women prepared food ahead of time so they would not have to work on the Sabbath, but fewer families observe this custom today.

Other Adventist groups worship on Sunday.

Adventist worship services may include hymns, prayers, special music, a sermon and an offering. No creeds are recited.

Adventists observe two sacraments:

• Baptism, by immersion after confession of faith.
• The Lord's Supper of bread and grape juice, symbolizing Jesus' last meal with his disciples. In Adventist churches, this is usually served to people as they sit in the pews, and is open to all Christians. In Seventh-day Adventist churches, the Lord's Supper is preceded by feet-washing, which is regarded as a rite, not a sacrament. Members gently bathe and dry each others' feet. This is often called "the little baptism." Feet-washing is a symbol of service to others, based on the New Testament account of Jesus' washing of his disciples' feet. As part of this rite, participants are expected to confess and make restitution to anyone they have wronged.

Non-members are welcome at Advent worship services. Visitors are free to participate in whatever elements of the service they wish. Communion is open, so anyone who desires may partake. The foot-washing is also open to visitors who wish to participate.

DRESS

Seventh-day Adventist statements of belief call for dress that is "simple, modest, and neat, befitting those whose true beauty does not consist of outward adornment." While few Adventists would wear gaudy jewelry, many wear watches and wedding bands. Cosmetics, if used, are usually not applied heavily.

DIETARY LAWS

Seventh-day Adventist statements of belief specifically call for refrain from alcohol, tobacco, narcotics and "unclean foods identified in scripture." These are listed specifically in Leviticus 11 and include pork and shellfish. Many Adventists are vegetarians and also avoid caffeine.

When entertaining an Adventist, one should not serve pork or shellfish, and should avoid serving meat unless other dishes are unavailable or it is known that the Adventist is not a vegetarian. Beverages other than coffee and tea should be available. One should not give gifts of alcohol, coffee or tea to an Adventist family.

PLACE OF CHILDREN

Adventists do not baptize children. Instead, children are expected to make a confession of faith and request baptism at an age when they are old enough to understand the commitment they are making.

ROLES OF MEN AND WOMEN

In the Seventh-day Adventist Church, women can be ordained by the local congregation to serve as elders in a local congregation; whereas a man's ordination is recognized by the entire Adventist church, a woman's is limited.

Adventists are generally taught that a man is head of the family.

HOUSEHOLD

There are no particular religious objects in an Adventist home. In the kitchen of a Seventh-day Adventist family, however, there may be an abundance of health foods. The church publishes its own cookbooks to promote a healthy diet, and the denomination sells food along with books in its denominational stores.

If being entertained in an Adventist home, do not request coffee or tea unless it is offered. Never smoke or use tobacco products in a Seventh-day Adventist home.

MILESTONES

Birth—Many Adventist hold a baby-dedication service when their child is a few weeks or months old. A minister officiates, and the ceremony is usually part of a regular worship service. The parents bring their child to the front of the church; the minister usually reads some scripture and offers some words of encouragement; then, the family dedicates their child to God.

Marriage—Adventists encourage marriage within the denomination, but do accept marriage between Adventists and other Christians. A Seventh-day Adventist minister would not perform a wedding between an Adventist and a non-Christian, although some other Adventists might.

Weddings usually include music, scripture, an exchange of vows, a short sermon and prayer, and are usually followed by a reception. In very strict families or churches, there will be no exchange of rings, since they are considered adornment.

Fornication is considered the only grounds for divorce by a Seventh-day Adventist church member, and only the wronged party of a marriage separated by fornication is permitted to remarry within the church.

Death—Adventists believe that people do not go immediately to heaven or hell when they die, but are simply unconscious and will remain so until Jesus comes again.

Adventist funerals are arranged according to the wishes of the family with the advice of the minister. They are likely to include music, scripture, prayer, remarks about the person who has died and expressions of condolence and reassurance to the family.

CONVERSION

A person becomes an Adventist by accepting the doctrine of the church and being received into membership if previously baptized by immersion in another Christian denomination. New converts to Christianity must be baptized.

MAJOR ORGANIZATIONS

Advent Christian Church
P.O. Box 23152
Charlotte, N.C. 28227

Church of God General Conference
P.O. Box 100,000
Morrow, Ga. 30260

The Church of God (Seventh Day)
330 W. 152nd Ave., P.O. Box 33677
Denver, Col. 80233

Christadelphian Action Society
1000 Mohawk Drive
Elgin, Ill. 60120-3148
(847) 741-5253

Seventh-day Adventist Church
12501 Old Columbia Pike
Silver Springs, Md. 20904-6600

FURTHER READING

Bull, Malcolm, and Lockhart, Keith. *Seeking A Sanctuary—Seventh-day Adventism & the American Dream.* San Francisco: Harper & Row, 1989.
Land, Gary, ed. *Adventism in America—A History.* Grand Rapids, Mich.: William B. Eerdmans Publishing Company, 1986.
Linden, Igmar. *The Last Trump—A historico-genetical study of some important chapters in the making and development of the Seventh-day Adventist Church.* Frankfurt am Main, Bern, Las Vegas: Peter Lang, 1978.
Rice, Richard. *The Reign of God—An Introduction to Christian Theology from a Seventh-day Adventist Perspective.* Berrien Springs, Mich.: Andrews University Press, 1985.
"Seventh-day Adventists Believe . . . ," Idagerstown, Maryland: Review and Herald Publishing Association, 1988.

ANABAPTISTS

ORIGINS

THE Anabaptists were given that label by their critics. The name comes from Greek terms meaning to baptize again. Anabaptists believed that only people old enough to understand their beliefs should be baptized; thus, anyone baptized as a child had to be rebaptized. Although few people identify themselves as Anabaptists today, many of the original beliefs persist in the Amish, Mennonite and Hutterite communities, all branches of Anabaptism.

The Anabaptists were generally regarded as the radical left of the Protestant Reformation. Sects of Anabaptists grew up in several places across Europe in the 16th century. One of the earliest and most significant events in the development of the Anabaptist movement occurred in Switzerland on Jan. 21, 1525, when a small group of men gathered at the home of Felix Manz.

The men had been followers or students of Ulrich Zwingli, a Catholic priest who became a Reformer in Zurich. Zwingli had supported some changes in the church, but he would not repudiate the tithe—a government tax of ten percent to support state-sanctioned churches. His refusal to go along with his followers on this and other issues prompted the meeting at Manz's house. A leader of the small band of rebels was Conrad Grebel, a young aristocrat. On the winter night at Manz's home, Grebel baptized George Blaurock, a former priest, who baptized the others. This simple act started the Anabaptist revolution.

Michael Sattler, a former monk and associate of the Zurich rebels, formulated the doctrines of the Anabaptist faith.

His beliefs and articles called for a Lord's Supper free of sacramentalism, baptism of believers but not infants, pacifism, separation from civil politics, non-resistance to violence, simplicity in lifestyle, refusal to take oaths and strong church discipline, including excommunication.

In Germany and Moravia, the work of the first Anabaptists was built on the foundation of Thomas Muntzer, a Reformer who around 1520 rejected Luther's ideas in favor of a more radical stance. Also influential was Jacob Hutter, an Anabaptist preacher who established the first church in his native Puster Valley in 1529. Quite an evangelist, he drew crowds of followers and the attention of authorities. For protection, he sent some of his followers to Moravia, and when things became too difficult, followed them himself in 1533, seeking refuge with a community at Austerlitz.

In his honor, the Brethren community of Austerlitz took his name and became the Hutterites. They gradually established themselves in Moravia, sent out missionaries and expanded into dozens of communities with thousands of members despite the fact that most of the missionaries were executed.

The best known of the Dutch Anabaptists is Menno Simons, who came to the faith in the mid-1530s. An ordained priest, he had begun to disagree with the doctrine of transubstantiation that says the bread and wine of communion, when consecrated, become the actual body and blood of Jesus, and questioned the idea of infant baptism. Simons agreed with leaders of the Reformation on the authority of scripture, but he thought that only adults should be baptized and he advocated freedom of choice of religion.

His followers became known as Mennonists, and finally, Mennonites. Some of their numbers came to North America to establish churches and communities, drawn by the idea of religious freedom. Some individual Dutch Mennonites came to New Amsterdam in the 1640s. The first whole community arrived October 6, 1683, settling in Germantown outside Philadelphia.

DIVISIONS

Amish—In general, the Amish are the strictest of the Anabaptist groups. They originated in 1693 in a split led by Jacob Amman from Swiss Mennonites. In the United States, the Old Order Amish with their rejection of modern conveniences, including the automobile and the telephone, and their adherence to centuries-old dress customs have become tourist attractions in their communities.

Hutterites—Also known as the Hutterian Brethren, this group is of Moravian origin. The most distinguishing characteristic of Hutterites is their practice of living communally, sharing all goods and duties.

Mennonites—The largest general group of Anabaptists in the United States, the Mennonites also vary greatly in their lifestyles, from rural farm communities that stress plain dress to city churches whose members are typically dressed urban dwellers.

DOCTRINES SPECIFIC TO ANABAPTISTS

Most Anabaptists reject the idea of original sin brought on by humans' first disobedience of God. They believe a person is responsible not for an inherited sinful nature but only for sins committed. They also believe people who accept new life in Christianity can overcome most temptation to sin.

The Christian denominations in the Anabaptist family are sometimes known as "peace churches" because many of them oppose war and require that members serve only as conscientious objectors. They are also likely to refrain from direct political involvement or public office.

Anabaptist teaching renounces extravagance and advocates a simple lifestyle.

They have a strong commitment to spread the faith and believe that only adults can be baptized because infants cannot make a free-will commitment to Jesus. They also feel that community, or a fellowship of like-minded believers, is essential for humans to live in God's will.

TITLES

Bishop or Elder—An ordained minister who officiates over the church in a particular geographic area. Usually addressed simply as "Brother" or "Sister" with a first name.

Preachers or Ministers—In some traditions, the preacher is called "Pastor," but usually is simply called "Brother" or "Sister" with a first name.

Deacon—In some churches they assist the minister, oversee charitable efforts, visit the sick and ascertain the spiritual health of the congregation. Usually addressed as "Brother" with his first name.

Deaconess—Women, usually in a ministry to the poor or sick; in some groups, the wife of a deacon. Usually addressed as "Sister" with a first name.

"Brother" or "Sister" is an appropriate form of address for any Anabaptist. These denote a certain kinship, however. Anyone not comfortable using them can use "Mr.," "Mrs." or "Miss."

COMMUNITY WORSHIP

There have been some disputes over the years between Anabaptists who favor observing the traditional Old Testament Sabbath on Saturday and those who insist on keeping the Lord's Day on Sunday. The Sunday Anabaptists far outnumber the Saturday Anabaptists.

Most Anabaptist churches or meeting halls are plain buildings with little decoration. Worship itself de-emphasizes the sacramental, focusing on internal changes, not external signs.

Among the Amish especially, worship can be lengthy, lasting several hours. Most other groups have much shorter services.

A service usually consists of some or all of the following elements: hymns, scripture, responsive readings, prayer (standing, sitting or kneeling, according to custom), special music, an offering. In some of the strictest groups, instrumental music is prohibited. Foot-washing may be a part of the service and may be performed by a team of people or by one worshiper on another. When communion is part of worship, some groups invite all members of their denomination, some invite all Christians, and others restrict it to only members of the congregation in good standing. Some use grape juice, some wine; some use a common cup, others individual containers; some serve worshipers in the pews, others require that the congregation file to the front of the church.

Since some Anabaptist groups practice closed communion, visitors should wait for an announcement that all are welcome before partaking. Foot-washing would probably not be restricted, and guests should participate in that and other parts of worship as fully as they feel comfortable.

DRESS

Over the years and through the many Anabaptist groups, there have been rules for almost every item of clothing from hats to shoes. Today, most Anabaptists wear no distinctive dress, but encourage simplicity and modesty. Some groups wear no jewelry—not even wedding bands. In very conservative Anabaptist communities, women wear long plain dresses with aprons or capes and cover their hair with bonnets or net caps. They wear no cosmetics or jewelry. Men in those very conservative communities dress simply, are always well covered and usually have beards. Some Anabaptists cover their heads for worship.

Anabaptists consider it inappropriate for anyone to adopt their dress who is not doing it for religious reasons. To attend an Anabaptist event, clean, modest clothes are always appropriate. Guests should avoid gaudiness or extravagance.

DIETARY LAWS

There are no specific laws governing food; in fact, many groups have a tradition of hearty, homemade cooking. Some groups prohibit the use of alcohol.

PLACE OF CHILDREN

Despite forbidding the baptizing of infants, Anabaptist groups regard children as heirs to the kingdom of God, citing Jesus' admonition to his disciples to be like children. The churches teach that parents should be loving but firm, providing training, discipline and education by example. Children are considered gifts from God, and some Anabaptist groups disapprove of birth control. Children may be baptized as early as age nine, but more often this occurs in their teens or even twenties. Baptism is regarded as the beginning of an adult journey of faith.

ROLES OF MEN AND WOMEN

Women are expected to work hard and live simply, but their duties may be different from those of men. In the more conservative groups, interaction between men and women outside the family occurs on a very formal level.

Hugging, kissing and outward shows of affection to an Anabaptist of the opposite sex might be offensive. Friendliness and courtesy, without physical contact, is advisable on first meeting of a member of a conservative Anabaptist group.

HOUSEHOLD

The distinguishing characteristic of traditional Anabaptist households is simplicity. In the most extreme groups, this means no electricity and no automobiles. Most observant Anabaptists, however, try to take advantage of modern conveniences without living wastefully or extravagantly.

MILESTONES

Birth—A new child is an occasion for joy in the family and in the church, but there is no religious ceremony to mark a baby's arrival. The absence of infant baptism is a defining principle of the Anabaptist movement.

Marriage—The strictest Anabaptist groups encourage or require marriage within the faith with the approval of the parents and the leaders of the church.

Weddings may include singing, prayer, scripture, remarks by the minister and exchange of vows. Some groups prohibit holding weddings in their church or meetinghouse; others permit simple, dignified ceremonies but discourage elaborate displays or receptions. Still others leave the wedding arrangements up to the taste of the bride and groom.

An Amish wedding is an all-day affair with several hours of religious service followed by a community feast.

Death—At the time of death, friends and neighbors traditionally come forward to help with arrangements for the funeral and burial as well as any chores or duties that must be done. Most Anabaptist funerals are simple ceremonies with closed caskets so as not to call attention to the body but to focus on the soul and spirit. Viewing may take place beforehand at the church, home or funeral home. Traditional services include singing, prayer, a sermon and a eulogy, and may close with worshipers filing past the closed coffin to pay their respects. A brief graveside service usually follows.

Some Anabaptists consider flowers an unnecessary extravagance. Cards, gifts of food before and after the funeral and memorial gifts to charity are appreciated.

CONVERSION

Baptism signifies acceptance into the faith, and usually consists of a series of questions during which the candidate is asked to renounce worldliness and to submit to the rules of the church. Some groups or ministers dip and pour; some pour; some sprinkle; and some immerse.

MAJOR ORGANIZATIONS

General Conference Mennonite Church
722 Main
Newton, Kansas 67114

Hutterian Brethren
Route 1, Box 6E
Reardon, Washington 99029

Mennonite Church
421 S. Second Street
Ste. 600
Elkhart, Indiana 46516

Old Order Amish Church
c/o Raber's Book Store
2467 C. R. 600
Baltic, Ohio 43804

FURTHER READING

Dyck, Cornelius V. *An Introduction to Mennonite History.* Scottdale, Pa.: Herald Press, 1967.
Estep, William R. *The Anabaptist Story.* Nashville: Broadman Press, 1963.
Friedman, Robert. *The Theology of Anabaptism.* Scottdale, Pa.: Herald Press, 1973.
The Mennonite Encyclopedia. Hillsboro, Kan.: Mennonite Brethren Publishing House; Newton, Kan.: Mennonite Publications Office; Scottdale, Pa.: Mennonite Publishing House, 1955.
Weaver, J. Denny. *Becoming Anabaptist.* Scottdale, Pa.: Herald Press, 1987.

BAPTISTS

ORIGINS

Jоны the Baptist baptized Jesus in the River Jordan, according to the gospels, and Baptists, the largest non-Catholic Christian group in the United States, follow his lead in emphasizing baptism by immersion in water as a ritual symbolizing entry into the kingdom of God.

Baptists are an independent lot by nature, and no Baptist has the authority to speak for another Baptist. They are congregational in their government, but have formed dozens of denominations, from the fifteen-million-member Southern Baptist Convention to the tiny Duck River (& Kindred) Association Baptists with a few dozen churches in Tennessee.

Although they claim their roots in the New Testament church, Baptists began to gain their identity in the Puritan Separatist movement of the 17th century.

In 1600, John Smyth, a young Anglican clergyman, was named to England's Cathedral of Lincoln. Within two years, he had stood in the pulpit to denounce the hierarchy of the Anglican church as unbiblical. The bishops of the church soon removed him from his post. He quickly found a more receptive audience in a congregation at Gainsborough that had separated from the Church of England but the group, feeling harassed by the Anglicans, soon moved to Holland. In 1606, his group was named the Second English Church in Amsterdam. Smyth urged his congregation to learn to read the scriptures in the original Hebrew and Greek, and prohibited any book besides the Bible from being used in worship, even hymnbooks. He also began to revise Anglican theology. If the church was to be made up of believers, he reasoned, then only believers should be baptized and any infant baptism was therefore invalid. Any baptism by a church that practiced false doctrine was also invalid, he decided. In 1609, he rebaptized himself and insisted that any member of his congregation whose baptism had been conducted by the Church of England also be rebaptized. Smyth performed the baptism in the Anglican method of the day—by pouring water over those to be baptized. His reconstituted congregation became the first Baptist church.

But the church soon split. One group stayed in Amsterdam with Smyth. Another returned to England with Thomas Helwys, who had been baptized by Smyth. Another group of Baptists with a different point of view grew up a few years later. A preacher named Henry Jacob formed an independent church in London in 1616, which, by the 1630s, had become Baptist. Because they believed only certain people will be redeemed by God—the so-called salvation of the elect—they came to be known as *Particular Baptists*. The Helwys Baptists, by contrast, were known as *General Baptists* since they believed salvation was open not to just particular people but to anyone. The two groups joined as the Baptist Union for Great Britain and Ireland in 1638. By then, most Baptists had adopted the Particular Baptist method of baptism by immersion.

Soon afterward, Baptists formed their first churches in the colonies out of reaction to the religious exclusivity promulgated in most settlements. Roger Williams, who founded the colony of Rhode Island as a refuge from religious persecution, was baptized in 1639 with a small group of friends and together they formed the First Baptist Church of Providence. In 1814, the Triennial Baptist Convention was founded, which, until 1845, encompassed most Baptist churches in America. A clash over slavery and organizational questions led a group of Southerners to separate from the convention at a meeting in Augusta, Georgia, in 1845. They formed the Southern Baptist Convention. Other Baptists continued to participate in the Triennial Baptist Convention until 1907, when the Northern Baptist Convention was formed. The name was changed to the American Baptist Convention in 1950, and to American Baptist Churches in the U.S.A. in 1972.

Many other separate Baptist groups also emerged. African Americans, many of them having first attended their owners' churches as slaves, began to form their own Baptist churches. The so-called Bluestone Church, founded in 1758 on the William Byrd plantation in Mecklenberg, Virginia, and the Silver Bluff Baptist Church, in South Carolina near Augusta, Georgia, were among the first. Silver Bluff, believed to have been founded between 1750 and 1775 by a slave named George Liele, is still in existence.

The first all-black Baptist local associations were formed in Ohio, Illinois and Michigan in the 1830s and 1840s. The first regional convention is believed to have been organized by the Abyssinian Baptist Church in New York City in 1840 to serve the New England and Middle Atlantic areas. After the Civil War, the group also sent missionaries to the South. During the first few years after the Civil War, black Baptist conventions developed in many states.

But after attempts to unite smaller associations into a broader convention had failed, the National Baptist Convention was born in 1895 at a gathering in Atlanta.

The national unity of black Baptists was short-lived. In 1915 a schism broke the group into the National Baptist Convention of America, Inc., and the National Baptist Convention U.S.A., Inc. In 1961, a second major schism over the role of black Baptists in the Civil Rights movement resulted in formation of the Progressive National Baptist Convention.

DIVISIONS

There are many groups of Baptists as well as independent Baptist churches. Among the largest groups are:

The Southern Baptist Convention—The second-largest religious group in the United States, the SBC claims some fifteen million members in almost forty thousand churches.

National Baptist Convention, U.S.A., Inc.—The convention is not only the country's largest black Baptist group, it is the largest African-American organization of any kind with more than eight million members in more than thirty thousand congregations. The denomination has national headquarters in Nashville.

National Baptist Convention of America, Inc.—With more than 3.5 million members, this group, originally known as the National Baptist Convention, Unincorporated, is the second largest of the black Baptist bodies.

American Baptist Churches in the U.S.A.—The former Northern Baptist Convention is generally less conservative than the Southern Baptist Convention. With more than 1.5 million members, it is among the country's major religious groups.

National Association of Free Will Baptists—The result of a merger of several groups of Arminian Baptists, this association claims more than 200,000 members in 2,500 churches. Emphasis of this group is on the theological point of view of James Arminius, that Jesus died for everyone, not just a chosen group, and that everyone has the free will to choose salvation through Jesus.

National Missionary Baptist Convention of America—This group resulted from a dispute within the National Baptist Convention of America, Inc., in 1988 and claims 2.1 million members, largely in the Far West.

National Primitive Baptist Convention of the U.S.A.—Black and largely Southern, this group was formerly known as the Colored Primitive Baptist Church. It now claims a membership of about a million.

Primitive Baptists—Because they profess opposition to church organizations, Primitive Baptists do not keep reliable national statistics on membership and churches. And because there is no national body to take positions, church doctrine is generally set by congregations and their ministers, usually called elders. Primitive Baptists are regarded as generally Calvinist in their views, preaching a corrupt human nature with the possibility of salvation of the elect by grace alone.

Progressive National Baptist Convention, Inc.—This black Baptist group was founded in 1961 by Martin Luther King Jr. and other leaders in the civil rights movement who were dissatisfied with what they saw as the lack of response to the movement among leaders of the National Baptist Convention. With 2.5 million members in two thousand churches, it claims some of the largest and most prominent congregations.

DOCTRINES SPECIFIC TO BAPTISTS

Most Baptist churches have little liturgy and do not emphasize the liturgical seasons. Baptists teach the doctrine of Priesthood of the Believers, which means everyone can approach God without going through clergy and that every believer is responsible for ministering in the name of God. Baptists also generally emphasize evangelism, citing Jesus' "great commission" instructing his disciples to go into the world and make believers of all people.

TITLES

Baptist clergy are called ministers or pastors and are usually addressed as "Pastor" or "Reverend." If they have doctoral degrees, they may be addressed as "Doctor."

Baptist churches usually have elected boards of deacons who are responsible for the physical plant and programs of the church. In some congregations, it is customary to address them as "Deacon," but many churches do not use this courtesy title.

COMMUNITY WORSHIP

The sanctuary, or main worship hall, of a Baptist church usually has no religious icons. In many churches, there will be a baptistry, or pool of water, often behind a curtain; other churches may have separate areas for baptism, and a few even perform outdoor baptisms in nearby lakes or rivers.

Baptist worship services usually include hymns, readings from the Bible, prayers, an offering and a sermon. Some services include an opportunity for people to give personal testimony to their faith or to request prayers for a particular situation or person.

Some Baptist services include the Lord's Supper, also called communion, a baptism. Baptists prefer to call these "ordinances" rather than sacraments, since they see the rituals as symbolic and not sacred in and of themselves.

- **Lord's Supper**—The communion elements usually consist of some form of bread and grape juice—seldom wine—which are passed down the pews or served from the front of the church. Usually only those who are baptized Christians are invited to participate. Some Baptist churches open the invitation to those of any Christian denomination, while others restrict it to people baptized by immersion after making a profession of their faith. A few churches restrict communion to members of the specific congregation.

• **Baptism**—Baptists consider baptism an act of confession, indicating their acceptance of Jesus as Lord and their desire to affiliate with a Baptist church. Since the mid-1600s, Baptists have baptized by immersion, completely dunking a newly confessed Christian underwater to symbolize turning away from an old way of life. A prospective member will be asked by a minister to reply to certain questions by declaring belief in the basic tenets of the Christian faith, then will be immersed.

Many Baptist services close with an invitation for those who have not yet committed themselves to Jesus to come forward.

Visitors are welcome to participate in worship as they feel comfortable. If communion is offered, guests should listen to the invitation to see whether all, or only Baptists or church members, are allowed to partake.

DRESS

There is no universal dress code for Baptists, but some more conservative churches do not allow women to wear slacks to services. In most churches, men wear ties and women wear modest dresses or suits.

DIETARY LAWS

Many Baptists abstain from alcohol.

Alcohol is not a wise gift for Baptists.

PLACE OF CHILDREN

Many Baptist churches have elaborate children's programs including Sunday School, choirs, youth groups and a summer Bible School and camp.

There is no specific coming-of-age ceremony in Baptist churches. Children are expected to join the church and be baptized when they feel ready.

ROLES OF MEN AND WOMEN

In many Baptist churches, especially those of the Southern Baptist and National Baptist conventions, women are not allowed to serve as deacons or ministers. Some Baptist congregations do ordain women to the ministry, however.

Baptist women and men should be treated equally. A woman invited to address a Baptist church should be aware, however, that in some congregations she will not be allowed to speak from behind the pulpit.

MILESTONES

Birth—Baptists do not baptize infants. Increasingly, however, Baptist churches are having infant-dedication services during which parents and the congregation acknowledge their responsibility for raising the child.

Marriage—A Baptist wedding is seen as a covenant between the bride and groom and between the couple and God. The basic ceremony usually consists of a processional, followed by scripture readings and words of advice from the presiding minister, an exchange of vows and rings, prayer and the pronouncement that the couple is husband and wife. Different forms of music may be used throughout the service, but some churches require that only Christian music be played in the church.

Death—Baptists regard the death of a believer as passage to a better life with God. Baptist funerals are usually very much like a worship service and may include songs, prayers, a sermon and remembrances of the deceased. Baptist ministers may also emphasize the need of those in the congregation to repent of their sins and accept Jesus so that they will be assured of life after death.

CONVERSION

Baptists believe that one must profess faith in Jesus Christ, ask forgiveness for sins and be baptized in order to join the church. Some groups and congregations are stricter than others about accepting new members.

MAJOR ORGANIZATIONS

American Baptist Churches in the U.S.A.
P. O. Box 851
Valley Forge, Pennsylvania 19482

National Baptist Convention, U.S.A., Inc.
1700 Baptist World Center Drive
Nashville, Tenn, 37207

Progressive National Baptist Convention, Inc.
601 50th St. N.E.
Washington, D.C. 20019

Southern Baptist Convention
901 Commerce St.
Nashville, Tennessee 37203

FURTHER READING

Leonard, Bill, ed. *Dictionary of Baptists in America.* Downers Grove, Ill.:
    InterVarsity Press, 1994.
Mullins, E. Y. *Baptist Beliefs.* Valley Forge, Pa.: Judson Press, 1925, revised 1991.
Shurden, Walter B. *The Baptist Identity.* Macon, Ga.: Smyth & Helwys Publishing,
    Inc., 1993.
Skoglund, John E. *The Baptists,* pamphlet. Valley Forge, Pa.: Judson Press, 1967.
Tuck, William Powell. *Our Baptist Tradition.* Macon, Ga.: Smyth & Helwys Pub-
    lishing, Inc., 1993.

BRETHREN

ORIGINS

In the Palatinate region, the Reformed church was the church of the establishment during the 17th century but a nobleman and Radical Pietist evangelist named Ernest Christoph Hochmann von Hochenau advocated non-participation in state churches. He gained many followers but many Radical Pietists, subject to persecution, were forced to flee to the area of Schwarzenau. Out of this group emerged the Brethen.

In the summer of 1708, five men and three women were baptized as Brethren, with a former Calvinist, Alexander Marck, as their leader. Their number began to grow and they sent missionaries out to form churches. For their efforts, they were sometimes arrested and imprisoned. Some moved to the Netherlands in 1720, where they remained until Mack led a party to Pennsylvania in 1729. Other Brethren from a satellite church had already arrived in North America and by 1740, most of the Brethren remaining in Europe had followed.

In the 1800s, Brethren spread across the country emphasizing the need for simple living. This sometimes led to legalistic prohibitions—such as those recorded against everything from liquor to wallpaper.

Despite their dispersion, Brethren were united under the official name German Baptist Brethren. They held an Annual Meeting each year at Pentecost. Unlike many denominations, the Brethren did not split during the Civil War, partly because the church had always prohibited holding slaves, but they did split twenty years later amid disputes over innovations such as revival meetings and Sunday schools that were proposed by the more progressive among them. In 1881, several thousand conservatives who had withdrawn from the fold formed the Old German Baptist Brethren. On the more liberal side, supporters of Henry R. Holsinger, a Progressive Brethren publisher, pulled out in 1883 to form the Brethren Church, now regarded as more conservative than the Church of the Brethren.

In 1908, the remaining centrist body changed its name to the Church of the Brethren, which continued to add members and remains the largest of the three groups.

DIVISIONS

Major groups of Brethren include:

Church of the Brethren—The largest of the Brethren groups, this denomination is known for its relief services around the world. It combines congregational and presbyterian government. With headquarters in Elgin, Ill., it claims more than 150,000 members in more than one thousand congregations.

Fellowship of Grace Brethren Churches—Incorporated in 1987, this group of Brethren is more Calvinist in its theology than some other Brethren groups. It is the larger of two branches of the Brethren Church that split from the main body of Brethren in 1883. Headquartered at Grace Theological Seminary in Winona, Indiana, the Fellowship claims about forty thousand members. The smaller branch is the Brethren Church (Ashland), headquartered in Ashland, Ohio, with about three thousand members.

DOCTRINES SPECIFIC TO BRETHREN

Humankind—Humans are created in the image of God. Brethren reject the idea of predestination, and the idea that everyone is born into sin because of Adam and Eve's fall from grace in the Garden of Eden.

Sin—People sin, but God forgives. Through sanctification—or the process of becoming more holy—people can overcome much of the temptation to sin.

Hell—Eternal separation from God is hell—although Alexander Mack taught that everyone will be redeemed eventually.

Brethren have no creeds or oaths, but do have several areas of emphasis:

Industry—hard work.
Simplicity—lack of excess.
Temperance—usually interpreted as abstinence from alcohol, drugs and tobacco.
Peace—refraining from combat.

RELIGIOUS FESTIVALS AND HOLIDAYS

For many years, most Brethren did not celebrate any special days, claiming that all days are holy. Today, many Brethren celebrate Christmas, Easter and other holidays, although sometimes with less commercialism than much of the culture.

Love Feast—For churches in the Brethren tradition, the Love Feasts, usually held by many groups on the Thursday before Easter and on World Communion Day in October, are the largest celebrations of the year. Brethren tradition calls for a full meal to celebrate the Lord's Supper—not just token bread and wine. For Brethren, the Love Feast is a combined observance of all the meals in the New Testament, from Jesus' last meal with his disciples to the shared meals of the early church.

A Love Feast is a lengthy, multi-part worship service that includes prayer, a simple meal and reading of scripture. Foot-washing is also part of the service. Following Jesus's example of washing his disciples' feet, celebrants wash each other's feet, sometime divided by gender, sometimes in family groups, sometimes in no particular order. Bread and wine—or usually grape juice—are consumed at the end.

Brethren congregations have open communion. Non-Brethren may participate in the Love Feast or communion service to the extent they feel comfortable.

TITLES

Brethren regard clergy and laity as equal. Most clergy do not use any particular title, but Brethren refer to each other as "Brother" and "Sister."

COMMUNITY WORSHIP

Most Brethren observe Sunday as the Lord's Day, but there are a few Seventh-day Brethren who observe Saturday.

Brethren houses of worship are usually now called churches, but in earlier times were known as meetinghouses. They are usually plain buildings. Worship is usually not highly liturgical, and may include songs, scripture, a sermon and responsive reading, but will not include any recitation of a creed.

Most Brethren churches emphasize baptism and the Love Feast. Some also practice foot-washing, anointing of the sick with oil and the laying on of hands. A particularly Brethren greeting, sometimes used during worship, is the Holy Kiss. Usually one person will grasp another's hand in a handshake, and lean forward to place a kiss on the cheek, which is reciprocated. Although some very traditional groups may still forgo instrumental music, most Brethren have accompaniment with their singing.

At most Brethren churches, to be baptized, a believer kneels in water, makes a confession of faith, pledges to be faithful and is dipped forward three times, once each in the name of the Father, the Son and the Holy Spirit. In many congregations, the minister then lays hands on the person's head and prays for the Holy Spirit to come in.

Guests may participate in worship to the extent they are comfortable. A visitor who is uncomfortable with the idea of the Holy Kiss should step back slightly and extend a hand at arm's length.

DRESS

Historically Brethren men were bearded and tieless, and women wore dark bonnets and plain dresses. This is seldom practiced today. Most Brethren dress according to the culture they are in, although perhaps somewhat modestly. In very traditional congregations, women still wear prayer coverings—or net caps—over their hair for worship. Some Brethren women wear such coverings at all times.

DIETARY LAWS

Many Brethren interpret the denomination's emphasis on purity to mean they should refrain from alcohol and tobacco.

Alcohol and tobacco are not appropriate gifts for Brethren. If entertaining Brethren, hosts should provide non-alcoholic beverages.

PLACE OF CHILDREN

Children are expected to profess their faith in Jesus Christ and join the church when they feel ready and can accept the responsibilities of membership. Some congregations have classes for children to prepare them for coming into membership.

ROLES OF MEN AND WOMEN

Women have been involved in Brethren worship and service since the earliest days of the movement. In fact, Brethren in Germany were criticized for allowing women to teach and to act as their husbands' equals. Also, two women were among the first half-dozen people baptized in America.

But some people have complained about the role of women in the church. At times women have been prohibited from holding the offices of deacon or minister, and therefore were unable to serve communion. Today the Church of the Brethren ordains women, but some more conservative groups do not.

Men and women should be treated equally within the laity. In some churches, during the Love Feast men and women will be expected to separate for foot-washing. Guests should follow the lead of the church.

HOUSEHOLD

While there are no specific religious objects required in Brethren homes, most Brethren would not allow any guns or objects of military service or war. Children would not be permitted to play war games. Some homes also avoid television and other similar forms of entertainment.

Guests should show respect for Brethren views and not give children any toys of violence or bring anything with military association into a Brethren home.

MILESTONES

Birth—Brethren do not practice infant baptism. They believe infants are born into God's grace without original sin. Some among the more progressive churches have infant consecration services as part of a regular worship service. Parents pledge to raise the child in the faith and the congregation vows to offer support and encouragement. The pastor may put his hand on the child's head and pray.

Marriage—Simplicity is the rule of Brethren weddings, but the plans are up to the bride in consultation with the minister. Some groups do not allow weddings in the meetinghouse; others have an extemporaneous service. In most Brethren congregations, weddings resemble those of other Christian groups.

Death—Historically friends and neighbors helped a family who had experienced a death with work as well as with arrangements for the funeral. The funeral itself is usually simple and follows the form of a worship service with scripture, singing, prayer and a eulogy. A memorial service with cremation is quite common. Brethren de-emphasize the body itself.

Many Brethren consider flowers wasteful and prefer memorials to charities such as Brethren service groups. Visits to the family are appropriate, as are cards and calls with expressions of sympathy. It is also appropriate to take food to families in mourning.

CONVERSION

To join a Brethren church, a person must make a confession of faith and be baptized. Even adults may be asked to go through classes to learn about the faith before they are baptized. Brethren consider joining the church to be a commitment to a new lifestyle as a follower of Christ.

MAJOR ORGANIZATIONS

Church of the Brethren
1451 Dundee Avenue
Elgin, Ill. 60120

Fellowship of Grace Brethren Churches
P.O. Box 386
Winona Lake, Ind. 46590

FURTHER READING

Bowman, S. Loren. *Power and Polity Among the Brethren.* Elgin, Ill.: Brethren Press, 1987.
The Brethren Encyclopedia. Elgin, Ill.: Brethren Press, 1983.
Durnbaugh, Donald F., ed. *Church of the Brethren Yesterday and Today.* Elgin, Ill.: Brethren Press, 1986.

CATHOLICS

ORIGINS

THE Catholic Church claims roots going back to Jesus' disciple Peter. According to the New Testament, Jesus said of Peter, "Upon this rock, I will build my church." Catholics consider Peter to have been the first pope, or Holy Father of their church.

Although Christians were at first persecuted, the Roman emperor Constantine became a Christian, and in 313 granted freedom of worship to all religious groups in the empire. With Constantine's recognition, the church grew in influence and number. With the collapse of the Western Roman Empire, barbarian kings ruled western Europe. In the absence of an emperor, the church set out to play a more central role in the region and to convert other people to Christianity. Religious orders and/or monasteries were established, giving the church a stable presence in many communities. When parts of Europe were fighting Muslims and Vikings, the church provided a unifying force.

In those days there was a single church with several geographic branches. Each country's church had its own language and style of liturgy. But differences started to grow. The Eastern and Western branches of the church were at odds over the *filioque* clause (which means "and from the son" in Latin), an amendment to the Nicene Creed. The creed originally said the Holy Spirit "proceedeth from the Father." The addition said, "from the Father and the Son." The Roman church accepted the change; the Greeks and others rejected it, saying God alone was the origin of all things, including Jesus. Photius, Patriarch of Constantinople, and the Roman church's pope, John VIII, agreed in 880 to keep the creed as originally adopted, but political rivalry and ecclesiastical competition continued.

By 1054, relations were so bad that the head of the church of Constantinople and the head of the church of Rome issued anathemas, or formal orders of excommunication, against each other. In 1965, Pope Paul VI and Patriarch of Constantinople Athenagoras I finally cancelled the anathemas, but the churches remain separate.

HOLY TEXTS

The Catholic Church accepts the Christian Bible including the thirty-nine books of the Old Testament and the twenty-seven books of the New Testament, but adds more text in Esther and Daniel and seven books in the Old Testament that are called by Catholics the Deuterocanon.

DIVISIONS

A majority of the world's Catholics are Roman Catholics. There are, however, other branches of the church, still a part of the Catholic Church, still under the authority of the pope, but with their own customs and bishops. More than twelve million Catholics belong to these churches. As Christianity spread throughout the world, some cities became centers of Christian thought and the churches around them developed customs in keeping with the local culture. Many of these churches in countries east of Rome left the Catholic Church for the Orthodox Church during the schism that created the two branches. Those churches that remained a part of the Catholic Church, or left and returned, kept their own rites and patriarchs. As people from those countries moved around the world, the churches spread as well. The rites they use include:

Alexandrian Rite—Includes two main branches, the Coptic, or Egyptian, and the Ethiopian, or Abyssinian.

Antiochene Rite—Includes the Malankarese of India, the Maronites of the Middle East, and the Syrians of Asia and Africa.

Armenian Rite—Used almost exclusively by those of Armenian heritage.

Byzantine Rite—Originating in Constantinople, which was previously known as Byzantium, this is the second most popular Catholic rite. Those who practice it include the Albanians, Bulgarians, Byelorussians, Georgians, Hungarians, Italo-Albanians, Melkites (Greek Catholics), Rumanians, Russians, Slovaks, Ukrainians and Yugoslavs, Serbs and Croatians.

Chaldean Rite—A derivation of the Antiochene Rite, this is practiced by the Chaldeans in the liturgical languages of Syriac and Arabic, and by the Syro-Malabarese, situated mostly in the Malabar region of India.

DOCTRINES SPECIFIC TO CATHOLICISM

The Catholic Church has several elements of doctrine not shared by many other major Christian groups. The specifics relate to:

Scripture—While many Christians believe they can interpret scripture for themselves, Catholics are taught that the church must always have the final word on what the Bible means.

Papal Infallibility—The pope, the temporal head of the church, is a human sinner; however, Catholics believe that he will be prevented by God from doctrinal error. Therefore, his teachings are regarded as infallible, although his behavior is not.

Purgatory—The Catholic Church recognizes the existence of purgatory, a temporary state of punishment for sins not serious enough to condemn the sinner to hell but not yet forgiven through repentance. Not everyone bound for heaven must go through purgatory, but many people must. And everyone who passes through purgatory will eventually make it into heaven. The existence of purgatory is part of the official church doctrine. (Some Catholics also accept a state of limbo, where unbaptized infants are said to go after death. This is not official church doctrine, but was espoused by some theologians.)

Mary—The Catholic Church pays special attention to Mary, the mother of Jesus, known to Catholics as Our Blessed Mother and Mary, the Mother of God. Catholics believe she has a special place in their devotion, but they do not worship her. They believe she always points the way to her son Jesus; was conceived and born without original sin and never committed sin; was a virgin before and after giving birth to Jesus and remained a virgin for the rest of her life; and did not experience mortal death, but was assumed into heaven with Jesus without dying.

- *Immaculate Conception*—The Catholic church teaches that Mary herself was conceived and born without the taint of original sin and that she never committed sin. This doctrine was proclaimed by Pope Pius IX in 1854.
- *Perpetual Virgin*—The church teaches that Mary was a virgin before and after giving birth to Jesus and for her entire life.
- *The Assumption*—In 1950, Pope Pius XII proclaimed as church doctrine the belief that Mary did not experience mortal death but was assumed into heaven with Jesus without dying.

Religious Orders—The Catholic Church has dozens of religious orders for men and women who pledge poverty, chastity and obedience. Some are cloistered and have little interaction with the outside world. Some are devoted primarily to study; others serve the poor. Some are teachers, some are nurses, some are priests. The orders usually bear the names of saints of the church or of aspects of Mary or Jesus.

Saints—The Catholic Church recognizes as saints some people who died as martyrs of the faith or who lived exceptional lives. The process of being declared a saint is called canonization. At first anyone with a strong enough following informally became a saint; but for the last thousand years, the church has followed a formal procedure under which only the pope can declare a person a saint. Catholics believe they can petition saints to intercede with God on their behalf. Days are set aside for devotion to certain saints, and specific saints are regarded as looking out for specific groups of people or geographic regions.

Transubstantiation—Catholics believe in the actual presence of Jesus in the bread and wine of the eucharist, or communion elements. When the elements are consecrated, they retain their material form but become the real blood and body of Christ.

RELIGIOUS FESTIVALS AND HOLIDAYS

Besides the major liturgical observances that occur on Sundays—such as Easter, celebrating Jesus's resurrection—the Catholic Church in the United States observes several Holy Days of Obligation during which church members are expected to partake of the eucharist and give special devotion. These are:

The Nativity—Christmas, Dec. 25.
Solemnity of Mary, Mother of God—Jan. 1.
Ascension Thursday—The sixth week after Easter, marking the day Jesus ascended into heaven after his resurrection.
Mary's Assumption—Aug. 15.
All Saints Day—Nov. 1.
Immaculate Conception—Dec. 8.

If attending Catholic Mass on a feast day or holy day, guests may participate in any part of the service to the extent they feel comfortable except communion. A guest who wishes to receive a blessing from a priest should step forward with arms across the chest.

TITLES

Deacon—The diaconate is the only Catholic office widely open to married men—although if a deacon's wife dies, he must remain celibate and cannot remarry. The deacon is responsible for assisting bishops and priests in the celebration of the sacraments and for helping to carry out the charitable work of the church. Deacons are usually addressed as "Deacon" or the "Rev. Mr."

Sister—Women who enter religious orders, or pledge their lives to service for the church, make vows of poverty, chastity and obedience. They are considered married to the church, or to Jesus. There are many different communities of women with many different functions. Some orders specialize in education, some in health care, and some devote their time to prayer and contemplation. A nun is addressed as "Sister."

Brother—Some men devote their lives to the church and take vows of poverty, chastity and obedience, but do not enter the priesthood. They live in communities with many different roles. Some teach, some are missionaries, some spend their lives in meditation. Some well-known orders for men include the Christian Brothers, the Benedictines and the Franciscans.

Priest—The Catholic clergy is all male, and all men who enter the priesthood must vow lifelong celibacy. (Exceptions are a few former Episcopal priests who were received into the Catholic Church after being married.) Some Eastern Rite churches ordain married men, but require that if their wives die, they remain celibate and unmarried. Priests serve parishes as administrators, and pastors, administering the sacraments and tending to the needs of the community. A priest is addressed as "Father." Priests may be part of a religious order or directly under a diocese or archdiocese.

Monsignor—Monsignor is an honorary title given to a priest for special service. A priest with this honor is addressed as "Monsignor."

Bishop—The Catholic Church considers bishops direct successors to the apostles. Bishops must be unmarried and celibate. Bishops are appointed by the pope, the temporal head of the church. The geographic area for which a bishop is responsible is called a diocese. Some bishops serve in Vatican agencies or in other administrative positions. A bishop is usually addressed as "Bishop" or as "Your Excellency."

Archbishop—The first among equal bishops in a particular geographic area is designated archbishop and the area for which he is responsible, the major diocese in a area, is an archdiocese. Archbishops are named by the pope. The proper terms of address are "Archbishop" or "Your Excellency."

Cardinal—The pope names a certain number of archbishops and leading bishops as cardinals. Cardinals serve as special advisors to the pope and, in the event of the death of the pope, elect his successor. Those with the title cardinal are usually addressed as "Cardinal" or "Your Eminence."

Patriarch—In Eastern Rite Catholic churches, the patriarch is bishop of a leading city of the church, the first among equals of the bishops of the Rite. Patriarchs are addressed as "Patriarch."

Pope—The church's Holy Father, the pope is considered the successor to Peter, Jesus's apostle, whom Catholics believe had a special place in Jesus's plan. Peter became Bishop of Rome and was martyred. The pope is likewise Bishop of Rome, but he is considered chief spokesman for the world's Catholics and chief pastor to the church. The doctrine of papal infallibility, accepted by the Catholic Church, means that God will not allow the pope to lead the church astray in doctrine, not that popes never make mistakes. Usually upon being elected, a pope will choose a new name, honoring some saint or figure in church history. The Pope is known with the title Pope and his newly adopted first name only. He is addressed as "Your Holiness."

COMMUNITY WORSHIP

Catholics distinguish Sunday from the Sabbath of the Old Testament, which they acknowledge is Saturday. They consider Sunday not the Sabbath of God's original covenant with the Israelites, but the Lord's Day, the day of Jesus' resurrection. Observance of Sunday honors the covenant God made with believers of Jesus. Church doctrine says Catholics should partake of the eucharist and rest on Sunday, considered by the church "the foremost holy day of obligation."

Religious services and sacraments may vary between the Roman church and the Eastern Rite churches. Most major elements are similar, however.

The Catholic Church holds that there are seven sacraments, divided into three groups:

SACRAMENTS OF INITIATION

Baptism—Catholics baptize either children or adults. Ordained clergy—deacon, priest or bishop—can administer the sacrament of baptism. Baptism may be done by immersion, but in most cases, it consists of pouring water over the head of the candidate three times, baptizing "in the name of the Father, Son and Holy Spirit." Candidates for baptism are dressed in white. In a full service of baptism, the person being received is accompanied by sponsors from the faith who are expected to serve as mentors in the church. The sponsors of an infant are known as godparents. The presiding clergy anoints the candidate with chrism which has been blessed at a special service on the Thursday before Easter for sacramental use throughout the year. It is olive oil, with balsam and other scents. The candidate lights a candle—or an infant's parents light a candle—from the Easter candle, and the priest reminds them that anyone in Jesus' fold walks in the light of Christ. The priest touches the candidate's ears and mouth and prays that the candidate's ears be open to hear the word of God and mouth be open to proclaim the faith. The priest then charges the newly baptized person to live with Christian dignity in God's love. Any baptized Christian can baptize another person in danger of death.

Confirmation—The rite of confirmation consists of the anointing of the forehead of the person being confirmed with sacred chrism, and the laying on of hands by the priest or bishop officiating. Confirmation is sometimes celebrated with baptism. When it is not, it begins with the renewal of baptismal vows and the profession of faith by those being confirmed. For those not baptized as infants, confirmation is somewhat a coming-of-age ceremony, recognizing that they are at the age of reason to reaffirm their commitment to the church and their faith in God. Those being confirmed have a sponsor in the church. Many Catholics take a confirmation name, the name of a saint who is expected to serve as a heavenly model and protector.

Eucharist—The eucharist is celebrated daily in most Catholic churches. The Liturgy of the Eucharist, also called Mass, is the regular worship service of the Catholic Church. The eucharist reenacts Jesus' last meal with his disciples before his crucifixion. The Catholic Church attaches special significance to the eucharist, believing that after a priest consecrates the bread and wine, Christ is actually present in them.

The Catholic Church urges its members to partake of the eucharist regularly, and requires them to receive the body of Christ, in the form of the bread and wine, at least annually. But the church restricts the actual consumption of the eucharist to those who are considered in a state of grace, having confessed any sins and living within the law of the church. Catholics are also supposed to fast for an hour before communion. The Catholic church restricts consumption of the elements of the eucharist to baptized Catholics and to members of Eastern Orthodox churches who request to partake. Although not prescribed as part of the Mass, most people who enter the church dip their hands in holy water and make the sign of the cross, with the open palm of their right hand touching the forehead as they say, "In the name of the Father," then moving the hand to the chest as they say, "and the Son," then touching the left shoulder then the right shoulder and saying, "and the Holy Spirit. Amen." They may genuflect, or bend the right knee and bow slightly facing the altar, before entering their pews.

SACRAMENTS OF HEALING

Penance or Reconciliation—Formerly known as confession, this sacrament allows baptized Catholics to meet with Jesus in the form of one of his ordained priests to be assured of forgiveness. Confession is necessary before taking communion in cases of mortal sin, and a child must go to confession before the first communion.

The sacrament of penance or reconciliation is usually carried out in a special part of the church where the confessor is assured privacy. Older churches have small booths in which the priest and the penitent are separated by a curtain or screen. Once the person confesses any sins, the priest imposes a penance—prayer, an offering, self-denial or service—and confers absolution. The sacrament ends with a prayer or blessing by the priest.

Anointing of the Sick—This sacrament can be celebrated at a home, hospital or church, or anywhere a person is sick or injured. A priest or priests silently lay hands on the ill person and pray, then anoint the person receiving the sacrament with blessed oil. This sacrament is sometimes followed by the eucharist.

SACRAMENTS OF VOCATION AND COMMITMENT

Marriage—A wedding is usually celebrated in the context of a Mass, or celebration of the eucharist. The couple exchanges vows and rings, then, if both are Catholic, shares communion. If only one spouse is Catholic, only that person receives communion. The wedding may have special readings, prayers or music chosen by the couple and approved by the presiding priest.

Holy Orders—The sacrament of ordination for deacons and priests varies some by culture and rite. In all cases, however, a bishop places his hands on the head of the person being ordained and asks God to consecrate him for the office.

Non-Catholics are invited to participate in every part of worship except communion. Many churches provide an outline of the Mass in the back of the hymnal. A caution: When praying the Lord's Prayer aloud, Catholics ordinarily stop after "deliver us from evil." Other Christians use a longer version. Only Catholics are allowed to receive the elements of communion at Mass. Non-Catholics should sit quietly in their pews, or if they wish to be blessed by the priest, move forward with arms crossed across the chest.

PRIVATE WORSHIP

Rosary—Many Catholics use a rosary—which takes its name from Holy Rose, or Rose of Sharon, both of which are names for Mary, or from "rose garden," a name for a collection of devotions—as an aid to prayer. The rosary is a string of beads with a crucifix; each bead represents a prayer.

Stations of the Cross—Especially during Lent, many Catholics pray the Stations of the Cross. Each of the fourteen stations represents an event beginning with Jesus' condemnation to death and ending with his being placed in the tomb. These are depicted in a series on the church walls.

Sacramentals—Some Catholics wear medals, carry holy cards or use other religious objects that have been blessed or that represent a saint or an event in the life of the church. These are not considered lucky charms but are used as reminders of divine grace or of the courage of a particular person in the life of the church.

Non-Catholics should show respect for religious objects. Anyone may wear a medal, carry a holy card or pray the rosary. Priests will bless objects for Catholics and non-Catholics alike.

DRESS

Although before 1962 women were expected to cover their heads in church, such rules are no longer generally observed.

Priests do often wear distinctive garments: most especially the Roman collar, a narrow, standing white collar or black collar with white under the chin. In worship, deacons, priests and bishops all wear clerical vestments.

No special dress is required for non-Catholics attending Catholic events except that men should never cover their heads in church.

DIETARY LAWS

Catholics in the United States are obligated by directive from the National Conference of Catholic Bishops to fast on Ash Wednesday, the first day of Lent, and on Good Friday, commemorating the days Jesus was crucified. When fasting, Catholics are allowed one full meal a day, plus two smaller meals that do not add up to a full meal.

American Catholics are also supposed to abstain from meat on Ash Wednesday and on Fridays during Lent. The bishops urge Catholics not to eat flesh on any Friday during the year, to commemorate Jesus' crucifixion on a Friday, although this is not an obligation. The law of abstinence from meat takes effect on the day of a person's fourteenth birthday. The law of fasting takes effect on the eighteenth birthday and lasts until the day after the fifty-ninth birthday.

Non-Catholics should be supportive of Catholics during fast days. If entertaining Catholics during Lent, friends should ascertain if possible whether any fasting rules apply. If this is not possible, provide a variety of foods. Do not be offended if a Catholic turns down meat.

PLACE OF CHILDREN

The Catholic Church places a high value on children, born and unborn. The church disapproves of artificial birth control and condemns abortion. The church's regard for children is apparent in its practice of infant baptism, during which parents bring their children before the congregation and pledge to bring them up in the faith. The widespread system of Catholic elementary schools and high schools also shows the church's commitment to children.

Children are urged to participate in the worship of the church by assisting the priest at the altar. Recently, the church has also begun to accept girls in this role, adding altar girls to the tradition of altar boys. Although they are a part of the church, children cannot take communion, or actually consume the elements of the eucharist, until they reach the age of reason, usually seven years old. A formal first communion is celebrated. Boys are dressed in nice clothes, while girls are usually outfitted in white dresses with short veils over their heads, resembling bridal veils.

Children who are old enough to understand the significance are educated in the faith and go through a confirmation ceremony, renewing any vows that may have been made by parents. This usually takes place when the child is fourteen years old.

A small gift of a religious nature is appropriate when a child is confirmed. Guests attending a confirmation ceremony should participate to the extent they feel comfortable during the congregational portions, but may not take communion.

ROLES OF MEN AND WOMEN

While women have their own religious orders and carry out many of the ministries of the church, women cannot be ordained to the priesthood.

HOUSEHOLD

Most Catholic households have religious objects or icons, but nothing is required.

MILESTONES

Birth—Catholics regard infants' baptism as a symbol of their being embraced in God's unearned love. This can be done during a regular Mass or as a separate ceremony. It can involve one or more infants and adults. At the time of baptism, a child's parents promise to bring the baby up in their faith. Some Catholics believe that infants who die without baptism go neither to heaven nor hell, but to limbo, a place of eternal peace that is not in God's presence, as heaven is. This is not official church doctrine, however.

Gifts are appropriate for the baptized baby. Non-Catholic guests at an infant baptism should not take communion.

Marriage—Catholics are expected to marry only Catholics and are supposed to have church permission to marry anyone not a member of the Catholic church. If they marry outside the church, even to other Christians, they are obligated to bring their children up as Catholics.

The Catholic Church considers matrimony a sacrament and married people bound for life. Under serious circumstances—such as physical abuse—the church condones physical separation and civil division of property and child custody. But if a Catholic is divorced civilly, no remarriage is recognized by the church unless the first marriage is annulled, or declared invalid. The remarried spouse whose previous mate is still alive is excluded from communion until and unless an annulment is granted. This requires an often lengthy process.

Gifts for the bride and groom are appropriate.

Death—Funeral rites vary according to the culture in which they take place. The Catholic Church does not consider a funeral itself a sacrament, since the person who has died has already gone on to be with God. Most funerals include expressions of condolence to the family, the reading of scripture, the celebration of the liturgy of the eucharist if the service takes place in a church and an expression of farewell to the one who has died.

Cards offering condolences are appropriate. For a small donation, a Mass can be said in honor of the deceased.

CONVERSION

For adults not baptized in the church who want to become Catholic, the church, in 1972, created a program called Rite of Christian Initiation for Adults, or RCIA. Candidates pass through this process, learning church doctrine and practice, before being received as members. The process is usually timed to end at Easter with reception into the church and administration of three sacraments: baptism, confirmation and the eucharist. The four stages of the process are:

Pre-Catechumenate—This is a period of inquiry, during which, for several weeks or months, candidates begin to learn about the church and explore their own spiritual state.

Catechumenate—Those who wish to continue begin a more intense period of learning about the church's liturgy and beliefs. Those who complete this stage usually move on to the next step at Lent, or the period leading up to Easter.

Purification—A preparation of intense prayer and study, this is the last step before reception into the church at the Easter vigil.

Post-baptismal Catechesis—Already a part of the church, the new member is expected to continue study from Easter to Pentecost, focusing on Christ's death, resurrection and ascension.

Christians who have been previously baptized in other denominations do not go through baptism, but are expected to follow much of the study plan to be thoroughly familiar with Catholic doctrine before they accept the eucharist.

MAJOR ORGANIZATIONS

United States Catholic Conference
3211 Fourth Street
Washington, D.C. 20017-1194

FURTHER READING

Catechism of the Catholic Church. Liguori, Mo.: Liguori Publications, 1992.

Foy, Felician and Avato, Rose M., eds. *The 1997 Catholic Almanac,* Huntington, Ind.: Our Sunday Visitor Publishing Division, 1997.

Johnson, Kevin Orlin, Ph.D. *Why Do Catholics Do That?* New York: Ballantine Books, 1994.

Keating, Karl. *What Catholics Really Believe—Setting the Record Straight.* Ann Arbor, Mich.: Servant Publications, 1992.

Lukefahr, Oscar, C.M. *"We Believe"—A Survey of the Catholic Faith.* Liguori, Mo.: Liguori Publications, 1990.

McBrien, Richard P., ed. *The HarperCollins Encylcopedia of Catholicism,* San Francisco: HarperSan Francisco.

McBrien, Richard P. *Inside Catholicism—Rituals and Symbols Revealed.* San Francisco: Collins Publishers, 1995.

Noonan, James-Charles, Jr. *The Church Visible—The Ceremonial Life and Protocol of the Roman Catholic Church.* New York: Viking, 1996.

Richstatter, Thomas, O.F.M. *Sacraments—How Catholics Pray.* Cincinnati, Ohio: St. Anthony Messenger Press, 1995.

CONGREGATIONALISTS

ORIGINS

THE Congregationalists—who take their name from the belief that power should reside in the local church—grew out of the Separatists within the Church of England during the reign of Elizabeth I.

In 1580 in Norwich, England, Robert Browne organized a Congregational church. Browne, about thirty years old at the time, had been educated at Cambridge and had worked with men and women who were unhappy with the Church of England. They were known as Puritans because they united to purify the church of perceived corruptions such as liturgy and clerical robes. Browne organized a church around the belief in congregational government and the personal relationship between each person and God. He was imprisoned in England for his views, but soon recanted them and came back into the Church of England's fold.

Although Browne did not last, his Congregational movement did. In the 1590s, postmaster William Brewster and a Separatist pastor named John Robinson built a congregation. At the time, Anglicanism was still strictly enforced by penalty of imprisonment. Out of fear that they would be discovered, they fled England and eventually sailed to the New World. Their ship, the *Mayflower*, anchored at Cape Cod. They drew up the Mayflower Contract and began to organize themselves to build a new community. Ironically, this group, which came to be known as the Pilgrims, did not set up a church.

A few years later, a second group of settlers arrived not too far away in Massachusetts Bay. These were non-Separatist Puritans who retained their hope of reforming the Church of England. Their leader was John Winthrop. The two groups soon joined forces.

A major split within Congregationalism came as some of the more liberal churches began leaning toward Unitarianism, or the denial of the Christian doctrine of the Trinity that places Jesus and the Holy Spirit equal to God. Differences came to a head in 1819 when William Ellery Channing, minister of the Federal Street Church in Boston, preached a sermon espousing Unitarianism in Baltimore. Liberals rallied behind him and established the American Unitarian Association, which drew more than one hundred Congregationalist churches.

Congregationalists merged with the General Convention of the Christian Church, a non-creedal group of about 100,000, in 1931 and became known as Congregational Christian Churches. In 1957, most Congregational Christian Churches joined with the Evangelical and Reformed Church to form the United Church of Christ.

DIVISIONS

United Church of Christ—This is by far the largest body with Congregational roots, although it is the product of mergers with bodies from other traditions. In 1957, it was constituted from two groups—the Congregational Christian Churches and the Evangelical and Reformed Church. Today, the United Church of Christ has about 1.5 million members in the United States.

Conservative Congregational Christian Conference—This organization, with about thirty thousand members, was formed in 1948 by evangelicals in the Congregational Christian Church. Churches in this group sometimes use the name Community or Bible Church.

National Association of Congregational Christian Churches—Formed in 1955 by delegates from Congregational Christian Churches who did not want to merge into the United Church of Christ, this group represents about seventy thousand members.

DOCTRINES SPECIFIC TO CONGREGATIONALISM

Belief in the autonomy of the local church is the doctrine for which the Congregationalist movement is named.

TITLES

Pastor—The clergy of a local church. Is addressed as ''Pastor,'' ''Reverend,'' or if appropriate, ''Doctor.''

The United Church of Christ also has three nationally elected officers: *President*—addressed as President; *Secretary*—no special form of address; *Treasurer*—no special form of address.

COMMUNITY WORSHIP

Congregationalist church services vary greatly since each congregation can set its own form. The movement has a tradition of simplicity in worship, with less liturgy and an emphasis on prayer, singing and preaching. There might be a prayer of confession or a responsive reading. Some congregations are becoming more liturgical, however.

Congregationalists observe two sacraments: *Baptism*—usually by sprinkling of water on the head in the name of the Father, Son and Holy Spirit, and *Communion*—sharing of bread and wine or grape juice to commemorate Jesus's last meal with his disciples during which he gave them bread, saying, "This is my body," and wine, saying, "This is my blood." Most churches practice open communion, but it is left up to the individual congregation whether children and non-members are invited.

Guests should participate as they feel comfortable. Visitors should listen carefully to the invitation before communion is served to see whether they are included.

PLACE OF CHILDREN

Congregationalists recognize infant baptism, although some churches prefer to hold dedication services for infants with baptism to follow later, usually in the early teens. When children are old enough to make the decision on their own, they may come forward, affirm their intention to follow Jesus and care for others and join the church. They will be baptized if they were not as infants, and they may kneel while the minister lays hands on their heads and prays. They are then regarded as full-fledged members of the church.

ROLES OF MEN AND WOMEN

The United Church of Christ ordains both men and women. Both genders can play any part in the church.

HOUSEHOLD

There are no special requirements for Congregationalist households, although some families might have crosses or religious art in their homes.

MILESTONES

Birth—Churches have either infant baptism, during which a child is sprinkled with water in the name of the Father, Son and Holy Spirit, or infant-dedication services during which parents pledge to raise their children in the church until the children can make the decision on their own to be baptized. These are usually held as part of a regular worship service. During such services, the congregation also promises to support and encourage the family.

If communion is offered at a baby-dedication service, visitors should listen carefully to see whether they or their children are included.

Marriage—A wedding in the Congregationalist tradition or the United Church of Christ is essentially a worship service with music, scripture and remarks by the minister, as well as an exchange of vows and rings by the couple. A recent development in some churches is that weddings are actually held as part of a Sunday worship service.

Death—Funerals in the Congregationalist tradition and in the United Church of Christ are Christian worship services that may include music, scripture, prayer and remarks by the minister. A second brief service may be held at graveside.

CONVERSION

Adults coming into Congregational or United Church of Christ churches often go through classes for new members to get to know the tradition. If not previously baptized, they are baptized before being taken into membership.

MAJOR ORGANIZATIONS

United Church of Christ
700 Prospect Avenue
Cleveland, Ohio 44115

FURTHER READING

History and Program—United Church of Christ. Cleveland, Ohio: United Church Press, 1991.

Horton, Douglas. *The United Church of Christ—Its Origins, Organization, and Role in the World Today.* New York: Thomas Nelson & Sons, 1962.

My Confirmation—A Guide for Confirmation Instruction (Revised and Updated). Cleveland, Ohio: United Church Press, 1994.

Paul, Robert S. *Freedom with Order—The Doctrine of the Church in the United Church of Christ.* New York: United Church Press, 1987.

Shinn, Roger L. *Confessing Our Faith—Interpretation of the Statement of Faith of the United Church of Christ.* New York: The Pilgrim Press, 1990.

Starkey, Marion L. *The Congregational Way.* Garden City, N.Y.: Doubleday & Co. Inc., 1966.

Youngs, J. William T. *The Congregationalists.* Westport, Conn.: Greenwood Press, 1990.

DISCIPLES AND CHRISTIANS

ORIGINS

Barton Warren Stone was ordained a Presbyterian minister in 1798 in Cane Ridge, Kentucky, but he was uncomfortable with certain aspects of Calvinism. He refused to accept parts of the Westminster Confession, a basic document of Presbyterianism, especially the idea of salvation and eternal life only for those elected in advance by God.

In 1801, a religious revival came to Cane Ridge, following other examples of spiritual outpourings in the late 1790s. After participating in the ecumenical Cane Ridge Revival, Stone and some fellow Presbyterian clergy withdrew from the Presbyterian Synod of Kentucky over the doctrine of predestination, and formed their own Springfield Presbytery. A few months later, they rejected all ideas of Presbyterianism and called themselves "Christians only." Thus, they referred to their church as the Christian Church or the Church of Christ, using the terms interchangeably.

While Stone was building a movement in Kentucky, another Presbyterian was making his way to southwest Pennsylvania. Scots-Irish Presbyterian Thomas Campbell arrived in the United States in 1807, and was soon renounced by his Irish denomination for fraternizing with other Presbyterians. He formed an association with a call for a return to primitive Christianity. Two years later, the rest of Campbell's family, including son Alexander, arrived. Alexander, also a clergyman, assumed leadership of his father's group and emphasized the need to restore the church to New Testament purity.

Campbell's movement, known as the Reformers or Disciples, spread and inevitably met Stone's. They agreed on many matters of faith and practice, but not on a name. Not surprisingly, Stone advocated calling the group Christians while Campbell insisted on Disciples. They also disagreed on whether instrumental music should be part of the service, and disagreements over mission societies aggravated the differences. In general, those who opposed instrumental music also opposed any mission organization other than the local congregation.

The division became official in 1906 when Churches of Christ—the non-instrumentalists—were listed as a separate group from the Disciples of Christ.

About half a century later, another split occurred—one that had started to develop as early as the 1920s. Conservative congregations, upset with the perceived liberalism in the denomination's colleges, universities and mission efforts, formed the Christian Restoration Society in 1925 as a fellowship within the Disciples.

In the 1960s, when the Disciples began a lengthy reorganization process that resulted in their identity as Christian Church (Disciples of Christ), some three thousand churches, representing more than 750,000 members, officially withdrew. By 1971, the Christian Churches and Churches of Christ was a separate category in denominational listings from either the Christian Church (Disciples of Christ) or the Churches of Christ. Combined, the various factions of the Christian Church and Churches of Christ make up the largest religious group founded in America.

DIVISIONS

Christian Church (Disciples of Christ)—Considered the most liberal of the three groups that grew out of the Stone-Campbell movement, the Disciples of Christ are now also the smallest, with about 606,000 full members in the United States. The denomination is headquartered in Indianapolis.

Christian Churches and Churches of Christ—The churches that are part of this group do not consider it a denomination. Government in these churches, which represent about one million people, is strictly congregational.

Churches of Christ—With an estimated 1.3 million members, the Churches of Christ are the largest of the Stone-Campbell groups. There is no headquarters. Most churches still do not use musical instruments in worship.

DOCTRINE SPECIFIC TO DISCIPLES AND CHRISTIANS

The churches of the Stone-Campbell movement are non-creedal, trusting in the priesthood of all believers, or the ability of individuals to interpret scripture for themselves.

With roots in what is widely known as the Restoration Movement, Christians and Disciples hope to restore the church to its pure New Testament state. Within and between the different groups of the movement there is disagreement about exactly what that means. Christians and Disciples emphasize communion. Congregations usually have the Lord's Supper, with wine or juice and bread representing Jesus' blood and body, on a weekly basis.

TITLES

Minister—Disciples use "Reverend," or "Doctor" for pastors with doctorates, to address ministers, except for some very traditional churches, which call ministers "Elder"; Churches of Christ reject the title "Reverend" (citing Psalm 111:9, which gives God the name "reverend"), and call pastors "Brother" or "Mr." since no women are pastors.

COMMUNITY WORSHIP

Worship among Christians and Disciples varies greatly. All churches are likely to have preaching, prayer and weekly communion. While Disciples now use instruments, congregations in the Churches of Christ still do not, but congregations sing without instrumental accompaniment.

Guests may participate in the worship service to the extent they are comfortable. Guests are also invited to receive communion with Disciples and Christians.

PLACE OF CHILDREN

Disciples and Christians do not baptize infants. Children are encouraged to come forward, be baptized and join the church when they are old enough to understand the significance of the act. Some churches have membership classes to prepare children for this step.

ROLES OF MEN AND WOMEN

In Disciples churches women can hold any role, including that of senior pastor. Churches of Christ do not permit women to be pulpit preachers or to hold the office of elder, which is a member of the church's governing body.

MILESTONES

Birth—Disciples and Christians do not baptize babies. Disciples churches may have a baby dedication as part of a regular worship service during which parents and godparents pledge to raise the child in the faith. Churches of Christ may have a Sunday service with an emphasis on children during which parents are invited to make a commitment on behalf of their children. In Churches of Christ, parents are welcome to walk down during any service and dedicate their children to Jesus.

Marriage—A wedding in a Disciples or Christian church usually has all the elements of worship with music, scripture, prayer, remarks by the minister as well as the exchange of vows by the couple. In Churches of Christ, couples may use instrumental music for their weddings despite the prohibition on instruments during worship.

Death—Funeral arrangements are up to the family, in consultation with the minister. Funerals usually include music, scripture, prayer, remarks by the minister and may include eulogies by family members or friends. In Churches of Christ, musical instruments may be permitted for a funeral at the family's request, although they are used infrequently.

CONVERSION

Christians and Disciples emphasize the importance of baptism by immersion, but Disciples will accept people baptized by other modes. Churches of Christ will baptize by immersion anyone who wishes to join and has been sprinkled or baptized as an infant in another church. Some congregations hold classes to prepare candidates for baptism.

MAJOR ORGANIZATIONS

Christian Church (Disciples of Christ)
130 E. Washington Street
P. O. Box 1986
Indianapolis, Indiana 46206-1986

Christian Churches and Churches of Christ
North American Christian Convention
4210 Bridgetown Road
Box 11326
Cincinnati, Ohio 45239

Churches of Christ
c/o Gospel Advocate
P. O. Box 726
Kosciusko, Missouri 39090

FURTHER READING

Allen, C. Leonard, and Hughes, Richard T. *Discovering Our Roots—The Ancestry of Churches of Christ.* Abilene, Texas: ACU Press, Abilene Christian University, 1988.

Cartwright, Colbert S. *People of the Chalice—Disciples of Christ in Faith and Practice.* St. Louis: CBP Press, 1987.

Cummins, Duane. *A Handbook for Today's Disciples.* St. Louis: The Bethany Press, 1981.

Foster, Douglas A. *Will the Cycle Be Unbroken—Churches of Christ Face the 21st Century.* Abilene, Texas: ACU Press, Abilene Christian University, 1994.

Hughes, Richard T. *Receiving the Ancient Faith—The Story of Churches of Christ in America.* Grand Rapids, Mich.: William B. Eerdmans Publishing Company, 1996.

McAllister, Lester G., and Tucker, William E. *Journey in Faith—A History of the Christian Church (Disciples of Christ).* St. Louis: Chalice Press, 1995.

Olbricht, Thomas H. *Hearing God's Voice—My Life with Scripture in the Churches of Christ.* Abilene, Texas: ACU Press, Abilene Christian University, 1996.

Randall, Max Ward. *The Great Awakenings and the Restoration Movement.* Joplin, Mo.: College Press Publishing Company, 1983.

EPISCOPALIANS

ORIGINS

In 1534, Henry VIII of Great Britain wanted to divorce his wife, Catherine of Aragon. Catherine had borne him five children, but only one, Mary, was alive and Henry desperately wanted a son. One thing stood between Henry and marriage to Anne Boleyn—the Roman Catholic Church's stance against divorce. Henry urged Parliament to pass two acts in 1534. One declared that the Roman Catholic pope had no authority in England. The other established the Church of England with the monarch at its head. Those who opposed the split were executed.

Henry was succeeded by nine-year-old Edward VI in 1547. His closest advisors supported church reform efforts by Thomas Cranmer, the Archbishop of Canterbury. Cranmer wrote two versions of what became the Book of Common Prayer, one in 1549 and one in 1552. He held worship services in English, not Latin. Clergy were allowed to marry. And in 1553, Cranmer wrote the forty-two "Articles of Religion" to be avowed by the clergy and the faculty and students of Oxford and Cambridge universities. The articles were never enforced because Edward died the same year. His successor, Mary Tudor, was a staunch Catholic determined to restore the country to what she saw as the true church. Under her reign she executed so many Protestants—including Cranmer—under newly revised heresy laws that she earned the nickname Bloody Mary.

When she died in 1558, Mary was succeeded by her half-sister Elizabeth I, who sought to form a church that was neither too Catholic nor too Protestant. In 1571, the Thirty-Nine Articles were issued, based on Cranmer's earlier Articles.

These set up the hierarchy of bishops, priests and deacons and allowed clergy to marry. They rejected the idea that the bread and wine of the communion service actually become the body and blood of Christ as taught by the Catholics, but also denied that the communion service is simply symbolic. Elizabeth died in 1603, having reigned long enough to give the infant Church of England a solid foundation.

The Scottish King James VI, who succeeded Elizabeth, supported a new but not significantly altered 1604 Prayer Book, called a convocation that produced a Book of Canons and, most significantly, supported a new translation of the Bible. The Authorized Version, which came out in 1611, is widely known as the King James. James's successors pulled the country back and forth toward and away from Catholicism until the rule of Queen Anne, who came to power in 1702. Since her reign, all English monarchs have been of the Church of England.

The Church of England came to North America with explorers sent by Elizabeth, bringing with them chaplains. With the settlement of Jamestown in 1607, the Church of England gained a firm foothold in North America. Early church leaders sought to bring the Native Americans they found into the church. Probably their most famous convert was the maiden Pocahontas. The colonial church remained firmly under the English church and the Bishop of London. Even during the American Revolution, some Anglican clergy, because of their oaths of ordination swearing allegiance to the monarchy, continued to pray for the king while the colonies were fighting him.

Efforts to form an American church became serious around 1782 when the Rev. William White, rector of Christ Church of Philadelphia and a former chaplain of the Continental Congress, made a proposal for a United States Church. Over the next two years, his idea was approved by clergy in Maryland, Pennsylvania, New Jersey and New York. But in the meantime, Connecticut clergy struck out on their own, electing Samuel Seabury to be a bishop. Seabury went to England to attempt to be consecrated, but English bishops refused. He then went to Scotland, where bishops there, not under the crown, obliged. Seabury returned to the United States in 1785 and quickly ordained more than two dozen priests for parishes up and down the Atlantic coast.

Also in 1785, delegates from seven states met in the first General Convention of the church in Philadelphia. They began work on a constitution and an American version of the Book of Common Prayer. The mainline church in America was known as the Protestant Episcopal Church—from its commitment to having bishops and its distinction from the Catholic Church—until 1967, when it became known simply as the Episcopal Church.

There are several other Anglican bodies in the United States as well. Disputes within the church over doctrine, ordination of women and prayer book revision have led to splits, but all the other bodies are much smaller than the Episcopal Church.

DIVISIONS

Episcopal Church—The mainline Anglican church in the United States and the only one recognized by the international Anglican communion, the Episcopal Church has about 2.5 million members. Several small conservative groups have split away from the Episcopal Church in the United States, many in the last few decades over ordination of women and changes in the prayer book, but it remains by far the largest denomination.

One of these offshoots is:

Anglican Orthodox Church—Although it has only a few thousand members inside the United States, the Anglican Orthodox church has more than 300,000 worldwide. It was organized in 1963 by James Parker Dees, a former North Carolina Episcopal priest dissatisfied with what he saw as the liberal leanings of the church.

DOCTRINES SPECIFIC TO EPISCOPALIANISM

The Episcopal Church is similar to the Catholic in its structure but admits women to every level of office and allows priests to marry.

The church believes in the apostolic succession of bishops—that the consecration of bishops leads back to Jesus' apostles.

The Episcopal Church emphasizes liturgy as the core of life and faith.

Episcopalians do not accept the doctrine that the bread and wine of communion actually become the body and blood of Christ, but neither do they regard the elements as symbolic, as many churches do. Episcopalians believe in the "real presence" of Christ in the elements of the eucharist, without defining that any further.

TITLES

Although many of the titles are the same, as in the Roman Catholic Church, unlike the Catholics the Anglican-Episcopal churches do not require a celibate clergy.

Bishop—serves as the head of a diocese, or the churches in a geographic area; also is a member of the church's House of Bishops, one of two houses in a bicameral legislative body. Addressed as "Bishop" or "Right Reverend."

Bishop Coadjutor—an assistant bishop elected to assist the diocesan bishop and become bishop when the diocesan bishop retires. Addressed as "Bishop" or "Right Reverend."

Dean—The chief priest at a cathedral. Addressed as "Dean" or "Very Reverend."

Canon—A clergy member of the cathedral staff. Addressed as "Canon."

Rector—The chief priest in a parish. Addressed as "Father" or "Mother."

Priest—A member of the Episcopal or Anglican clergy. Addressed as "Father" or "Mother."

Deacon—Provides service such as work with the poor; can baptize. Most deacons are later ordained to the priesthood. Addressed as "Deacon."

Warden—Chief of the vestry, or congregational governing body. No special form of address.

Sexton—Responsible for church property and physical plant. No special form of address.

COMMUNITY WORSHIP

Many Episcopal worship services are highly liturgical. They usually begin with a processional in which a cross is held high in front. All those who will participate in conducting the worship service follow. Incense is frequently carried in the procession and used in the worship service.

Episcopalians are guided in their worship by the Book of Common Prayer. They stand whenever the gospel is read and to sing, and may kneel or stand to pray.

Episcopalians recognize two sacraments:

Baptism—Often baptisms take place at the Easter vigil, the night before Easter, and on Pentecost, All Saints' Day and the first Sunday after Epiphany, which is known as the Feast of the Baptism of Jesus. Baptism in the Episcopal Church may be by immersion or by pouring of water over the head. As parents make pledges on behalf of their babies, or older children and adults confess their faith, Christians in the congregation are expected to renew their own baptismal vows.

The Eucharist—Also known as the Lord's Supper or Holy Communion, this is "the principal act of Christian worship on the Lord's Day and other major Feasts," according to the Episcopal Church's Book of Common Prayer. The eucharist commemorates Jesus' last supper with his disciples, when he offered them bread and wine as his body and blood. Episcopalians recognize the "real presence" of Christ in the elements of the eucharist. In the Episcopal church, communion wine is usually presented in a chalice for all to drink. Some churches—and some parishioners within churches—use intinction, or dipping the wafer of bread into the wine before eating it.

Non-Episcopalians are welcome to participate in any congregational part of worship or sacraments. All Christians are welcome to take communion in the Episcopal Church.

PRIVATE WORSHIP

Episcopalians follow the long-standing Anglican tradition of matins and even-song, or morning and evening prayers. The Book of Common Prayer provides prayers to be used each day, either individually or communally.

DRESS

There is no dress code in the Anglican or Episcopal church. Most clergy wear distinctive collars to signify their office. Episcopal clerical worship vestments resemble those of Catholic clergy.

PLACE OF CHILDREN

The Episcopal Church baptizes infants. When children are older, they generally attend a series of classes to learn about the faith, and are accepted as full members of the church in a ceremony that includes the reaffirmation of baptismal vows and a blessing.

ROLES OF MEN AND WOMEN

In Episcopal and Anglican churches, attitudes toward the role of women vary. In the mainline Episcopal Church, women are ordained and even serve as bishops, although this practice is not universally accepted. The Church of England also now ordains women to the priesthood. But some Anglican branches in the United States still have an all-male priesthood.

MILESTONES

Birth—Episcopal and Anglican churches baptize babies. Parents and godparents make the baptismal promises on behalf of the baby.

Marriage—The marriage ceremony is considered a sacramental rite—not a sacrament—but marriage is regarded as a covenant blessed by God. The wedding rite usually takes place with the celebration of the eucharist. Ministers are usually vested in white. The service may include a processional, music, prayer, scripture and a sermon or homily. It always includes an exchange of vows and a blessing of the marriage. If the eucharist is not being celebrated, the blessing by a priest or bishop, sometimes with holy water, ends the service.

Many people who worship in the Anglican tradition follow the custom of publishing banns announcing a forthcoming marriage on three Sundays before the wedding.

Death—When a person is near death, a priest may visit and serve the eucharist, hear confession and/or anoint the person with oil. Confession, or reconciliation, is a rite, not a sacrament in the Episcopal church. Confession may be heard any time by any Christian but only a priest may pronounce absolution. A Litany, or responsive recitation, may be said with friends and family, asking for divine mercy on the one who is dying, followed by the Lord's Prayer and a prayer by the priest. If a priest is present when death occurs, the priest says a prayer for the departing soul and a prayer commending the soul to God.

When the body is brought to the church before the funeral, the priest receives it with a prayer and precedes it into the church. The coffin remains closed during the service. The church offers a choice of rites that include music, scriptures, prayer, the eucharist and litanies. A committal service, either at the end of the funeral or at the graveside, follows. The priest may use incense or holy water to bless the coffin. The priest says words of reassurance, commits the body to the ground and the soul to God, and prays.

On All Souls Day, on November 2, a memorial is held for all those who have died in the past year. In every eucharist, there is a place to remember those who have died.

CONVERSION

The Episcopal Church requires that people who are coming into the church have classes to familiarize them with the faith before they are baptized. The extent and form of the classes vary from parish to parish. The Episcopal Church recognizes the baptisms of other Christian bodies.

MAJOR ORGANIZATIONS

The Episcopal Church
815 Second Avenue
New York, N.Y. 10017

FURTHER READING

An Outline of the Faith Commonly called The Catechism, compiled and edited by Leo Malania. New York: Church Hymnal Corporation, 1977.

The Book of Common Prayer and Administration of the Sacraments and Other Rites and Ceremonies of the Church. Church Hymnal Commission and the Seabury Press, 1979.

Holmes, David L. *A Brief History of the Episcopal Church.* Valley Forge, Pa.: Trinity Press International, 1993.

Holmes, Urban T. III. *What Is Anglicanism.* Harrisburg, Pa.: Morehouse Publishing, 1982.

Prichard, Robert W. *A History of the Episcopal Church.* Harrisburg, Pa.: Morehouse Publishing, 1991.

Wall, Rev. John N. Jr. *A New Dictionary for Episcopalians.* San Francisco: Harper-San Francisco, 1985.

LUTHERANS

ORIGINS

Although Catholic monk Martin Luther never intended to form his own church, millions of Christians around the world are now in a family of denominations that bear his name.

Luther was born Nov. 10, 1483, in Eisleben in Saxony, near the Czech border. Frightened by a severe thunderstorm while on a walk at age twenty-one, he promised to devote his life to God by becoming a monk. Through his study, Luther became convinced that faith alone—through the power of Jesus—brings about salvation. This position placed him directly in opposition to the church's practice of selling indulgences, or grants of forgiveness of sin. Some church officials sold indulgences even for sins yet to be committed, giving church members a license to sin for a price. They also accepted gifts as payment for getting dead relatives out of purgatory.

The more he studied, the greater Luther's frustration became until, on October 31, 1517, he nailed his ninety-five Theses to the door of the Wittenburg Castle church.

Among the principles of the theses are:

- The pope cannot remit any penalties except those he imposes.
- Only God can remit guilt and does so only with repentance.
- The church has no authority over purgatory.
- Those who rely on indulgences for salvation are damned.
- Christians have the blessings of Christ without indulgences.

• Assisting the poor is better than buying indulgences.
• One cannot transfer divine merit or credits to others.

Luther maintained that the document was intended only to stimulate discussion within the church, but it set off a furor that reached the Vatican. Many Germans regarded him as a hero for standing up to what they saw as an oppressive religious system.

Luther proposed a reduction in the pomp and wealth of the church and in the number of sacraments. He advocated keeping only baptism and communion of the seven. He also rejected the doctrine of transubstantiation that holds that during communion the bread and wine actually become the physical body and blood of Christ. Luther said that Christ is present in the bread and wine, but that they remain in their physical state of bread and wine.

In October 1520, an order from the pope reached Luther, demanding that he recant his position within sixty days. Sixty days later, on December 10, Luther threw the pope's demands into a bonfire during a public demonstration with students and faculty at Wittenburg University. Luther was excommunicated on January 3, 1521, by the pope, who called him "a boar in the vineyard of the Lord." Luther continued to teach and preach.

To deal with the spread of Luther's influence, a parliamentary assembly was convened at Augsburg in 1530. To state their side, Lutherans submitted a statement of faith that came to be known as the Augsburg Confession. On August 3, 1530, theologians appointed by Emperor Charles V rejected major articles of the confession. However, Lutheranism still flourished even after Luther's death in 1546.

Although Luther advocated reform within the Catholic Church, the deteriorating relationship between the church and his followers ensured that the Lutherans had to leave the church in order to carry out their teachings. Some German princes declared Lutheranism the official religion of their territories, and Lutheran churches formed in other parts of Europe. In 1580, the Book of Concord brought together the major writings of Lutheranism as a common basis for the faith.

Lutheranism continued to spread, and came to North America in the 1600s through Dutch and Scandinavian immigrants to the Hudson and Delaware River valleys. Lutheran congregations were formed throughout the New World, and through the years many different branches of Lutheranism developed.

A series of mergers in the 20th century has attempted to bring together Lutherans of various roots into a unified church. The most recent major merger came in 1988 when three large Lutheran bodies—the American Lutheran Church, the Lutheran Church in America and the Association of Evangelical Lutheran Churches—joined to form the country's largest Lutheran group, the Evangelical Lutheran Church in America.

DIVISIONS

Although there are several small Lutheran bodies active in the United States, a series of mergers has reduced the major groups to two:

Evangelical Lutheran Church in America (ELCA)—A product of the merger of three major Lutheran groups in 1988, this is the country's largest Lutheran body with more than five million members in eleven thousand churches.

Lutheran Church, Missouri Synod—This more conservative Lutheran group is the second largest in the country with some 2.6 million members in more than five thousand churches. Although it did not merge into the Evangelical Lutheran Church in America in 1988, the Missouri Synod church cooperates with the larger ELCA in many endeavors.

DOCTRINES SPECIFIC TO LUTHERANISM

Justification by Faith—Martin Luther's most distinctive teaching says a person is saved to eternal life and made holy by faith in Jesus Christ and God's grace, not by acts, deeds or thoughts

RELIGIOUS HOLIDAYS AND FESTIVALS

Reformation Day—Some Lutheran churches have special services around October 31 to commemorate Luther's nailing of his theses to the church door, beginning what became the Protestant Reformation.

TITLES

Bishop—A pastors' pastor and head of a geographic area of the church. Addressed as "Bishop."

Pastor—Spiritual leader of a congregation. Addressed as "Pastor," "Reverend," or "Doctor" if he or she has a doctorate.

COMMUNITY WORSHIP

Lutheran worship is community oriented, focused on the altar and is usually liturgical—that is, it follows a fairly set form—although this may vary somewhat from congregation to congregation and service to service. Generally, worship emphasizes preaching and sacraments and also consists of hymns, a dialog (or responsive reading), canticles, Old Testament and New Testament readings, prayers and a sermon. The Lutheran Book of Worship, used by most Lutheran churches, includes specific responses between congregation and minister to follow certain parts of the service.

The Lutheran church observes two sacraments:

Holy communion—When this is a part of the worship service, the minister explains the significance of the shared bread and wine, using words set forth in the Book of Worship for the occasion, blesses the bread and wine and tells those taking communion as they are served, "The body of Christ, given for you" and "The blood of Christ, shed for you."

Baptism—Described in the rites of most Lutheran churches as "the door to life and the kingdom of God," baptism signifies entrance into the life of Christ. To be baptized, a Lutheran must profess faith in Jesus Christ, reject sin and Satan, and confess the faith of the church. A sponsor from the congregation presents each candidate for baptism, and the minister asks the candidates if they desire to be baptized. Sponsors pledge to help the candidates live in the faith. The minister prays, with congregational responses. Candidates are then asked prescribed questions about their readiness for baptism, and about their specific beliefs. With the congregation, they may reply to some of these with excerpts from the Apostles Creed. The minister actually baptizes each candidate in the name of the Father, the Son and the Holy Spirit, pouring water over the candidate's head three times, once after naming each member of the Trinity. The newly baptized people kneel at the altar and the minister lays both hands on each one's head and says a prayer. The minister then makes the sign of the cross on the forehead of each, pronouncing them "sealed by the Holy Spirit and marked with the cross of Christ forever." When all have received the sign of the cross, they stand. In some churches, they are given a lighted candle, to represent the light of their faith that should shine in the world.

Non-Lutherans are welcome in worship but should not receive communion in some Lutheran churches. The ELCA invites all who believe in the actual presence of Christ in communion to partake.

PLACE OF CHILDREN

Lutherans baptize infants presented by their parents in preparation for the day when the children can come forth and proclaim their own faith. In the case of infant baptism, the parents hold children and promise to support and teach them in the faith.

ROLES OF MEN AND WOMEN

Specific strands of Lutheranism vary in their attitude toward the ordination of women to the clergy. The ELCA ordains both men and women to the ministry. The Missouri synod ordains only men.

MILESTONES

Birth—Shortly after birth parents may present their child for baptism at a worship service, promising to raise the child in the faith.

Marriage—A Lutheran wedding is much like a worship service with prayer, scripture, music and ministerial advice. The couple exchanges vows and rings and is pronounced husband and wife. The service may conclude with the Lord's Prayer. Communion may also be a part of a Lutheran wedding.

Non-Lutheran guests at a wedding should listen carefully to the invitation to determine whether they should partake of communion. Gifts for the bride and groom are appropriate.

Death—Lutheran funerals usually begin with a procession into the church with the minister preceding the coffin. A funeral or memorial service is regarded as worship and contains many of the same elements as any worship service, with the addition of prayers for the mourners, remarks about the deceased person and the commendation of the person's soul to God. The funeral concludes with a recessional with the minister again preceding the coffin. A brief graveside service usually follows.

CONVERSION

To become a Lutheran, one must renounce sin, accept Jesus Christ and be baptized into the church.

MAJOR ORGANIZATIONS

The Lutheran Church, Missouri Synod
International Center
1333 S. Kirkwood Road
St. Louis, Missouri 63122-729

Evangelical Lutheran Church in America
8765 W. Higgins Road
Chicago, Illinois 60631

FURTHER READING

Bodensieck, Julius, ed. *Encyclopedia of the Lutheran Church*. Minneapolis: Augsburg Publishing House, 1965.
Gritsch, Eric W. *Fortress Introduction to Lutheranism*. Minneapolis: Fortress Press, 1994.
Lutheran Book of Worship. Minneapolis: Augsburg Publishing House; Philadelphia: Board of Publication, Lutheran Church in America, 1978.
Pfatteicher, Phillip H. *Commentary on the Lutheran Book of Worship*. Minneapolis: Augsburg Fortress Press, 1990.
Stump, Joseph. *Luther's Catechism with an Explanation*. Philadelphia: The United Lutheran Publishing House, 1935.

METHODISTS

ORIGINS

ANGLICAN clergyman John Wesley is credited with starting the Methodist movement, but his younger brother Charles, famous for his Protestant hymns, actually
convened the first meeting of the club that fostered the movement.

Charles Wesley started a Holy Club of three young men at Oxford University.
When his older brother John returned to Oxford in 1729 after a two-year absence,
he became part of the group and took over its leadership. Following the goals he
attempted to live up to in his own life, John led the group to apply a pattern, or a
method, to their daily lives as well as to their corporate worship. The group acquired several nicknames, but the one that stuck was The Methodists. In 1738,
John had what is known as the "Aldersgate experience"—a renewal of faith that
compelled him to preach with new enthusiasm. He gained many followers.

By 1769, England's Methodists were ready to try sending ministers to the
colonies. Richard Boardman and Joseph Pilmore were the first to make the trip.
They were followed in 1771 by Richard Wright and Francis Asbury, who became
known as the "Wesley of America" and who is credited with setting up the structure of the Methodist church in America. While the other ministers sent by Wesley
returned to England during the Revolutionary War, Asbury stayed, riding thousands
of miles on horseback to spread the gospel and set up Methodist societies. After
the Revolution, the bishop of London refused to send more men to minister in
America, and John Wesley decided to ordain some ministers for the mission himself

in 1784. The decision marked the separation of the Methodists from the Church of England.

Over the years, divisions over issues such as slavery caused several splits among Methodists, eventually followed by some mergers and reconfigurations. Black believers started their own churches, which developed into separate Methodist denominations. In 1939, three major predominantly white groups united to form the Methodist Church. On April 23, 1968, they were joined by the Evangelical United Brethren, to become the United Methodist Church, the country's largest Methodist body. But several predominantly black Methodist groups and several smaller organizations calling themselves Methodist or Wesleyan continue to hold separate conferences and function as separate identities.

DIVISIONS

There are many Methodist bodies in the United States. Among the larger groups are:

United Methodist Church—By far the largest of many Methodist denominations, this is a majority-white, mainline Protestant group of more than eight million members. Caucuses within the denomination range from liberal to conservative. The church has worldwide missions and an extensive social ministry within the United States.

Free Methodist Church of North America—Organized in Pekin, New York, in 1860, this conservative body formed in protest to what organizers saw as liberal leanings in the larger Methodist church. It is an international church with more than 300,000 members worldwide, about eighty thousand in the United States.

African Methodist Episcopal Church—The A.M.E. church began in 1787 when former slave Richard Allen, a licensed preacher, and several other black worshipers walked out of St. George's Methodist Episcopal Church in Philadelphia after being chastised for being in a gallery they did not know was white-only. The same year, Allen and Absalom Jones formed an aid society called the Free Africa Society, which soon took on religious overtones. The original building of the Free Africa Society became the mother church of the new African Methodist Episcopal Church. It is the largest of the predominantly black Methodist denominations with more than three million members.

African Methodist Episcopal Zion Church—The A.M.E. Zion church grew out of the John Street Methodist Episcopal Church in New York City in 1796 when a group of black members formed their own chapel. Chief among them was former slave Peter Williams, an employee of the church. The chapel was incorporated in 1801 as the African Methodist Episcopal Church (Called Zion) of the City of New York. It is now the second-largest black Methodist denomination with more than 1.2 million members.

Christian Methodist Episcopal Church—In 1870, white members of the Methodist Episcopal Church, South agreed to a proposal by black members to form a separate denomination. The group they formed was known as the Colored Methodist Episcopal Church until 1954. Today it claims some 800,000 members.

DOCTRINES SPECIFIC TO METHODISM

John Wesley preached that everyone can accept Jesus Christ as Lord, repent of past sins and thus have eternal life. This teaching differs from some Christian groups which believe that God pre-ordains, or elects, people for salvation.

Methodists believe in the scripture as interpreted through tradition, experience and reason. Methodism teaches that disciplined, holy living leads believers toward perfection—with God's help. It emphasizes the relationship between faith and works, or the social application of one's Christian beliefs.

As taught by Wesley, Methodism combines piety with knowledge and supports an educated clergy. It stresses the need for a connectional church, or congregations in communion with each other through a church hierarchy.

Many Methodist denominations expect their clergy to be itinerant, or temporary, subject to reassignment by the bishop, so that the congregation's allegiance is to the church and not to the particular clergy person and so that no clergyperson becomes too entrenched in a particular congregation.

TITLES

Deacon—In the United Methodist Church, a person ordained to a special ministry such as music, education, or social service. Deacons are allowed to conduct worship and preside over weddings and funerals, but do not have the authority to administer the sacraments alone. Deacons are usually addressed as "Reverend."

Elder—A fully ordained minister in the Methodist church. Among Methodists, most elders are itinerant, and may be moved at the will of the district superintendent and bishop. Elders are addressed as "Reverend" or, if they have doctorates, as "Doctor."

District Superintendent—An elder appointed by a bishop to oversee the clergy and churches in a designated geographic area. Addressed as "Reverend" or "Doctor."

Bishop—An elder elected to oversee a specific conference, consisting of several districts, and to be a member of the council of bishops that oversees the entire Methodist denomination of which he or she is a part. Unlike some Christian groups, Methodists do not see their bishops as part of an apostolic succession reaching back to Peter in the New Testament, but as a leader among clergy. Addressed as "Bishop."

COMMUNITY WORSHIP

Methodist worship usually includes prayer, scripture readings, congregational hymns, responsive readings, special music, a sermon and an offering.

Methodists recognize two sacraments:

Baptism—Most Methodists today baptize by sprinkling, although a person can ask to be immersed. When infants are baptized, their parents or sponsors make commitment to God in the children's names and promise to raise the children in the faith. The congregation also acknowledges a responsibility to support the parents and the child in their efforts.

Adults or older children who were not baptized as babies are usually asked to go through a series of classes during which they explore their own faith and the beliefs of Methodism. At baptism, they make a commitment to obey God's will and affirm their faith in Christ. During the ceremony, the minister usually describes the significance of baptism and says a prayer that those to be baptized are forgiven of their sins. The minister asks the people to be baptized a series of questions to which they give answers affirming their faith. The minister then baptizes each person in the name of the Father, Son and Holy Spirit, dipping a hand into a font of water and placing it on each person's head. The minister may close the baptismal portion of the service with a prayer or blessing.

Communion, or the Lord's Supper—Representing Jesus' last meal with his disciples before his crucifixion, the Lord's Supper is an important reenactment for Methodists. The minister usually opens the communion portion of a worship service with a prayer of thanksgiving; there may be a responsive reading or prayer of confession read by the congregation. The minister breaks the bread or picks up a piece of bread off a tray, explaining that it is representative of Christ's body. The minister then lifts the chalice or cup, explaining that it signifies Jesus' blood. In Methodist churches, grape juice is almost always used instead of wine in celebrating communion so that alcoholics and children can participate freely. Usually members of the congregation come to the front of the church to receive communion, sometimes taking time to kneel at the altar and pray before returning to their seats. Communion is usually followed by a prayer and a blessing. All Christians are invited to receive communion in Methodist churches, and Methodists may take communion in other churches when they feel comfortable.

Visitors may participate in worship as they are comfortable, and all Christians may take communion at Methodist churches.

PLACE OF CHILDREN

Usually within the first few weeks or months of an infant's life, Methodist parents bring the child for baptism and christening, or naming, at a regular Sunday morning church service. In the United Methodist Church, a baptized baby is listed on the "roll of baptized members" until he or she makes a profession of faith and becomes a "professing" member. Children are allowed to partake of communion, or the Lord's Supper, in Methodist churches.

Most Methodist churches have a variety of programs for children and youth, from Sunday School to summer camp.

ROLES OF MEN AND WOMEN

Women are ordained to the ministry and serve as district superintendents and bishops in the largest Methodist group, the United Methodist Church. Other strands of Methodism are divided in their positions on whether women should be ordained.

MILESTONES

Birth—Within a few weeks or months of birth, parents may present their infants for baptism, or christening. The parents pledge to bring the child up in the faith; the congregation pledges to support the parents and child, and the minister dips a hand into a baptismal font and sprinkles the baby's head with water.

Marriage—Marriage is regarded as a covenant between a man and a woman, and between the couple and God. All plans for the wedding ceremony must be approved by the minister who is performing it. Weddings are regarded as worship services that include the affirming of the marriage bonds. Therefore, scripture readings, hymns, prayers and a short sermon or message are sometimes included. Other special features may be added, such as a unity candle, a single candle which the bride and groom light from separate candles. During a wedding, the congregation may be asked to respond to questions from the minister requesting their blessings. Communion may be offered after the couple has exchanged vows. Often the wedding is followed by a reception, either at the church or elsewhere.

Non-Methodists should participate in the wedding service as they are comfortable. All Christians may receive communion if they choose.

Death—Funeral or memorial service plans are made by the family with the approval of the minister who will conduct the service. Any additional elements of the service besides Christian burial—military or Masonic honors, for instance—should be included in a way as to not interrupt the worship. In some cases, the coffin or urn is present in the church when the guests arrive. In others, it is carried in a processional and placed at the front of the church, usually behind the minister who is reading or reciting words of reassurance. For a memorial service, no coffin or urn will be present.

As services of worship, Methodist funerals or memorial services include prayer, scripture and hymns. The congregation may be asked to recite a prayer in unison or to respond to a responsive reading. Some funerals also include the sacrament of communion. A shorter service may follow at graveside. In this case, the minister usually reads from scripture or says a few words of assurance, says a prayer, then greets family members.

Specific services are included in the United Methodist Book of Worship for unexpected death, the death of a stillborn child and the death of a non-Christian.

Families may have visitation times at a funeral home or a family member's home within a few days before or immediately after the service.

Visitors may participate in a Methodist funeral as they feel comfortable. It is proper to visit with the family before or after the service to offer condolences.

CONVERSION

Anyone not previously baptized in a Christian church is expected to be baptized in order to join a Methodist church. Those who were baptized as infants or have been baptized by another Christian body may join by answering affirmatively to a series of questions.

MAJOR ORGANIZATIONS

African Methodist Episcopal Church
1134 11th Street, N.W.
Washington, D. C. 20001

African Methodist Episcopal Zion Church
P.O. Box 32843
Charlotte, N.C. 28232

Christian Methodist Episcopal Church
First Memphis Plaza
4466 Elvis Presley Boulevard
Memphis, Tennessee 38116

United Methodist Church
475 Riverside Drive
New York, New York 10015

FURTHER READING

Allen, Charles L. *Meet the Methodists*. Nashville: Abingdon Press, 1986.
Colaw, Emerson. *Beliefs of a United Methodist Christian*. Nashville: Discipleship Resources, 1987, (revised 1994).
Custer, Chester E. *The United Methodist Primer,* revised edition. Nashville: Discipleship Resources, 1993.
Haskins, James. *The Methodists*. New York: Hippocrene Books, 1992.
McAnally, Thomas S. *Questions & Answers about the United Methodist Church*. Nashville: Abingdon Press, 1995.

Seasons of the Gospel—Resources for the Christian Year for the Use of United Methodists. Nashville: Abingdon Press, 1979.

Tuell, Jack M. ed., *The Organization of the United Methodist Church.* revised edition. Nashville: Abingdon Press, 1970.

Waltz, Alan K. *Dictionary for United Methodists.* Nashville: Abingdon Press, 1991.

ORTHODOX CHRISTIANS

ORIGINS

T HE Orthodox Church claims roots with the Apostle Paul, who established Christianity in Greece, Peter, who founded the church in Antioch, and other apostles. It takes its name from Greek words meaning "correct belief."

For the first thousand years after Jesus, his followers were loosely united. The five historic cities of Jerusalem, Antioch, Rome, Alexandria and Constantinople each had significant Christian communities established by disciples, and the churches in those cities were in communion and communication with each other. In 325, at a council in Nicaea, the church adopted a statement of faith known as the Nicene Creed that outlined its basic beliefs.

Differences started to grow in the 9th century, however. In 862, Nicoholas, Pope of Rome, refused to acknowledge Photius, the new Patriarch of Constantinople; Photius, in turn, excommunicated the Pope five years later. A major dispute between the two branches of the church was the *filioque* clause (*filioque* means "and the son" in Latin), an amendment to the Nicene Creed accepted by Rome and rejected by the Greeks and others. The creed originally said the Holy Spirit "proceedeth from the Father." The addition said "from the Father and the Son." The Greek-speaking church insisted that God alone was the source of all things, including Jesus; advocates of the *filioque* clause saw God and Jesus as equal.

Photius of Constantinople and the Roman church's pope, John VIII, agreed in 880 to keep the original creed, but their differences were far from settled. Increasing political rivalry was matched by ecclesiastical competition. By 1054, relations had deteriorated to the point that the head of the church of Constantinople and the head of the church of Rome issued anathemas, or formal orders of excommunication, against each other. This parting of the ways is known as the Great Schism.

Relations became even worse in 1204 when, during the Crusades, which were military expeditions ordered by the popes to reclaim the Holy Land from Muslim control, Constantinople was ransacked. In 1453, Constantinople fell to Turkish control and became known as Istanbul. It remains the seat of the patriarchy of the Orthodox Church and the Bishop of Constantinople is first among equals of the Orthodox world.

HOLY TEXTS

Orthodox Christians regard the Bible as sacramental. The Gospel book has a special place on the altar and is carried through the congregation in processions. People kiss it and bow to it. Branches of the Orthodox Church accept the Roman Catholic Bible with some additions.

DIVISIONS

There are national churches within Orthodoxy, organized by custom and language.

DOCTRINES SPECIFIC TO CHRISTIAN ORTHODOXY

- Jesus was born of Mary's flesh and blood, yet Mary remained a virgin after giving birth to Jesus. Mary is known as Theotokos, or God-bearer.
- Saints are people who have achieved sanctity and perfection. God is worshiped through the saints, who can intercede on behalf of humans.
- Icons are pictorial images of that which is immaterial. Icons themselves are not worshiped, but God is worshiped by using icons. Statues are not used.
- Relics of the saints are also endowed with holiness.
- The communal worship experience of the church is not only desirable but necessary for true Christianity.
- Angels are real. They are separate creations from humans, but are conscious persons. Some angels chose to rebel against God. Different angels, just as different humans, have different gifts and talents.

CALENDAR

Some Orthodox churches use the Julian, or so-called Old Style, calendar, which now lags thirteen days behind the Gregorian calendar. Each century, the calendars separate by another day. In the 21st century, they will be fourteen days apart.

The Orthodox ecclesiastical calendar begins on September 1. The church calculates days beginning at sunset.

RELIGIOUS FESTIVALS AND HOLIDAYS

Pascha, or **Easter**—Celebrates the resurrection of Jesus and is considered the most important day of the year. The Easter service actually begins at midnight Saturday before Easter Sunday. In a darkened church, the priest goes to the Holy Doors in the front with a lighted candle from which people light candles as he says, "Receive ye the light from the unwavering Light and glorify Christ who rose from the dead." They all leave the building, walk in procession joyfully around the outside of the church singing hymns and re-enter. After the worship liturgy, the priest proclaims "Christ is Risen." The people reply, "Truly He is risen." The service concludes with the distribution of Easter eggs dyed red. Worshipers tap their eggs against those of other worshipers to break them. The red color represents Jesus' blood, the shell his entombment and the breaking his release from death.

Orthodox Christians also celebrate the entire week leading up to Pascha.

In addition, the church celebrates twelve major feasts:

Nativity of the Mother of God—September 8. Honors Mary's birth.

Exaltation of the Cross—September 14. The cross is carried on a tray of flowers, placed in the middle of the church and raised by the priest toward the four directions of the compass, as he says a blessing three times in each direction and prays that God protect the authorities of the government and the church.

Presentation of the Mother of God in the Temple—November 21. A feast that probably originated in Syria, this day is one of four set aside to honor Mary.

Nativity of Christ—December 25. Christmas, or the Feast of the Nativity, is a joyful family feast that emphasizes children.

Baptism of Christ—January 6. Considered one of the major feasts of the year, this day in Orthodoxy honors Jesus' baptism in the Jordan River by John the Baptist, establishing his identity as the Son of God. After liturgy, priests bless waters to be used for baptism, and all water in the world. After the service, the priest sprinkles worshipers with water. Some worshipers take blessed water home with them.

Presentation of Our Lord in the Temple—February 2. Marks the day Mary and Joseph took the forty-day-old Jesus to the temple.

Annunciation of the Mother of God—March 25. A joyful day commemorating the message delivered by the Archangel Gabriel to Mary, telling her she would give birth to Jesus.

Entry of Our Lord into Jerusalem—also known as Palm Sunday. Seven days before Easter, this day commemorates Jesus' entry into Jerusalem before his crucifixion when he was greeted by crowds waving palm leaves. The priest may bless palm branches and distribute them to the people. After the liturgy, children walk around the altar carrying palm branches and singing a hymn.

Ascension of Our Lord Jesus Christ—The fortieth day after Easter. Celebrates Jesus' rising into heaven after his resurrection.

Pentecost—The fiftieth day after Easter. Commemorates the Holy Spirit's descent to guide the disciples after Jesus' ascension. Seven "prayers of kneeling" are read, signifying that the Easter Season is concluded.

Transfiguration of Our Saviour Jesus Christ—August 6. On this day, the church celebrates the harvest, prays for abundance and honors Jesus' ascent of Mount Tabor to pray with some disciples, who saw him transfigured and realized he was the messiah.

Falling Asleep of the Mother of God—August 15. Celebrates Mary's passage into heaven, regarded as a reunion with her son Jesus.

Non-Orthodox Christians are free to participate in most portions of worship, but should not take the bread and wine of communion commemorating Jesus' body and blood. During the period between Easter and Pentecost, no one should kneel in an Orthodox church.

ATTITUDE TOWARD OTHER HOLIDAYS

Birthdays—Orthodox Christians celebrate as they wish, but some ignore birthdays in favor of name days, celebrating the anniversary of the giving of their name in the church. On this day, after the liturgy while serving communion, the priest may say a special office or prayer sanctifying the day to their saint.

TITLES

Bishop—A leading clergyman over other clergy in an area. Cannot be married at consecration or after taking office, but can be a widower. Addressed as "Bishop" or "Your Eminence."

Priest—The basic order of Orthodox clergy. "White" priests are married. "Black" priests are unmarried. Addressed as "Father."

Deacon—Responsible for helping the community, leading the litany in worship and handling the incense. Addressed as "Father Deacon."

In addition, clergy may be given the following honorary titles of office:

Ecumenical—Patriarch of Constantinople, considered first among equal heads of branches of the Orthodox Church. Addressed as "Ecumenical" or "Your All Holiness."

Patriarch—The head of most branches of the Orthodox church. Addressed as "Patriarch" or "Your Holiness."

Pope—The head of some branches of the Orthodox church. Addressed as "Pope" or "Your Holiness."

Metropolitan—Originally the bishop of the capital of a province; a church official over archbishops. Addressed as "Metropolitan" or "Your Eminence."

Primate—Usually the top bishop in a country. Addressed as "Primate" or "Your Eminence."

Archbishop—A high-ranking bishop; in the Greek church, ranks above metropolitan; in the Russian church, is an honorary title given to a patriarch or bishop of distinction. Addressed as "Your Eminence."

COMMUNITY WORSHIP

Orthodox Christian architecture and art contribute significantly to the worship experience. Most Orthodox churches are constructed cross-shaped on an east-west plane, with the entrance to the church facing west and the sanctuary facing east. The symbolism is that of going from the darkness of the west to the light of the east. Most Orthodox churches have at least one cupola, or dome, with crosses on top. The crosses may have different forms in churches with different ethnic roots.

Pictorial icons, many elaborate, in stained glass, metals, tiles and other forms, are found throughout Orthodox churches. Orthodox Christians light candles before icons, kiss them and bow before them. Orthodox Christians regard the Bible as an icon.

In some Orthodox churches, worshipers stand throughout the service. In others, they may stand, kneel, bow, lie prostrate and cross their arms and pound on their chests at different parts of the liturgy. In some traditions, worshipers buy candles and bread outside the church; the candles will be lighted before icons while the bread will be given to the priest to be soaked in consecrated wine and returned to the worshiper for consumption at home later.

Upon entering a church, a worshiper may spend time before several icons, kissing them, making the sign of the cross, or bowing to show reference. Orthodox Christians also make the sign of the cross at the mention of the Trinity during worship. They make the sign with the right hand, thumb and first two fingers touching to represent the Trinity, and touch the forehead first, followed by the breast and the right and left shoulders.

The Orthodox Church recognizes seven sacraments, with the eucharist and baptism regarded as the most important:

Anointing of the Sick—By praying and anointing the sick with oil, the church believes it ministers to both body and soul.

Baptism—Infants and new converts to the church are immersed three times in water, for the Father, Son and Holy Spirit, in an Orthodox baptism. Baptism cannot be repeated.

Chrismation (confirmation)—Usually immediately after baptism, the priest anoints the newly baptized person with blessed, scented oil and calls the Holy Spirit to be present. After baptism and confirmation, a person is allowed to take the eucharist, or Holy Communion. Even infants are confirmed and given communion, usually with a spoon.

Confession—Usually before partaking of the eucharist, an Orthodox Christian will confess sins and shortcomings. This is not done in a closed confessional, as in some Roman Catholic Churches, but may take place in any part of the church. Both priest and penitent may stand or sit, with the penitent facing a cross and an icon of Jesus or a bible to emphasis that it is God to whom the confession is actually being made. Before and after confession, the penitent kisses the icon. The priest may, but does not have to, prescribe a penance.

Eucharist (Holy Communion)—Bread and wine that, according to Orthodox tradition, actually become the body and blood of Christ through consecration. Some branches of the church offer the eucharist weekly, but in some traditions Christians only partake four times a year: Easter, Christmas, the Assumption and a person's feast day. Strict Orthodox Christians consume only water from the previous midnight until the time they take the eucharist to break their fast, and they confess their sins before partaking.

In the Orthodox Church, clergy eat the bread from their hands and sip the wine from a chalice three times, but the eucharist is administered with a spoon to the laity after the bread is put into a chalice of wine. After the eucharist, congregants receive the *antidoron,* a small piece of bread that is blessed but not consecrated, as the bread of the eucharist is. People who do not take communion are also given the *antidoron.* At the end of the eucharistic liturgy, congregants may approach the priest to kiss his hand and request a blessing.

Holy Orders—The Orthodox Church recognizes three major orders (bishop, priest and deacon) and two minor orders (subdeacon and reader). Ordinations or, in the case of bishops, consecrations, to major orders are always performed in the context of the liturgy and only one person can be ordained to each order at any liturgy.

Ordinations are performed by bishops. Ordination of bishops is performed by at least two other bishops.

Marriage—The Orthodox Church regards married life as a special vocation that must be confirmed in a sacrament.

Only Orthodox Christians can take communion in an Orthodox church. Otherwise, visitors may participate in any part of the service. Orthodox Christians in some churches often enter and leave the church during services and do not consider it rude for guests to do the same.

PRIVATE WORSHIP

Churches provide guides for private morning and evening prayers. Daily scripture readings are also provided.

During prayer before meals, an Orthodox family is likely to face the family icons rather than bowing with their eyes closed.

Orthodox Christians may use the "Jesus Prayer" many times a day in private devotions in the midst of any kind of activity. It says simply, "Lord Jesus Christ, Son of God, have mercy on me a sinner." Instead of a beaded rosary, some Orthodox Christians use a silent, wool cord with their prayers.

If entertaining Orthodox Christians for an extended period, hosts should offer a time and a place for morning and evening prayers.

DRESS

Orthodox men except for clergy do not cover their heads in worship. Traditionally, women do, although this practice is no longer followed in many churches.

Priests and bishops wear elaborate vestments for worship and clerical collars for street wear. Priests and bishops usually have beards and may not cut their hair, tucking it up instead.

Male guests should not wear hats to an Orthodox church. Loose clothing is probably best in cases where worshipers may be kneeling. Women should wear modest dresses that cover their arms and knees. Women may be asked to cover their heads in some churches.

DIETARY LAWS

There are no forbidden foods in Orthodox Christianity, but during certain periods of the year, Orthodox Christians are expected to fast. Almost all Wednesdays and Fridays, special fast days and the periods of Lent, the Fast of the Apostles, the Assumption Fast and the Christmas Fast are observed by the strictest Orthodox worshipers. Other Orthodox Christians may observe some of these times—especially the first week of Lent and the week before Easter. The strictest Orthodox rules of fasting require abstaining from meat, fish, wine, oil and all dairy products.

If entertaining an Orthodox Christian, a host should determine whether any fast is being observed and plan the meal accordingly. Orthodox friends who are fasting should be encouraged and supported, not tempted with violations of fasting rules.

PLACE OF CHILDREN

Orthodox children may receive communion from the time they are able to eat and drink it. When they are old enough to distinguish right from wrong on their own, usually at age seven, they are expected to also confess their sins and repent.

ROLES OF MEN AND WOMEN

The Orthodox Church does not ordain women to the clergy.

HOUSEHOLD

Many Orthodox Christians have icons in their homes and may carry personal icons with them. Icons in the home may be lighted with lamps or candles and should be shown the same respect as those in a church. Family members often kiss them and make the sign of the cross or bow before them. They also pray before them, sometimes using incense.

Often Orthodox families have their homes blessed by a priest. The house is considered a satellite of the church.

MILESTONES

Birth—In some Orthodox traditions, a baby is baptized between one and two years after birth and is not given a name until baptism. The name is revealed during the ceremony itself. A priest will anoint the baby with oil on the forehead, cheek, hands and feet. The service is not a part of regular worship, and is often held on Saturday. The next time the child is in church during the eucharist, he or she may be given communion.

Many families bring their baby to the church forty days after birth for a service of thanksgiving, in honor of the baby Jesus' presentation at the temple by Mary and Joseph. In some traditions, baptism and naming are done at this time. Many Orthodox Christians begin calling their children by their names at birth and the ceremony formalizes the name and officially links it to a saint.

Marriage—Two formerly separate services are now usually performed together in the Orthodox Church:

- *The Office of Betrothal*—It consists of blessing and exchanging rings and may take place before the procession into the church.
- *The Office of Crowning*—Unique to the Orthodox church, this service culminates with the priest placing crowns on the heads of the bride and groom—groom first. In the Greek church, these are usually made of greenery or flowers; in the Russian church, they are actual crowns.

At the end of the wedding, the couple shares a cup of wine to symbolize their common life and walks in a circular procession, symbolizing their unending union.

Death—Some Orthodox Christians keep the bodies of loved ones in their homes until time for the funeral, some use funeral homes and many have the body placed in the church from the time it is prepared for burial until after the funeral. Some families have a memorial service in the evening before the funeral with readings and prayers, then take turns staying up to pray with the body before the funeral service the next day.

The funeral may include scriptures, prayer, songs and remarks by the priest. In the Orthodox church, the casket is generally left open until after the funeral. Men are usually buried with an icon of Jesus on their chests; women have an icon of Mary.

To pay their last respects, family members and friends may walk by the casket, taking time to bow, kiss the icon and, if they wish, the forehead of the person, and say a brief prayer asking for forgiveness for any wrong committed against the dead. At the end of the funeral service, the priest anoints the body with oil and wine; the casket is closed and taken to the grave.

The graveside service is brief. The priest pronounces the casket sealed until the last judgment, and it is lowered. In some cases, those present step forward to drop dirt onto the casket; sometimes the priest starts the process with charcoal from the censer, or incense pot, used during the service.

Guest should kiss the forehead or the icon of the deceased person if they wish, but should not feel obligated to do so. They may simply pass by and look or just stay at their seats.

CONVERSION

A person joins the Orthodox Church by being baptized by immersion three times in water, in the name of the Father, Son and Holy Spirit, by an Orthodox clergyman. Priests vary in how much preparation they require of a candidate before performing baptism.

MAJOR ORGANIZATIONS

There are many branches of Orthodox Christianity in the United States. Here are some of the larger ones:

Antiochean Orthodox Christian Archdiocese of North America
358 Mountain Road
Englewood, N. J. 07631

Greek Orthodox Archdiocese of North and South America
8-10 East 79th Street
New York, New York 10021,

The Orthodox Church in America
6850 North Hempstead Turnpike
P. O. Box 675
Syosset, New York 11791-0675

Russian Orthodox Church Outside of Russia
75 East 93rd Street
New York, New York 10028

FURTHER READING

Benz, Ernst. *The Eastern Orthodox Church*. trans. Richard and Clara Winston. Garden City, N.Y.: Anchor Books, Doubleday & Company, 1963.

Constantelos, Demetrios J. *The Greek Orthodox Church—Faith, History and Practice*. New York: Seabury Press, 1967.

Cross, Lawrence. *Eastern Christianity—The Byzantine Tradition*. Sydney and Philadelphia: E. J. Dwyer, 1988.

Gillquist, Peter E. *Becoming Orthodox—A Journey to the Ancient Christian Faith*, revised and updated. Ben Lomond, Cal.: Conciliar Press, 1992.

Meyendorff, John. *The Orthodox*. Minneapolis: Light and Life Publishing Co., 1966.

Waddams, Herbert, Canon of Canterbury. *Meeting the Orthodox Church*. London: SCM Press, 1964.

Ware, Timothy. *The Orthodox Church*. revised edition. London, New York: Penguin Books, 1993.

FOR CHILDREN

Roussou, Maria, and Papamichael, Panos. *I am a Greek Orthodox*. London and New York: Franklin Watts, 1985.

PENTECOSTALS

ORIGINS

Pentecostals take their name from the day of Pentecost, or the day chronicled in the New Testament Book of Acts when the Holy Spirit descended on Jesus' disciples and enabled them to speak and understand strange languages, prophesy and heal people.

The modern day Pentecostal movement began around the beginning of the 20th century, growing out of the Wesleyan Holiness movement. There are various opinions as to which event should be considered the beginning of the movement. Some people put it as early as 1896 when, at a revival in Cherokee County, North Carolina, led by four ministers including R. G. Spurling Jr., founder with his father of the Christian Union, people began speaking in unknown tongues. The Christian Union evolved into the Cleveland, Tennessee-based Church of God. Others say Charles Fox Parham was the father of modern Pentecostalism. In 1885, Parham became a Congregationalist and came to believe in divine healing. By 1893, he had become pastor of a Methodist church, where he was influenced by the Holiness movement, and in 1895 he left the Methodists to become independent. In 1900, Parham toured several Holiness ministries, where he heard reports of speaking in unknown tongues. He became convinced that this was a manifestation of the Holy Spirit. By 1901, Parham and several of his students had begun speaking in tongues.

After a rocky start, Parham's new ministry began to spread. He went into Texas, where he established a Bible training school. Among those who attended was William J. Seymour, a student who later surpassed his teacher in renown.

Parham's ministry began disintegrating in 1907 when he was charged with sodomy. Although the charges were later dropped, he lost much of his following. He died in relative obscurity in 1929. Seymour, meanwhile, went on to Los Angeles, where he conducted Bible studies at 312 Azusa Street, an address now widely known as the birthplace of Modern Pentecostalism. By the end of 1906, Seymour had officially incorporated as the Pacific Apostolic Faith Movement. Soon he was holding meetings there three times a day, seven days a week, drawing thousands of worshipers—black and white, some from outside the United States—who took the stories of their experiences home and influenced others.

However, dissenters eventually weakened the ministry. A major split came when William H. Durham began teaching that Jesus' death on the cross guaranteed both forgiveness of sins and sanctification. Thus, after accepting Jesus, believers only had to gradually claim their sanctification. He and his followers formed what became the Assemblies of God.

Another Pentecostal offshoot was started by Charles Harrison Mason, founder of the Church of God in Christ, incorporated as a denomination in Memphis in 1897. In 1907, Mason and some of his fellow elders began speaking in tongues—a practice they tried to take back to the Church of God in Christ. The denomination split as a result. The majority, who rejected the practice, became the Church of Christ (Holiness) U.S.A. The rest remained with Mason in the Church of God in Christ. The first Pentecostal General Assembly of the Church of God in Christ was convened by Mason in Memphis later in 1907.

DIVISIONS

There are many small Pentecostal groups throughout the United States, some with only a few dozen members. Here are the major bodies:

Assemblies of God—The largest, predominantly white Pentecostal denomination, the Assemblies of God organized in 1914 in Hot Springs, Arkansas. It later moved its headquarters to St. Louis. Today the Assemblies of God has about 2.3 million members.

Church of God—The Church of God began in Monroe County, Tennessee, as the Christian Union in 1886 under the leadership of two Baptist preachers, Richard G. Spurling Sr. and Jr. They emphasized the right of each person to interpret scriptures. After the father died, the son carried on. When a revival broke out at Camp Creek in Cherokee, North Carolina, ten years later, Spurling and his followers moved their church there. By the end of 1896, more than a hundred people were said to have begun speaking in tongues and miraculous healings were reported. In 1902, Spurling's followers formed guidelines and named themselves the Holiness Church at Camp Creek. Soon additional congregations were formed. By 1906, the existing congregations began to form a denomination which, a year later, was named the Church of God. The Church of God continued to grow and organize, evolving from a rural movement to an international denomination with more than 700,000 members. This group should not be confused with the 200,000-plus Church of God headquartered in Anderson, Indiana, which is not Pentecostal.

Church of God in Christ—The largest Pentecostal body in the world, this predominantly black group was founded by Charles H. Mason. Removed from his Baptist church in Arkansas because he preached the Wesleyan doctrine of sanctification, consecration and purification as a work of God's grace following conversion, Mason struck out on his own conducting revivals. In 1907, a denomination was incorporated in Memphis as the Church of God in Christ.

Mason attended the Azusa Street revival conducted by William Seymour in Los Angeles in 1907 and began speaking in tongues. But when Mason and his friends returned from Los Angeles to share their experience, a majority of COGIC members rejected the practice and split away to form the Church of Christ (Holiness) U.S.A. Mason presided over those who remained in the first Pentecostal General Assembly of the Church of God in Christ in 1907. Today, COGIC claims some 6.5 million members internationally, with 5.5 million of them in the United States.

Church of God of Prophecy—A. J. Tomlinson was head of the Church of God, but was impeached in 1923 because of misappropriation of funds. He went on to found this group. Once known as the Tomlinson Church of God, this denomination officially became known as the Church of God of Prophecy in 1952. It now claims about seventy thousand members in the United States.

International Church of the Foursquare Gospel—Born of a woman—the famous Aimee Semple McPherson—this Los Angeles-based denomination has more than 200,000 members in the United States. "Sister" McPherson and her husband Robert Semple were ordained by Assemblies of God founder William H. Durham in 1909, and worked with Durham in Chicago for a year before becoming missionaries to China.

McPherson later returned to the States, conducted a series of revivals and began to write and publish a monthly magazine. She opened the Angelus Temple in Los Angeles in the early 1920s, planned as a headquarters from which she would travel. By 1927, the ministry had grown to include a radio station, Bible college and office tower, and was incorporated as the Church of the Foursquare Gospel.

Pentecostal Assemblies of the World—This predominantly black but integrated group is the largest of the so-called Oneness Pentecostal groups with about a million members. Oneness Pentecostalism teaches that there is only one divinity—that Jesus is the Father, Son and Holy Spirit.

United Pentecostal Church International—A Oneness Pentecostal group, this denomination resulted from the merger in 1945 of The Pentecostal Church, Inc., and the Pentecostal Assemblies of Jesus Christ. It has about half a million members.

DOCTRINES SPECIFIC TO PENTECOSTALISM

Humankind—Many Pentecostals see three parts of human nature: soul, spirit and body. The spirit is potentially divine.

Baptism in the Holy Spirit—The doctrine most widely associated with Pentecostalism is Baptism by the Holy Spirit. Pentecostals believe that the events recorded in the New Testament Book of Acts, when the Holy Spirit descended on Jesus' followers after his ascension into heaven, are possible today. Thus, they accept the ideas of miraculous healing, prophecy and *glossalia,* also known as speaking in tongues.

Baptism in the Holy Spirit comes after conversion, or after one has accepted Jesus as savior, although the two events can seem simultaneous. Glossalia is the most obvious of the signs of Baptism in the Holy Spirit. Believers begin to speak in seemingly unintelligible syllables, or unknown tongues, usually during a state of ecstasy.

Messiah—Jesus is coming back and there are indications it may be soon. In fact, Pentecostals see the manifestations of the Holy Spirit in their worship as evidence of the imminence. Most Pentecostals are premillennialists, believing that Jesus will return to earth and establish a thousand-year reign. Most also are pretribulationists, expecting believers to be taken into heaven in an event known as the Rapture, before a time of tribulation that the earth must undergo before Jesus returns—although some believe Christians also will have to endure the tribulations.

TITLES

Pastor—Title and form of address for most Pentecostal ministers.

Bishop—A few Pentecostal groups have bishops who oversee groups of pastors. Addressed as "Bishop."

COMMUNITY WORSHIP

Pentecostal worship services are usually joyful and offer opportunity for spontaneity. They include music—sometimes with the accompaniment of electronic and percussion instruments—as well as scripture, prayer and a sermon. Congregants may hold their hands out, palms up, during music or prayer. Some may clap, dance in the spirit or burst into spontaneous vocal expressions, including speaking in tongues. An altar call at the end of a worship service is common among Pentecostals. The minister invites anyone who wants to express their faith in Jesus or to be baptized and join the church to come forward.

Most Pentecostal groups recognize two ordinances, which some do not call sacraments because they do not believe the practice itself is sacred or brings about spiritual change.

Baptism—As in all Christian denominations that practice water baptism of believers, Pentecostals expect a person to repent of sin and claim Jesus Christ as savior before being baptized. All major Pentecostal groups baptize older children and adults by immersion, although some also recognize sprinkling if a worshiper prefers. They do not baptize infants, and some even require that anyone who was baptized as a baby be rebaptized. While most Pentecostal groups baptize in the name of the Father, the Son and the Holy Ghost or Holy Spirit, so-called Oneness Pentecostals baptize in Jesus' name only.

Communion—Pentecostals serve the Lord's Supper, usually using bread and grape juice—although at least one group uses wine—to remember Jesus' sharing of a cup and loaf with his followers, proclaiming the elements to be his body and blood.

Some Pentecostal groups also practice foot-washing, washing of each other's feet in remembrance of Jesus' washing his disciples' feet. Some also have altar calls at the end of each service, inviting those in need of special prayer or ministry to come forward. And some have healing services, either at separate times or as part of each worship service, during which people with physical or emotional problems may come forward and be blessed by the minister.

Guests may participate in worship services to the extent they feel comfortable. Most Pentecostal churches have open communion and anyone may receive it.

DRESS

Historically many Pentecostal groups insisted that women wear modest dresses, avoid pants or shorts, keep their hair long and forgo jewelry or makeup. In all but a few groups, those rules are no longer observed.

PLACE OF CHILDREN

Pentecostals do not baptize infants, but expect children to come forward and join the church when they are old enough to realize the significance. Many churches have a variety of activities for children from Sunday School to choirs.

ROLES OF MEN AND WOMEN

Early Pentecostalism in America pioneered the idea of leadership roles for women in the church. Among Assemblies of God today, for instance, women have the same offices as men including preaching. Some other groups do not allow women to preach. There are very few women preachers in the Church of God in Christ, for example.

MILESTONES

Birth—Some churches may have dedication ceremonies for new babies. These consist of the parents bringing the child forward for blessing by the minister. The congregation may also be asked to affirm its intention to support the parents and the child in the Christian faith.

Marriage—Wedding ceremonies vary widely and are generally planned by the bride in consultation with the minister. They usually include elements of worship such as scripture, prayer, music and remarks by the minister as well as an exchange of vows. Some also include communion.

Death—Funerals follow the usual Protestant Christian style with scripture, prayer, hymns and remarks by the minister.

CONVERSION

Pentecostals believe in baptism of believers following confession of faith. People may be baptized once they express their faith in Jesus. After baptism, they are considered full members of the church.

MAJOR ORGANIZATIONS

Assemblies of God
1445 Boonville Avenue
Springfield, Mo. 65802

Church of God (Cleveland, Tenn.)
P. O. Box 2430
Cleveland, Tenn. 37320

Church of God of Prophecy
P. O. Box 2910
Cleveland, Tenn. 37320-2910

International Church of the Foursquare Gospel
1910 W. Sunset Boulevard
Suite 200
P. O. Box 29602
Los Angeles, California 90026-0176

Pentecostal Assemblies of the World
3939 Meadows Drive
Indianapolis, Ind. 46205

United Pentecostal Church International
8855 Dunn Road
Hazelwood, Missouri 63042

FURTHER READING

Burgess, Stanley M., and McGee, Gary, eds. *Dictionary of Pentecostal and Charismatic Movements.* Grand Rapids, Mich.: Regency Reference Library, Zondervan Publishing House, 1988.

Conn, Charles W. *Like a Mighty Army—A History of the Church of God.* Cleveland, Tenn.: Pathway Press, 1977.

Cox, Harvey. *Fire from Heaven.* New York: Addison-Wesley Publishing Company, 1995.

Durasoff, Steve. *Bright Wind of the Spirit—Pentecostalism Today.* Englewood Cliffs, N. J.: Prentice-Hall, Inc., 1972.

Paris, Arthur E. *Black Pentecostalism.* Amherst, Mass.: University of Massachusetts Press, 1982.

PRESBYTERIANS AND REFORMED

ORIGINS

P RESBYTERIANS take their name from the Greek word *presbyteros,* or elder, used in the New Testament. The Presbyterian form of church government relies on elders—some clergy, some lay. But Presbyterians are of the Reformed school of theology, referring both to roots in the Protestant Reformation and also to the idea that Christian faith and life, and thus the church, must be constantly reformed by the grace of God. So some churches call themselves Reformed. But all are part of the same branch of the family tree of the Christian faith.

The father of the Reformed tradition is John Calvin. In 1536, at age twenty-seven, he published his "Institutes for the Christian Religion," advancing the idea of the elect, the concept that God first chooses people for eternal life before they decide to follow God. For his ideas, he was run out of France and spent several years living in various places, sometimes under assumed names, and writing. With William Farel, another Reformer, Calvin wrote a catechism, a confession of faith and a book of discipline for the church. He became a teacher for Reform-minded clergy throughout Europe.

John Knox, a Catholic priest from Scotland, was one of those who studied under Calvin. He established the Presbyterian church in Scotland and in 1560, persuaded the parliament of Scotland to renounce Catholicism in favor of the Reformed Church. A conference in England gave the Church the Westminster documents, which serve as the foundation for the faith in the English-speaking world.

A clergyman named Francis Makemie is often called the Father of American

Presbyterianism because of his efforts to organize the church in the colonies. Makemie, who emigrated from Ireland, founded a church at Rehoboth, Maryland, in 1683. In 1706, with six other ministers, he organized the first long-standing American presbytery.

But over the next few years, schisms, reunions and expansion made the church an ever-changing entity. With the new country came a new denomination. In 1788, ministers from sixteen presbyteries adopted the name The Presbyterian Church in the United States of America and amended the Westminster documents to reflect the American view of separation of church and state. Like many American denominations, Presbyterians were divided over the issue of slavery revival and missions, and by 1861, there were four different branches of the 1788 Church, two each in the North and the South. After the war, the two Southern branches merged, as did the two Northern branches.

Over the years, smaller Presbyterian groups were formed; some came into the fold of either the Northern or the Southern church. But it was not until 1983, at a gathering in Atlanta, that the main branches of the church came together again. The former Southern church, the Presbyterian Church U.S., and the former Northern church, the United Presbyterian Church in the United States of America, became the Presbyterian Church (U.S.A.) Although it is the largest Presbyterian denomination today, it is far from the only one. Other Presbyterian and Reformed groups are thriving.

DIVISIONS

Some of the larger Presbyterian and Reformed bodies are:

Presbyterian Church (U.S.A.)—The largest of the Presbyterian and Reformed bodies with almost three million members, the P.C.(U.S.A.) is the product of more than a century of divisions and mergers.

Reformed Church in America—Established in 1628 by early settlers in New York as the Reformed Protestant Dutch Church, this group claims to have the longest continuous ministry of any Protestant denomination in North America.

Cumberland Presbyterian Church—This ninety-thousand-member Presbyterian Church, organized in Dickson County, Tennessee, in 1810, was a product of the so-called Great Revival of 1800. Its founders disagreed with the Calvinist doctrine of predestination. Some members joined with the mainline Presbyterian Church in 1906; the remaining Cumberland churches cooperate with the Presbyterian Church (U.S.A.) in some efforts, including publications.

Christian Reformed Church in North America—Formed in Michigan in 1847, this group was briefly affiliated with the Reformed Church in America. It now has more than 300,000 members.

Presbyterian Church in America—This 200,000-member conservative denomination was formed in 1973 as a splinter group of the Southern branch of the mainline Presbyterian Church in protest of what organizers saw as liberalism within the denomination. In 1982, the Reformed Presbyterian Church, Evangelical Synod joined the P.C.A. Unlike the larger Presbyterian Church (U.S.A.), the P.C.A. does not ordain women.

Evangelical Presbyterian Church—Since its founding in 1981, the conservative E.P.C. has grown to more than fifty thousand members.

DOCTRINES SPECIFIC TO PRESBYTERIANISM

Presbyterians are probably most identified with the idea of predestination, or the belief that God selects in advance those who will be saved.

Five principles of Calvinism are often memorized by theology students through the acronym TULIP:

Total Depravity—all human nature is tainted by the temptation to sin.

Unconditional Election—God determines who will be saved to eternal life on the basis of his own will, not his advance knowledge of how people will respond to him.

Limited Atonement—Jesus' death by crucifixion paid the price of sin only for the elect who were predestined by God for eternal life.

Irresistible Grace—Once God has determined that a person will have eternal life, God's will or grace cannot be refused but will eventually be accepted.

Perseverance of the Saints—The doctrine of "once saved, always saved" says once God has brought a person into his fold, that person cannot be drawn out.

TITLES

Minister—also called a teaching elder. Usually addressed as "Reverend."

Elder—member of the governing board of the local church, called the session. No particular form of address.

Deacon—member of the diaconate, or board of deacons, responsible for care of the congregation and property. No particular form of address.

Local congregations are members of a presbytery, or local governing body. Presbyteries make up synods, in the United States usually composed of several states. The highest governing body of the Presbyterian Church is the General Assembly, made up of representatives from all presbyteries in a country, which meets regularly to set policy.

COMMUNITY WORSHIP

The order of worship varies from church to church. Leaders of worship include the pastor, any assistant pastors and sometimes a lay leader or liturgist. The congregation sings hymns, recites responses and may have an opportunity to ask for special prayers.

Presbyterians may observe either or both of two sacraments at a service. They are:

Baptism—Presbyterians usually baptize, by sprinkling water rather than by complete immersion. Parents may bring their infants for baptism and promise to bring them up in the faith, or older children and adults may be baptized when they decide to join the church. In this case, they usually meet with the session—or ruling body of elders of the church—to discuss their faith and reason for wishing to be baptized. They will then be asked to publicly declare their faith by replying affirmatively to a series of questions from the minister during a church service. Finally, the minister will dip his hand in water and hold it on their heads, proclaiming them baptized in the name of "the Father, and of the Son and of the Holy Spirit."

Lord's Supper, or Communion—Presbyterians believe that the bread and the wine or grape juice of communion are symbols of Jesus Christ's body and blood. Jesus ate a meal with his disciples shortly before he was crucified, according to the New Testament, and told them to eat bread and drink wine in remembrance of him. The style of the communion service and the frequency vary from church to church. Sometimes bread and wine are passed down the pews; sometimes people are invited to the front of the church to receive them; sometimes there are individual pieces of bread and cups of juice; other times people break bread off a loaf to dip into the cup, a practice called intinction. In all cases, all baptized Christians, regardless of denomination, are invited to participate. The minister presides over the communion table, but elders or other lay members may help serve the elements.

Non-Presbyterians may participate in worship as they feel comfortable. All baptized Christians are invited to take communion in Presbyterian churches.

PLACE OF CHILDREN

Many Presbyterian churches have active Sunday Schools and youth programs for children. Those children who are baptized as infants are expected to make their own commitment to Jesus Christ and the church when they are older, along with those who were not baptized as infants. Many churches hold special classes for children to make sure they understand the commitment they are making. When they come into the church as older children or as teenagers, their reception into membership is called Confirmation.

In the Presbyterian church, children who were baptized as infants are allowed to participate in the Lord's Supper, or communion, but some parents prefer that their children wait until they are old enough to understand the sacrament.

ROLES OF MEN AND WOMEN

Within the various branches of the Presbyterian and Reformed faith, treatment of women varies tremendously. Many churches, such as those in the Presbyterian Church (U.S.A.), the country's largest Presbyterian group, ordain women to all offices in the church. Other churches, such as those in the more conservative Presbyterian Church in America, specifically forbid women to be ordained.

MILESTONES

Birth—A few weeks or months after birth, Presbyterian parents usually arrange to have their child baptized at a church service as "a sign and seal of God's promises to them." At a designated time, the parents bring the baby forward to the front of the church. The minister addresses questions to the parents, who will affirm their intention to bring the child up in the church. The congregation is asked to pledge its support to the family and the child. The actual baptism occurs when the minister sprinkles water on the infant's head and using its full name, proclaims it baptized.

Marriage—Weddings vary tremendously depending on the preferences of the bridal couple and the traditions of the particular church. Usually they include a processional, scripture readings, words of wisdom from the minister, special music, prayers, declaration of intent in which the minister tells the company why they have gathered, exchange of vows and rings and the proclamation by the minister that the couple is now husband and wife.

Death—Funerals usually begin with a procession bringing the coffin into the church and include the elements of a worship service, with the addition of expressions of love and concern for the person who has died and the family. One or more ministers may participate. The congregation may be asked to sing hymns. Literature for the Presbyterian Church (U.S.A.) and Cumberland Presbyterian Church calls for Romans 6:3-5 to be used at the funeral of every baptized person. In the New Revised Standard Version of the Bible, it says, "Do you not know that all of us who have been baptized into Christ Jesus were baptized into his death? Therefore we have been buried with him by baptism into death, so that, just as Christ was raised from the dead by the glory of the Father, so we too might walk in newness of life. For if we have been united with him in a death like his, we will certainly be united with him in a resurrection like his."

CONVERSION

To be baptized into the Presbyterian church, people must confess their sins, avow their faith in Jesus Christ and promise to live by the teachings of the church.

To join a particular church, they must be approved by the session, or board of elders.

MAJOR ORGANIZATIONS

Christian Reformed Church in North America
2850 Kalamazoo Avenue, S.E.
Grand Rapids, Michigan 49560

Cumberland Presbyterian Church
1978 Union Avenue
Memphis, Tennessee 38104

Evangelical Presbyterian Church
29140 Buckingham Avenue, Suite 5
Livonia, MI , 48154

Presbyterian Church in America
1852 Century Place
Atlanta, Georgia 30345

Presbyterian Church (U.S.A.)
100 Witherspoon Street
Louisville, Kentucky 40202

Reformed Church in America
475 Riverside Drive
New York, New York 10115

FURTHER READING

Angell, James W. *How to Spell Presbyterian.* revised. Louisville: Geneva Press, 1984.
Book of Order, Presbyterian Church (U.S.A.). Louisville: The Office of the General Assembly, Presbyterian Church (U.S.A.), 1994.
Calvin: Theological Treatises. Rev. J. K. S. Reid. ed., trans. Philadelphia: Westminster Press, 1954.
Christian Marriage, the Worship of God, the Ministry Unit on Theology and Worship. Presbyterian Church (U.S.A.), Cumberland Presbyterian Church. Philadelphia: Westminster Press, 1986.
Leith, John H. *Introduction to the Reformed Tradition.* Atlanta: John Knox Press, 1981.
Lingle, Walter L., and Kuykendall, John W. *Presbyterians—Their History and Beliefs.* Altanta: John Knox Press, 1988.

Liturgical Year—The Worship of God, the Ministry Unit on Theology and Worship. Presbyterian Church (U.S.A.), Cumberland Presbyterian Church. Louisville: Westminster John Knox Press, 1992.

Loetscher, Lefferts A. *A Brief History of the Presbyterians.* fourth edition. Philadelphia: The Westminster Press, 1978.

McKim, Donald, ed. *Encyclopedia of the Reformed Faith.* Louisville: Westminster/ John Knox Press; Edinburgh: St. Andrew Press, 1992.

Weeks, Louis B. *To Be a Presbyterian.* Atlanta: John Knox Press, 1973.

QUAKERS

∞

ORIGINS

As one story goes, the Society of Friends got the nickname of Quakers when founder George Fox appeared before a magistrate who warned him to tremble before the law. Fox, in turn, warned the judge to quake before God.

Fox was a Puritan born in 1624 in the British village of Fenny Drayton in Leicester. Around 1646, Fox had the first of a series of religious experiences that led him to recognize an "Inner Light" of Christ in himself and every person. As he became more involved with his religious beliefs, Fox began talking to people on the streets and speaking out at churches. He was not always well received. About 1652, Fox founded the Friends of the Truth, which later became known as the Society of Friends.

In keeping a careful record of his spiritual experiences, Fox recorded performing many miracles. Fox was arrested for blasphemy eight times and served several years in prison. Many of his followers were harassed and imprisoned. Among complaints against them were their refusal to remove their hats in the presence of officials, including royalty, while saying they would subjugate themselves only to God; their refusal to take oaths; and their propensity for interrupting religious services with their opinions. Quakers also argued against the state-supported Church of England with its elaborate religious rituals.

Despite the persecution, Friends continued to meet and to grow. Some began traveling to North America. They found themselves unwanted in several colonies.

Probably the most famous colonial Quaker was William Penn. Penn, a religious rebel in England, became a Quaker in 1665, and quickly began to espouse doctrine that got him thrown into prison. While in prison in 1669, he wrote "No Cross, No Crown," explaining the Quaker faith. When he was released from prison, he began planning an expedition to America to form a colony where religious freedom would prevail. In 1682, he finally acquired the proper authority and founded Pennsylvania.

Most Quakers refused to fight for the colonies, but their principle of equality made them great crusaders in the interest of abolition, women's rights, friendship with Indians and humane treatment of prisoners. But even the peaceful Quakers developed differences of opinion on theological and social matters that led to formation of different factions.

DIVISIONS

There are several Friends, or Quaker, organizations in the United States.

Friends United Meeting—The largest Friends organization in the United States, the United Meeting represents more than five hundred meetings, or congregations, and 55,000 members. It was organized in 1902 and known as the Five Years Meeting of Friends until 1963. Its international affiliates represent about half the Quakers in the world.

Friends General Conference—An organization of more than five hundred meetings, or congregations, with more than thirty thousand members, the General Conference was founded in 1900. It is primarily a service organization.

Evangelical Friends International, North America Region—This group is conservative in theology. Unlike traditional Quaker meetings, its two-hundred-plus meetings have pastors and generally conduct programmed worship services with scripture, sermons and songs. It represents more than twenty thousand Quakers.

Religious Society of Friends (Conservative)—A small group of only about twenty-seven meetings and two thousand members, this organization is also known as the Wilburites after John Wilbur, a Rhode Island Quaker who argued against what he saw as increasing creedalism among some other Quakers.

DOCTRINES SPECIFIC TO QUAKERISM

God—Many Quakers accept the unity of a Godhead—God, Jesus and the Holy Spirit. Everyone has direct and constant access to God, known traditionally as the Divine Light Within. Through this, they can discern good from evil.

Sin—Quakers have no doctrine of original sin, or humankind carrying the burden of the sin committed by Adam and Eve as told in the Old Testament Book of Genesis. They regard sin as being "out of the truth." Infants are born sinless, but humans are tempted to sin. Through Divine Light, or access to God, people are able to overcome the temptation to sin.

Quakers believe that the Divine Light is in everyone, not an elect or a group predestined by God. They oppose oaths in any form, as well as lawsuits and litigation. Quakers believe in plain dress, and early Quakers practiced "plain speech," avoiding the word "you" by saying "thee" and "thou."

There are no sacraments in the Quaker faith because they hold that all of life is sacramental.

CALENDAR

Quakers use the Gregorian calendar, but historically refused to use the common names of the days and months because the roots of their names are pagan. Thus, January becomes First Month and Sunday is First Day, etc.

RELIGIOUS FESTIVALS AND HOLIDAYS

Quakers traditionally do not observe Christmas, Easter or any special days other than First Days (Sundays). Modern Quakers who do observe holidays may do so simply, attempting to stay away from excess commercialism.

Most Quakers would not mind receiving holiday wishes, although they might choose to forgo parties, pageants and other celebrations.

TITLES

Presiding Clerk—selected by the meeting.
Recording Clerk—records the minutes of the business meeting.

Quakers traditionally do not use titles—Mr., Mrs., Miss or Ms.—to address each other, but use first and last names only.

The business of the Friends congregations is usually carried out at monthly meetings, but there is no voting. If a consensus is not reached, they simply postpone the item of business until they can agree. Quakers speak of achieving "unity," or a sense of common spiritual sense. Several congregations in an area may come together for a quarterly meeting, and the entire denomination gathers at a yearly meeting, but these can only advise; authority is vested in the monthly meeting.

Non-members are welcome at meetings.

COMMUNITY WORSHIP

Quakers meet on Sunday, which they call First-day. The weekly worship gathering is called a meeting, and the place of worship a meetinghouse. In many congregations, there is no clergy.

The foremost characteristic of Quaker worship is silence. Friends gather in a plain room with wooden benches and keep quiet. Occasionally someone may be moved to say a prayer, read scripture or make a statement. Otherwise, they sit together absorbed in silent communal worship until a congregational leader signals the end of the meeting by shaking hands with a neighbor. A particularly spiritually significant worship is called a Gathered Meeting.

Today, not all Quaker groups keep the silent meeting. Some have worship services with sermons and music, much like other Christian groups.

If at a silent meeting, sit quietly and enjoy the time away from the rush of the culture. If at a meeting where there is a sermon and music, participate if so inclined.

PRIVATE WORSHIP

Individual Quakers may have their own spiritual practices, or Friends may gather at a time other than First Day. Whenever two or more Quakers are gathered, a meeting may proceed.

DRESS

In a word, Quaker dress is plain. Traditionally, until early this century, the women wore gray dresses with white shawls and the men wore long coats with plain collars and hats. But since the principle behind the dress was not to call attention to oneself, when their clothing customs became so unusual as to draw notice, they abandoned them. Still, Quakers are unlikely to wear much ornamentation, very bright colors or distinctive styles of clothes. They usually keep their wardrobes simple.

Historically, Quaker men refused to take off or tip their hats except when in prayer, showing deference only to God. In keeping with the old custom, a few Friends wear hats to meetings and keep them on except for prayer.

If visiting a Quaker meeting, keep the clothing simple.

DIETARY LAWS

Some groups prohibit alcohol and tobacco.

If entertaining Quakers, have beverages other than alcohol available. Alchohol is not a good gift for Quakers unless you know that they drink.

PLACE OF CHILDREN

Quakers believe children are born innocent and should be brought up in an atmosphere of gentleness. There is no specific coming-of-age ceremony for Quaker children.

ROLES OF MEN AND WOMEN

Men and women are usually regarded equally among Quakers. Women have been among the best-known Quakers in endeavors from mission work to anti-slavery and equal rights crusades.

HOUSEHOLD

In living arrangements as in clothing, Quakers have traditionally preferred plainness and simplicity. The faith teaches that the style of life should be based on need, not wealth. Historically Quakers frowned on music, cards, games, sports and fiction. Few Quakers today completely avoid all those recreations, however.

MILESTONES

Birth—There is no ceremony for newborn babies, but the child is registered at the parents' meeting.

Marriage—The first step for an engaged Quaker couple is to bring a written statement of their intention to the meeting. Both sets of parents must also approve.

A Quaker wedding may be a part of a regular meeting or take place another time, but it closely resembles weekly worship. In a congregation that keeps silent meetings, friends and family are seated in the meeting hall. The bride and groom arrive, and all sit in silence until the bride and groom feel moved to stand and recite their simple vows. He goes first, pledging, "with divine assistance," to be a faithful husband. She in turn, promises to be a faithful wife. After they resume their places on the bench, silence resumes. Friends and family may interrupt it from time to time with blessings or words of advice. When the meeting is over, a brides-maid and a groomsman bring in a small table and a certificate of marriage. The couple signs the certificate, as does everyone who is present. A wedding is usually followed by a party.

Guests should observe the rules of a Quaker meeting. If it is a traditional "unprogrammed" meeting, visitors can offer a blessing if so inclined, but should otherwise keep silent. Visitors can sign the certificate if they desire. Gifts and cards are appropriate, but if the bride and groom are strict, traditional Quakers, household goods and appliances would be better choices than less practical gifts.

Death—Quakers regard death as deliverance from the world's trials. Usually a member of the meeting is commissioned to write a memorial to the deceased, which is read at a meeting.

Non-Quakers attending a memorial service should observe the rules of the meeting. If it is a traditional, unprogrammed meeting, guests may offer thoughts or prayers as they wish.

CONVERSION

After attending several meetings, a person interested in joining can make a written request. One or two members will meet with the candidate to discuss membership. Then, the new member is simply added to the records of the group. Quakers call converts "convicted" members and people born into the faith "birthright" members.

MAJOR ORGANIZATIONS

American Friends Service Committee
1501 Cherry Street
Philadelphia, Pennsylvania 19102

Evangelical Friends International, North America Region
5350 Broadmoor Circle, N.W.
Canton, Ohio 44709

Friends General Conference
1216 Arch Street, 2 B
Philadelphia, Pennsylvania 19107

Friends United Meeting
101 Quaker Hill Drive
Richmond, Indiana 47374-1980

Friends World Committee for Consultation
Section of the Americas
1506 Race Street
Philadelphia, Pennsylvania 19102

FURTHER READING

Cooper, Wilmer A. *A Living Faith—An Historical Study of Quaker Beliefs.* Richmond, Ind.: Friends United Press, 1990.

Ingle, H. Larry. *First Among Friends—George Fox and the Creation of Quakerism.* New York: Oxford University Press, Inc., 1994.

Newman, Daisy. *A Procession of Friends—Quakers in America.* Richmond, Ind.: Friends United Press, 1972.

Yolen, Jane. *Friend—The Story of George Fox and the Quakers.* New York: Seabury Press, 1972.

FOR CHILDREN

Elgin, Kathleen. *The Quakers—The Religious Society of Friends.* New York: David McKay Company, Inc., 1968.

BIBLIOGRAPHY

Anderson, Sir Norman, ed. *The World's Religions*. Leicester, England: Inter-Varsity Press, and Grand Rapids, Mich.: Wm. B. Eerdmans Publishing Company, 1975.

Bedell, Kenneth B., ed. *Yearbook of American & Canadian Churches, 1996*. Nashville: Abingdon Press, 1996.

Brosse, Jacques. *Religious Leaders*. Edinburgh, New York, Toronto: W & R Chambers Ltd., 1991.

Catoir, John T. *World Religions—Beliefs Behind Today's Headlines*. New York: Alba House, 1992.

Eliade, Mircea and Couliano, Ioan P. *The Eliade Guilde to World Religions*. San Francisco: HarperSan Francisco, 1991.

Eliade, Mircea, ed. *The Encyclopedia of Religion*. New York: MacMillan Publishing Co., 1987.

Hinnells, John R., ed. *A Handbook of Living Religions*. Middlesex, England: Penguin Books, 1984.

Hinnells, John R., ed. *Who's Who of Religions*. New York: Penguin Books, 1991.

Lewis, James F. and Travis, William G., *Religious Traditions of the World*. Grand Rapids, Mich.: Zondervan Publishing House, 1991.

Lincoln, C. Eric, and Mamiya, Lawrence H. *The Black Church in the African American Experience*. Durham, N.C.: Duke University Press, 1990.

Magida, Arthur J., ed. *How To Be a Perfect Stranger—A Guide to Etiquette in Other People's Religious Ceremonies*. Woodstock, Vermont: Jewish Lights Publishing, 1996.

McGrath, Alister E. *Christian Theology, an Introduction*. Cambridge, Mass.: Blackwell Publishers Inc., 1994.

Mead, Frank S. *Handbook of Denominations in the United States*. Revised by Samuel S. Hill, Nashville: Abingdon Press, 1995.

Neusner, Jacob, ed. *World Religions in America—An Introduction*. Louisville: Westminster/John Knox Press, 1994.

Occhiogrosso, Peter. *The Joy of Sects—A Spirited Guide to the World's Religious Traditions*. New York: Doubleday, 1994.

Ross, Floyd H., and Hills, Tynette. *The Great Religions by Which Men Live*. New York: Fawcett Premier, 1956.

Rosten, Elon, ed. *Religions of America—Ferment and Faith in an Age of Crisis*. New York: Touchstone, 1975.

Sacred Writings of World Religions. Chambers Encyclopedic Guides. Edinburgh: W & R Chambers Ltd., 1992.

Sadleir, Steven S. *The Spiritual Seeker's Guide*. Costa Mesa, Ca.: Allwon Publish Co., 1992.

Sharma, Arvind, ed. *Our Religions*. San Francisco: HarperSan Francisco, 1993.

Shumacher, Stephan, and Woerner, Gert, eds. *The Encyclopedia of Eastern Philosophy and Religion*. Boston: Shambhala, 1994.

Smith, Huston. *The World's Religions*. San Francisco: HarperSan Francisco, 1991.

Smith, Jonathan Z., ed. *The HarperCollins Dictionary of Religion*. San Francisco: HarperSan Francisco, 1995.

A Sourcebook for the Community of Religions. Joel Beversluis, project editor. Chicago: The Council for a Parliament of the World's Religions, 1993.

The World's Religions—Understanding the Living Faiths. Dr. Peter B. Clarke consulting editor. Pleasantville, N.Y.: Reader's Digest, 1993.

FOR CHILDREN

Jacobs, William J. *World Religions—Great Lives*. New York: Atheneum Books for Young Readers, 1996.

McElrath, William N. *Ways We Worship*. Hauppauge, N.Y.: Barron's Educational Series Inc., 1987.

Osborne, Mary Pope. *One World, Many Religions—The Ways We Worship*. New York: Alfred A. Knopf, 1996.

Ward, Hiley H. *My Friends' Beliefs—A Young Reader's Guide to World Religions*. New York: Walker and Company, 1988.

Welpy, Michael, and Makhlouf, Georgia. *The Human Story—The Rise of Major Religions*, Englewood Cliffs, N. J.: Silver Burdett Press, 1988.

The World's Great Religions. Special Edition for Young Readers, by the editorial staff of LIFE. New York: Golden Press, 1958.